Upland Bird Hunting

Joel M. Vance

Drawings by Tom Beecham

AN OUTDOOR LIFE BOOK

Outdoor Life Books
NEW YORK

E. P. Dutton & Co., Inc.
NEW YORK

Photo Credits

Bettmann Archive: page 276
John Davis: page 299
Pete Czura: pages 189, 199, 226, 238, 248
George Laycock: page 106
Leonard Lee Rue III: pages 191, 192, 197, 244
James Tallon: pages 130, 133

Library of Congress Catalog Card Number: 80-5886
ISBN: 0-525-93234-2

Manufactured in the United States of America

To the memory of my father, who first put a love of bird hunting in my heart, then a shotgun in my hand.

Contents

Acknowledgments

Special thanks are due to Mike McIntosh, who generously allowed me to use his copious files on shotguns and shotgun history, as well as his fine photographs of guns; to Russ Reagan and Carrie Stegner, who patiently printed a ton of photographs; to John Davis for the sensitive hunting-shack photo from *South Carolina Wildlife,* and to Pete Czura, George Laycock, Leonard Lee Rue III and Jim Tallon, superb photographers whose works illumine these pages. Finally, my sincere thanks and especially my affection to all the fine bird hunters I've shared field, forest and hunting shack with over the years. Bird hunting is fun any way you do it, but most of all when you share the trials and triumphs with good hunting pards. Foster and Spence and Mike and all the rest of you, this book is for you and about you . . .

1

On Being a Birdshooter

It starts in the late heat of summer, amid eddying pollen, hovering gnats, the endless rasp of cicadas, and ends three or more months later. A quarter of the year spent trudging from dust and sweat into what becomes a biting, mean winter wind that restlessly stirs thin snow among long-dead cornstalks.

There will be golden days, there will be desolate ones. Some days the air is filled with dirty cotton clouds, the color of grimy undershirts; some days it holds a winey sparkle that, were it bottled, would stop global wars.

But always there are the birds. That's why we go. For the birds that squat in the fencerows, that stalk the far, silent ridges, that sail endlessly in the protective arms of a prairie wind. Each has his talents, his subterfuges, his special savor on the dinner plate. Each is special, for I have lived with them, Tom-peeped their sexual antics, midwifed their births and assisted with unashamed gusto at their executions.

No matter the species, there are attributes that make it worth looking beyond the bead on the end of a trim double. Birdshooting is more than bird shooting—or should be. Any birdshooter should develop his overall knowledge of the bird he shoots. No one who measures his hunt by the bulge in his game bag should claim to be a birdshooter. That's not what it's all about.

Although outdoor pleasures are simple and basic, I accept the necessity of studying wildlife and habitat, even while I vaguely resent complicating my simple fun with statistics. Wildlife management is a young science, no more than fifty years old. Before that, it was only a concern, headed in the right direction, but composed of far more questions than answers. There still are a lot of unanswered questions. Wildlife doesn't hold still and wild things care not for our concern for them. You'll not find forest creatures lining up meekly to be counted, tagged, sexed and aged. Wildlife managers have had to invent every method they use today. Someone, for example, had the idea of using common old rural mailboxes to trap grouse. You fix up a trip pan inside the box, put a mirror in the back end. Set the box on a grouse drumming log. The randy cock grouse, thumping out his percussive challenge, peers into the strange-looking contraption that grew overnight on his log, sees what appears to be a belligerent bird glaring back at him, rushes in to do battle, trips the door . . . and is caught.

Some methods have proved wrong, no matter how logical they seemed. Nature loves the hidden flaw. But we, as hunters, should be interested in biological science for two reasons: (1) because we have, I think, an ethical obligation to acquire more than just a surface knowledge of our prey—after all, we're taking the most important thing it has to offer, its life, and that should give it enough stature to warrant our academic as well as our sporting interest; and (2) because behavioral knowledge can help our hunting success.

Wildlife management has been a roller coaster of triumph and pratfall. What passed for wildlife management a hundred years ago was the introduction of such lovelies as the English sparrow and the starling, not to mention the Gypsy moth and the German carp. We're still at it with grass carp and monk parakeets. All too few have been such triumphs as the brown trout, a native of Europe, or the ring-necked pheasant which started in Asia and, through introduction, made its way into Europe and finally to the United States.

If we're lucky, we come up with a pheasant. If we're at least not unlucky, the exotic fades away, as did the coturnix quail. Coturnix quail represent one of those dark chapters in the history of the agency I work for, the Missouri Conservation Department. The department led a national move (I'm tempted to say "craze") to stock coturnix quail in the late 1950s that, at best, can be characterized as an expensive flop. In brief, what birds didn't commit suicide by flying into trees or fences, or got caught by cats, dogs, hawks and just about anything else that eats meat, tried to fly back to the Old World, from whence they originally came.

Not being particularly strong flyers, they found the Atlantic Ocean a bit much and they vanished into the smudged pages of biological history. So, biologists are not always right—but they try and the ones I know try hard, with a professionalism that should be envied by other professions. It gripes me to hear drugstore cowboys take time out from second-guessing football coaches to lecture "the conservation" on how they ought to be running things. Maybe that's why I'm so strong on hunters taking a little time to stick their noses in some good books, to study their game outside the hunting season, to develop a healthy interest in what makes wildlife tick.

I fear our upland hunting is headed for grim times, mainly because of the American farmer. He likes to talk about his traditional independence, but he's in bondage to more masters than ever in his history. He's a slave to his gargantuan mortgage, to the sonorously repeated message that it is America's duty to feed the world. Perhaps—if all the food went to starving kids and not to our ideological enemies. Agribusiness dangles the luscious plum of Superprofit before the plow jockey's dazzled eyes and he stumbles into overproduction, overcowing, overuse of his only true heritage, his land. The bank account fattens perhaps, but the earth grows lean. Talk like this is not popular with farmers, but neither is telling friends they have spinach on their teeth. While I ache for the farmer and his economic problems (and, owning an interest in a farm, I share some of them), I can't believe the answer is to mine the land today only to leave it ravaged for tomorrow. Does it make sense to suck the water out of the West for today's fast buck when it's perfectly obvious that tomorrow the water will run out? Does it make sense to erode Iowa for Supercorn today, to leave hard-rock dirt for tomorrow's farmer? Not to me it doesn't—and a lot of farsighted farm spokesmen are beginning to say the same things. This isn't a treatise on good or bad farming, but the bulk of upland bird hunting is done in farm country, and what the farmer does with his land directly affects our sport.

The contrast between my uncle's hard-rock, gullied Chariton County Depression farm and today's typical Chariton County farm is staggering. He plowed his piddling tobacco patch on 160 acres with a horse, a knot-headed, muley old son of a bitch who, when I tried to ride her, regularly used to dump me on the yellow clay a mile from the house and leave me stranded there. There were plenty of quail on that farm because my uncle couldn't do much more than scratch the surface of 160 acres with a horse and plow.

Today's farmer has a $40,000 diesel tractor with stereo-in-cab that probably would, if you hooked it up right, pull the world inside out. You don't farm 160 acres with one of those big bastards, nor even if you own 1,000 acres do you farm small fields within it. No, you chop out the fencerows, fill in the gullies, flatten the whole 1,000 acres so you can put the spurs to that snorting monster and let 'er rip. And, of course, the quail in the brush patches, gullies and fencerows quietly vanish, victims of modern, clean farming. And if the hillside is too steep to run a tractor, why you spray the timber with Agent Orange, bulldoze the dead wood into a pile, burn it and seed the slope to fescue because cows have adjustable wheels.

This is modern agriculture and while I don't blame the farmer, I certainly don't sympathize with him. But I find it difficult to buy the argument that such farming is the only way to survive. I know farmers who survive quite well in harmony with nature. A fellow named Gene Poirot, down by Golden City, Missouri, bought a worn-out farm back in the 1920s with his last few bucks and has become a millionaire by dedicating himself to building the soil with nature's own tools. He's no empty-headed dreamer. Everything he does is easily done by any other farmer. Poirot has a wildlife paradise. The place swarms with quail, waterfowl, prairie chickens—you name it. Poirot's methods are too lengthy to go into here, but his book, *Our Margin of Life,* should be the only textbook used in every College of Agriculture in the country. Don't hold your breath.

Agriculture has been seduced into this self-destructive way of life by the basic American philosophy of "Bigger is Better" fueled by Vo-Ag teachers and college aggie professors who get their information from agribusiness. Farm broadcasts and farm publications almost inevitably are supported by (in some cases published by) the petrochemical and industrial giants of agriculture. My father couldn't believe it the first time he sprayed his corn with herbicides and there was no foxtail, no cockleburrs. It was a miracle.

This chemical legerdemain is touted constantly by the agribusiness advertisers. You get the feeling the use of herbicides and pesticides is a religious experience. Well, those chemicals have played hell with America's wildlife, both directly and indirectly. What they haven't poisoned outright, they've hindered by eliminating food and cover.

What we need to reverse the trend is a really good depression . . . or a war. Don't lynch me yet—I'm not advocating either. But wildlife made a startling comeback through the 1930s and 1940s because of two things. First, a depression drove thousands of farmers off their land and it grew up in foxtail, cockleburrs and quail. Second, a world war took a generation of hunters out of the fields long enough to give wildlife a chance to build the populations which only now are declining. The 1950s were a time of balance—growing wildlife populations, the stirrings of big time agriculture. The 1970s saw agribusiness come into its own. Missouri lost a million and a half acres of woodlands to pasture conversion in the 1960s, many more acres in the 1970s. Virtually all of it was to that rank, worthless wildlife plant, fescue, rather than the clovers and lespedezas and other legumes that characterized pastures in the glory years.

Well, maybe we'll survive modern agriculture. That is, maybe wildlife will. I'm not so sure about people. Land prices are horrifying, equipment costs staggering. As I write this in the summer of 1980, Texas, Oklahoma, Kansas are locked in 100-degree heat, dry weather—worst, they say, since the Dirty Thirties. Maybe not this time the Dust Bowl. Maybe not this time. But it's comin'. I can squat on the cracked sidewalk in front of the general store and dig at the tufts of crabgrass sprouted there with the honed-down tip of a Barlow blade and squint a rheumy eye into the hazy sunshine and opine about hard times with the best and/or the worst of them.

The wind will blow and the dust will fly and the crops will shrivel. And a bobwhite will sit on the rusty hood of a mouldering old diesel and talk to his lady love of good times to come . . .

Bird hunting has been a part of my life for about thirty years—some before that, actually, but something I looked forward to for that long. I've trudged into a keen north wind so vicious it made me scream curses at the unremitting irritation. I've hunted birds when it was so hot the dogs trailed foot-long tongues and could go no longer than half a day. I've watched the sun come up over the stark Flint Hills and heard the quick roar of an incoming prairie chicken. I've stood in pole thickets amid the twitter of woodcock, rising in helicopter ascent. I've jumped, spooked, as a ruffed grouse flushed with muffled thunder from a Minnesota alder swamp. The heathen Chinese pheasant has cackled hysteric harmony to accompany his iridescent, meteoric rise ahead of my gun. I've sweated in gnat-shrouded September cornfields, waiting for incoming dove flights.

Dogs trot briskly in and out of my memory. (And one slender lady Brittany whines and whuffs at this moment to get my attention, so she can sit in my lap and look to see what I'm writing about her.) The dogs range all the way from a feathery, lovely setter my father picked up as payment on a bad debt, thinking he was coming out ahead (he was incredibly wrong), to the brace of Brittanies who share my current bird fields and my sleeping bag. Some dogs have been egg suckers, others needed only opportunity to have brought home field trial trophies.

In my youth, I hunted with crinkled men, sparse of fat, who chewed vile home-grown and carried battered shotguns that would not have fetched boughten-plug money in any hock shop, but who could shuck three shots out in less time than it takes to write about it and put three birds on the ground.

Their dogs echoed their rake-ribbed personalities—their skeletal structure was plainly visible through taut, scarred skin. They were X-rays of a dog, thinly covered by whipcord muscles that carried them tirelessly all day over gullied Chariton County hills where broomsedge, tobacco and quail were the only viable crops.

I've never really learned to shoot, despite having fired thousands of rounds. Perhaps a good gunner could take me in hand and straighten out my faults, but I suspect it's too late for redemption. I still peek over the gun barrel, still miss shots that a five-year-old child, unencumbered by bad habits, could make with impunity. Yet, once in a while I make a few good shots and that keeps me hopeful. I shoot better alone, probably a psychological release from having had to shoot against those taciturn hillmen with whom I grew up. If you didn't rush your shot with them, there was little point in shooting at all, for the sky would be empty of birds. So, when I'm with others, I hurry my shots and miss a lot.

I haven't babied my guns and don't have an extensive collection of them. I've come to the ones I own now through a process of sifting, first taking what was available free—teenagers generally don't buy The Gun unless they're a whole lot richer than I was. They take whatever hand-me-down is stuck back in a corner of the closet, usually a Stevens single-shot or something comparable. I went through a period of yearning for the automatic shotgun, equating a lot of lead with successful shooting.

Now I'm down to three shotguns. I can shoot only one at a time anyway.

There is an old long-barreled Model 12 that my father bought second hand and which he handed down to me. It is my turkey shooter, long as a coastal defense gun, still as slick-smooth of operation as the day some lucky soul bought it, probably for $75.

My money is in two double-barreled guns. One is a Charles Daly over-and-under, bored improved cylinder and modified, field grade, with no barrel selector. The receiver is silvered where I have worn the blueing off with my carrying hand. The stock is dented and the finish chipped and it needs refinishing. It is plain old American walnut and not a particularly good grade at that. But it has chromed barrels and takes a minimum amount of care when encumbered with a maximum amount of abuse and I like it.

But the gun, The Gun, is a lovely old L.C. Smith side-by-side double, made in 1910, bored improved cylinder and modified, that takes 16-gauge shells. We fell in love at a gun show and a few days later I parted with enough money to send an idiot through Yale and now it is my bird gun.

I do not intend to baby it, even though each round pushed through it, each unavoidable scratch lessens its market value. It is my gun, fitted to me as if by a master gunmaker. When the gun speaks ancient thunder, birds rain from the sky. Not always—it isn't a magic wand—but more often than with any other gun I've ever shot. It is so beautiful as to be a distinct source of pleasure just resting in its gun case, never mind when it leaps to my shoulder and executes a juking woodcock. We'll talk about it and some of its elderly cousins later on.

When I uncase my gun, there is no doubt in anyone's mind that I am a bird hunter. Only long hours of handling will wear the blueing off the way mine is worn. I am no Johnny-come-lately to the briar hells, rigged out in stiff birdshooter britches still with the price tag, owner of a stiff-actioned gun in a carrying case whose lining hasn't yet ripped because the goddam bead catches it. I don't have to tell fellow bird hunters that I am one of them. They can look at my battered old guns and know it.

So, we're going to take a long trip, you and I, through a hundred fields, plains, gullies, willow breaks, up the long hill to home, where the light shines soft yellow. We'll meet some birds, a few over the bead of a gun, some very personally through their sex habits. We'll stick our nose in the mud with the bogsucker, drum with a cock grouse. We'll boom our brag a mile over grama grass with a prairie chicken, huddle on a starshot night so cold the telephone wires whine, with our butts nestled close to our quail coveymates.

Not to run down other birds, but upland birds are something special. That's why we're here: to celebrate the upland bird. So, let's get on with it. . . .

2

History of Shotgunning

History's first great wingshooter was Hercules, the famed Greek hero who, as one of the Twelve Labours with which he was charged, had to rid the swamps of Lake Stymphalos of a bunch of man-eating birds. These birds were even meaner than cock pheasants. Their feathers were so sharp they'd cut anyone on whom they fell.

Hercules dropped some with a slingshot, but also nailed some with bow and arrow, this being somewhat before the advent of gunpowder. But it was far from a sporting outing. The surviving birds flew to the island of Ares where they later dropped feathers on Jason and the Argonauts. Apparently, the Stymphalos birds couldn't adapt to change, for they're all gone today.

Too bad. It would make a hell of a bird hunt, going after birds that are going after you.

As a point of interest, Hercules was so popular with King Thespios on the island of Thebes, that the king let our first great birdshooter sleep with forty-nine of his fifty daughters. Only one resisted, for some reason not explained, and the rest had enough kids to colonize the island of Sardinia. This is only one of the possible rewards of becoming a fine wingshot.

One of the earliest smoothbore shooters was an obscure Czech warrior, lost in history, who frantically poured gravel and bits of metal scrap down the muzzle of his crude hand cannon as a brace of soldiers of the Emperor Sigismund hove on the scene, armed with swords sharp enough to skin a locomotive. Our Czech may have had one of the earliest shotguns, but he wasn't interested in sport hunting; only in saving his hide. And while our hero was a gunner of sorts, his smoothbore was as likely to kill *him* as it was anything else. Early guns, all smoothbores (rifling didn't appear until the first part of the 16th century), were used as much for their noise as for their lethal charge. A medieval warhorse, confronted with a hand cannon belching fire and noise, usually dumped his armored rider like a sack of galvanized shingles tossed down a coal chute.

Shotguns were around a long, long time before bird hunters developed any sense of ethics or sport about the use of them. By the 1500s, bird hunting was established,

Early wingshooters used a stalking horse who didn't mind being shot over or under, a moveable blind. Notice the spaniel crouching and preparing to retrieve.

but mostly as a food-gathering exercise. Most of the methods were beneath the dignity of the nobility, who were the only people with means enough to waste shot on flying creatures.

Some of the hunting methods were ingenious. One involved several hunters and a dog, usually a spaniel, the progenitor of my own two Brittanies. The dog would point a covey of quail, freezing them. At the same time, a hunter would fly a hawk or throw his hat in the air to simulate a hawk. Caught between a rock and a hard place (the hawk or the dog), the panicked quail would squat so tightly they were easy prey for a couple of men with a net.

Another odd method involved the hunter posing as a cow. The hunter draped a cowhide over himself and gently herded the scurrying birds into a hoop net.

Akin to that was the use of a "stalking horse," either a specially trained horse or cow, or a canvas blind painted to resemble an animal (or a tree or bush). The phony animal had its head down as if feeding and was light enough that the wildfowler could lift it with one hand. The hunter crept along behind the movable blind until he was close enough to poke his single-barrel matchlock or wheel-lock arquebus (which might have weighed fifteen pounds or more and could have been as much as nine feet long) through the blind so he could ground swat his prey. Some of the stalking horses even had switch tails so they were more realistic.

But the use of a stalking horse inevitably has many of the elements of low comedy and it's easy to see why fowling was considered a sport of the lower classes, too cloaked with buffoonery to be suitable for the nobility.

Some deadeyes in Poland developed a small wheel-lock rifle to pick off pheasants and other birds after the birds had been flushed into trees by dogs—an early example of today's dog-hunter relationship.

In 1621, Gervase Markham published a shooter's guide called *Hunger's Prevention, Or The Whole Art Of Fowling By Water And Land*. Included in his advice on taking wildfowl is a prescription for making birds snot-flying drunk after which

Wingshooting in the 1700s was tough with the long delay between the fall of the hammer and the explosion of the gun. This elegantly dressed shooter is using a flintlock. The dogs look very pointer-like. The birds probably are grouse. And the shooter probably missed.

A veritable army of early wingshooters creeps on this poor bunch of ducks. Notice the length of the barrels. This scene probably was in the early 1600s. And, already, the wingshooter had help from dogs.

you can have your will with them. The gruesome mixture includes lettuce, poppy, henbane, hemlock and wheat, boiled in the dregs of wine. I'm pretty sure I've been in a couple of taverns where they still serve this, only to visiting hunters instead of their prey.

By the mid-1500s, European gunners were potting birds on the wing and at the turn of the 17th century, Japanese hunters were dropping flying birds *from horseback* with quick guns. A Spanish book, written in 1644, comments on the decimation of partridges by Spanish gunners who shot them on the wing.

Louis XIV, one of history's most famed kings, who brought a Camelot charm to the French court and gave his name to a lot of furniture, also established a hell of a record as a wingshot. He once killed thirty-two flying pheasants with thirty-four shots.

Perhaps somewhere there is a link between Louis and the deposed and exiled English king of the time, Charles II, since Charles was in France during Louis' early reign. Charles left behind him a primitive form of bird shooting. Because of the limitations of the guns, the Englanders, more concerned with meat than esthetic satisfaction, were still bagging their birds on the ground. They were not inclined to waste shot and powder on speculation.

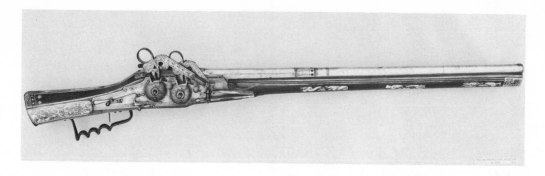

The first wingshooters were stuck with the awkwardness of wheellock guns. Most shots at birds in the wheellock era were in what a friend whimsically calls "the pre-flight position."

A gentleman wingshooter of the flintlock era with his dogs which look like spaniel-pointer crosses. The tiny little dog has the markings and shape of a Brittany, but one somehow shrunk to half-size.

A colonial wingshooter levels down on some ducks and drops two with one shot from his flintlock. The dogs are a duke's mixture—one pointer, one setter and one something else.

So it remained for the nobility to embrace and develop wingshooting. We can date the beginning of American upland bird hunting to 1660 when Charles II, the Merry Monarch, regained the throne of England after fleeing to France in 1651, pursued hotly and violently by Oliver Cromwell's no-nonsense soldiery. He loved dogs, hunting, sports and the good life. Only thirty when he regained his crown, Charles led an eventful life, fathering fourteen illegitimate children. He brought back to us from France one thing more important than his appetite for smooth skin—he had acquired a taste for the French sport of taking birds on the wing.

You'd think that the next logical step would have been a quick series of innovations in firearms, but it was about 200 years before much of anything changed. The only major change in shotgunning over that period was the introduction of percussion caps between 1805–1823. E. Goode Wright of Hereford, England, first

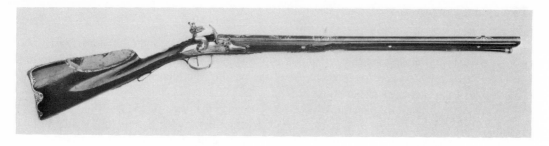

Flintlocks were some improvement over wheellocks, but not much. There still was a breathless moment between flash and firing when the gunner had just enough time to flinch and miss.

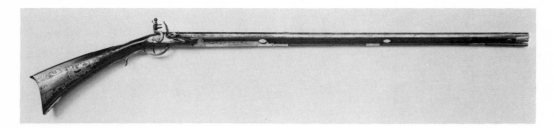

Flintlock rifle of late 18th century, called the Kentucky rifle.

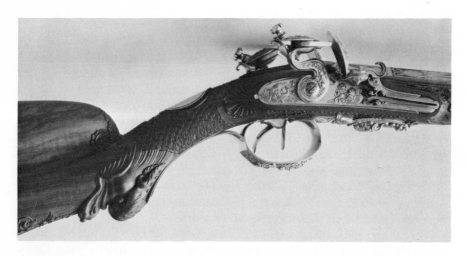

Gunsmithing of some of the early guns was remarkably lovely. Note the rich beauty of this double-barrel flintlock dating to 1801, made in Versailles by Nicolas Noel Boutet for presentation to Napoleon Bonaparte.

used fulminate of mercury, which was reliable, waterproof and fairly noncorrosive. Also eliminated by the percussion cap was most of the delay between spark and the gun's firing. Now the success of the passing shot depended more on the skill of the shooter than blind luck.

Multi-barreled guns came along fairly early in the game. In the late 18th century, there was a series of four-barrel French guns, but double barrels, either side-by-side or over-and-unders were (and are) the most popular.

Multi-barrels go back a long way. They were known in the 15th century and the 1547 inventory of Henry VIII's arms at Greenwich included "one dagge with two pieces and one stock." The gun probably was similar to the saddle pistol of Charles V of Spain. There were double-barreled wheellock rifles in the 16th century, but it wasn't until the second half of the 17th century that the double barrel developed into something very similar to what we have today.

The English, bless their granite conservatism, resisted the new-fangled idea as long as possible. R.B. Thornhill, in *The Shooting Directory* (1804), said double barrels had been introduced from France "as a great many other foolish things have been." Thornhill disliked doubles because he thought the extra barrel was extra weight, because sometimes it went off accidentally and because it could be dangerously double-loaded.

DEVELOPMENT OF BREECHLOADING

In 1812, a French gunmaker experimented with a type of breechloading gun with drop-down barrels, and in 1829 another inventor patented a metal and paper cartridge with a percussion cap in the base, but the world wasn't yet ready for the modern shotgun. In fact, there was a great deal of resentment toward the idea of breechloaders. The muzzleloader had been around since the 1300s, and what was good enough for great-great-great-great-great-granddaddy was good enough for the modern gunner. And such gunmakers as Joseph Manton created such gorgeous guns that it probably was difficult to visualize a crude breechloader as anything but the handiwork of a maniac and a damn troublemaker to boot.

But breechloader advocates persisted. Casimir Lefaucheux exhibited a pinfire cartridge gun in 1851, and within months, another gunmaker, Joseph Lang, had refined it. Charles Lancaster developed a centerfire cartridge gun with an extractor in 1852 and, for all practical purposes, shotgunning was jerked into modern times.

Not without a lot of bitching, though. Traditionalists cried that the breechloaders were dangerous. They did leak gas at the breech and, owing to design problems, were heavier than their muzzleloading counterparts.

On the other hand, a muzzleloading shotgun always had been like playing chicken with a mortar. There always was the possibility that the barrel you just loaded would go off accidentally while you were loading the second barrel. No experienced muzzleloader hung his nose over the loaded barrel while he charged the other tube, but there still were quite a few early birdshooters with less than the normal tally of fingers on the ramrod hand.

Another swell trick was to double-load a barrel. If that happened, the best you could hope for was a shoulder that felt as if Mean Joe Greene just gave you a Dutch rub. The worst that could happen was that the gun would imitate a fragmentation grenade an inch or two in front of your eyes.

Much of the opposition to breechloaders was more apathy than anything. The more technically minded gunners claimed that breechloaders needed more repair work than muzzleloaders, didn't last as long, weren't as accurate, were heavier, cost more, recoiled more, made more noise, and tended to blow up. The shells had to be loaded, which was (a) a lot of trouble and (b) dangerous. Fixed shells were cumbersome to carry, as opposed to loose shot and a powder flask. Paper shells often separated on firing and had to be picked out of the breech, a time-consuming process. Metal shells weighed a bunch.

There were other considerations. The muzzleloader is equivalent to the streamside fly vise. The shooter can adjust his load to hunting conditions while the shotshell man is limited to whatever loads he is carrying.

Many of the objections had validity. But had there been no advantages to breechloaders, we'd still be ramming charges down the muzzles of our shotguns. Obviously, there are some.

One, probably the best argument of all, was the quickness of reloading. No question that breechloaders are much quicker. Aside from the danger of explosion or gas leakage around a loose seal between barrel and receiver, the breechloader was (and is) far safer—no double charge, no accidental explosions from residual fire smouldering in the recesses of the muzzle.

Relative ease is the best argument for adoption of nearly every gadget that comes down the pike. Sometimes the argument is valid and the gadget is valuable; sometimes we get expensive junk that cheapens the sport.

Occasionally I hunt with a gent who uses a muzzleloading shotgun, and I haven't had as much fun since I got impetigo on my lower lip a week before the junior-senior high-school prom. We all thoroughly enjoy waiting as the flushed quail soar into the jillikins to vanish forever while our blackpowder pard recharges his artillery. It's a little hard to be gruff with him, though, since he's my boss.

By the 1880s, the first successful repeating shotgun, the Winchester Lever Action Repeater in 10 and 12 gauge, was on the market. Then along came the Model 97 Winchester as the first truly successful slide-action shotgun. The Remington Browning autoloader became the leader of that final shotgun type about 1911.

CHOKES

The idea of choking a shotgun to tighten the pattern occurred to various gunmakers as early as the late 18th century. However, it took almost a century before advocates of choking managed to convince shooters it was worthwhile. As an innovation in gunmaking, it beat some more esoteric ones, including a cocking device that emitted a musical note.

A French writer in 1788 noted that some gunsmiths narrowed the barrel of their guns in the middle while others narrowed it gradually from breech to muzzle in order to tighten the shot pattern. Many American gunmakers used some system of boring the barrel so it was constricted or choked near the muzzle. Jeremiah Smith of Smithfield, Rhode Island, bored barrels this way as early as 1827.

In 1866, William Pape, a Newcastle, England, gunsmith, took out a provisional patent on a choking process. He didn't follow up on the idea, but two other English gunsmiths, W. Scott and E. C. Green, sent guns bored with choked barrels to a trial in New York in 1873. The guns were successful. Another trial in England two years later finally resolved most experts' doubts about the value of choking a barrel.

Fred Kimble, an Illinois marker shooter and Renaissance Man, tinkered with a number of guns and, in 1868, finally stumbled onto a method of choking a muzzleloader. He apparently corresponded with W. W. Greener, famed gunsmith, and there's some dispute over whether Greener or Pape patented the first choke system. Greener claimed he was the first in 1868.

There were others who experimented with chokes, both successfully and unsuccessfully, and it really doesn't matter who did what, just that it was done and finally accepted by about 1875.

Kimble claimed not to be a gunmaker, merely a home workshop experimenter, while Greener was in business to make and sell guns. Both were fascinating characters, especially Kimble, who not only was a famed market hunter but also a competitive shooter, ranking with Captain Bogardus and Doc Carver, the most famous names in shooting history. Kimble also was a figure skater, and a violinist, and invented both a clay target and a trap for throwing it.

The spread of chokes today in a 12-gauge shotgun is some .036 inch, from .729 inch in cylinder (no choke) to .693 at full choke.

BARRELS

The other major improvement in the gun itself was the introduction of fluid steel barrels to replace the twist method of barrel construction. Twist barrels were first made by winding iron strips, later alternating strips of iron and steel, around a mandrel, their twists running in opposite directions. These ribbons of metal were then welded together. The finish was browned, a process in which acid rusts the metal slightly, leaving a brown finish, rather than the blued finish of modern guns. Since the steel fibers were harder than the iron, they stood out, leaving a distinctive woven pattern on the metal. Twist and Damascus construction have come to be used as interchangeable descriptions, though Damascus steel was one ingredient, rather than the generic term.

Any shooter today who has a shotgun with a twist barrel, no matter how attractive, should think twice, both times negatively, about shooting it with *any* kind of load. Rust is an insidious weakener and those welds between the twist strips, no matter how tight at manufacture, can contain almost microscopic pores that have invited deterioration in over the life of the gun.

Gun experts used to warn of the danger of shooting twist barrel guns with modern powder, but most said it was safe to shoot a Damascus gun in good condition with black-powder loads, especially low-power field loads.

Listen to my friend, Mike McIntosh, author of *The Best Shotguns Ever Made in America* (Scribners 1981) and make up your own mind: "A Damascus barrel is full of tiny air pockets in the welds; moisture condenses in these and rust begins from the inside out, leaving them riddled with unseen weak spots. The welds, moreover, tend to crystallize with time and use, making any twist barrel a potential disaster. Now, they aren't completely safe, even with black powder, and a smokeless powder shell can blow them to kingdom come."

McIntosh adds, "The most common place for a twist barrel to rupture is ten or twelve inches in front of the chamber; this is about where the shot charge is when a modern shell develops its peak chamber pressure. It's also the place where your forward hand is holding the gun. Personally, I need all the fingers I have. I've got none to spare in a round of Damascus Roulette."

Is that clear enough? Don't shoot twist barrel guns. Look at them, treat them as art objects—but don't shoot them. The ancient Chinese used tubes of bamboo as barrels to direct the fire of their primitive powder. Now, you wouldn't shoot a Double X Magnum out of a cane fishing pole. So don't do the equivalent by firing a twist gun.

Fluid steel barrels, infinitely stronger, replaced twist barrels, and while you should think twice about banging out a bunch of magnum loads in a seventy-year-old fluid-steel-barreled gun, a good one can shoot field loads almost forever. My 1910 L.C. Smith Grade Three double is as shiny up the tubes as it was the day it came from the factory. No rust pits, dents or bulges. It actually has fewer nicks and scratches than my Charles Daly 12-gauge, bought new in the 1960s. Apparently the various owners of the Smith didn't hunt briar hells with it. It originally was built for a skeet shooter and, I suspect, spent some years of its life laying idle in a gun collection. Most old doubles have been used, but there are a lot of very fine ones around. They'll cost some money, but give back far more than their intrinsic value in esthetic dividends.

McIntosh's book is a good reference on what guns to buy and how to buy them. In a moment I'll talk about the various great American doubles and how much you might have to pay, but first let's look at the development of the other two components involved in shotgun shooting—shot and powder.

SHOTSHELLS

The first guns were shotguns. They were loaded with metal scrap and rocks, but they weren't designed for bird hunting; they were to kill men with (or, as was more often the case, scare the hell out of them).

Early shot was made by cutting pieces of sheet lead, then tumbling the pieces to round them. They probably were ballistic horrors and, coupled with slow-burning

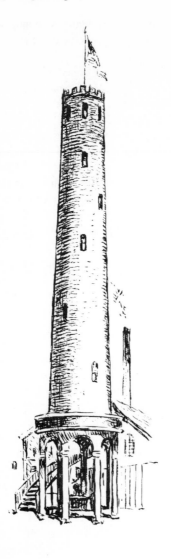

William Watts discovered the principle of dropped shot in 1769 and by the 1880s there were six shot towers in the United States, producing 5,000 tons of shot a year.

black powder and long, heavy guns, wingshooting must have been an incredible challenge, a luxury of the rich, considering that certainly there were far more misses than hits.

It wasn't until 1769 that William Watts, Bristol, England, discovered the principle of dropped shot. He dropped molten lead through a colanderlike sieve into cooling water and produced rounder, truer-shooting shot.

The diameter of the colander holes determines the size of the shot. Addition of a bit of arsenic to the lead encourages a rounder shot by increasing the surface tension of the molten metal. And addition of antimony makes the shot harder.

These shot tower workers are dropping molten lead through a colander-like device that sizes the drops. Gravity forms the falling pellets into round shape and a cooling tank at the bottom solidifies them.

Chilled shot actually is no colder than any other shot—it just has more antimony in it. BB-size shot is about the largest practical size for the drop method. Larger shot (certainly outside the upland gunner's needs, if not his interest) is made by a cold-forming operation called swaging.

Watts is alleged to have dreamed he was caught in a rainstorm of perfectly round shot (which damn sure *would* get your attention). It started him thinking about the problems of making the then-primitive dropped shot perfectly round. He began to experiment with dropping molten lead from progressively higher spots, seeking a height that would give the elusive perfect shot. He finally settled on a height of around 200 feet. The legend goes on to say that Watts sold his idea for 10,000 English pounds and then went out and had a classic high old time with the money. He faded from the shot picture, but the world had round shot. Though the process has been mechanized today, shot still is produced quite like it was in Watts' day.

Trap shooting proved to be a boon to the budding shotshell industry. Capt. Adam H. Bogardus, a legendary shooter who went from market hunting to international fame as an exhibition shooter, invented a trap that threw glass balls. It wasn't long before the idea of shooting flying targets caught on, to the extent that ammo manufacture became big business. Market hunting, done mostly with muzzleloaded shotguns, was fading, but the new sport certainly spurred shotshell production.

My home, Missouri, figured heavily in shotgun ammo, since it led the nation in lead production. The first shot tower west of the Mississippi River was built by John Macklot at Herculaneum in 1809. There were six shot towers in the country by 1883. Shot towers were just what their name implies—tall structures looking in some cases like smokestacks at the top of which molten lead is poured through sieves, then is cooled by falling into water.

The hardest shot is coppered by electroplating. It has two advantages: it doesn't foul the gun bore as much with lead and it doesn't deform as much, giving a better ballistic performance.

TRAP SHOOTING

Capt. Bogardus was born in 1834 and died in 1913. He won the U.S. live pigeon shooting championship in 1874, then went to England and beat the top guns there. A handsome man with a bushy mustache that looks as if someone threw a tiny schnauzer onto his face, he has the eye of a gyrfalcon.

Had he not invented the trap, someone else would have, but the invention was necessary, for there was increasing social pressure to ban live pigeon shooting. It was a time when militant anti-cruelty spinsters were belaboring burly teamsters with umbrellas for beating their dray horses.

So, shooting at clay or glass targets replaced live birds. Some of the lexicon, however, stuck with the tamed version of pigeon shooting. Ever since I was old enough to soak up shotgun lore, I've heard grizzled old Missouri gunners talk about shooting blue rocks when they referred to trap. Probably they meant the Blue Rock brand of clay targets, rather than the blue rock pigeon. (Blue Rocks and White Flyers are the best-known makes of clay birds.) Early clay-bird shooters called their targets muds, clay pigeons, asphalts, flying discs, river bottoms, baked birds, traps or blackbirds. Clay ''pigeons'' is a hangover from the old days, and the name ''trap'' shooting came from the boxlike wooden traps that, when tripped, fell apart with a clatter, frighting the pigeon inside into quick flight.

Pigeon shooting goes back to the 1850s in England. One famed pub was named the Old Hats because the pigeons used for the matches were put in holes in the ground under old hats. Blue rock pigeons came from the English chalk cliffs and flew about forty-five miles per hour. Frank Butler, Annie Oakley's husband, himself a fine shot, said the English blue rock doves beat anything on the American pigeon-shooting circuit for speed and elusiveness. Butler raved about the London Gun Club's elaborate grounds, which included a polo field, lawn tennis courts and other game fields. He also paid homage to the light, well-balanced English guns necessary to track the quick birds. ''Many remember the boast of Mr. Dougall, of London, in which he said, 'Ten English shots using 12-bore guns could beat ten Americans of equal skill using 10-bore guns,' '' Butler said. ''Of course, the Americans, I as well as the rest, laughed at the idea of such a thing being possible. But since I came here, I am inclined to think he was nearer right than we gave him credit for being.''

Originally, pigeons were released inside a half-circle with a radius of some twenty-five to thirty meters. The goal was to drop the birds inside that boundary. Pigeon shooting still is legal in many states, but is not advertised for fear of offending bird lovers. Competitive pigeon shooting today works like this: The shooter puts his pigeon chip, a coin-shaped device, in an automatic selector that chooses one of five traps to release a bird. The traps are small metal boxes in a row, a few yards apart. You stand on the firing line, tell the pull boy you're ready. He holds a sensitive microphone under your arm and at the first sound from you, the trap collapses and the bird flushes. You must shoot the bird, within two shots, so it falls dead within a fence 17½ yards away. Any bird, even a dead one, that falls outside the fence is counted lost.

The Swiss led the fight to ban live pigeon shooting and in 1912 prohibited it. England followed suit in 1921, fining a violator twenty-five pounds and sentencing him to three months in prison, perhaps at hard labor.

The first targets in the states were passenger pigeons. The first recorded U.S. pigeon match was held in 1831 at the Cincinnati Sportsmen's Club. Cost of the birds was from $1.20 to $2.40 a dozen. During the 1870s there were from 12,000 to 20,000 birds being held in coops in St. Louis and Cincinnati at all times for upcoming shooting matches.

Captain Bogardus could hit eighty-seven of one hundred live birds—not a great run on clay birds, but the best around on live ones. Lesser shooters hit three of four birds.

Sometimes shooters would bribe the trap boys to squeeze a bird to crush the rib cage and slow the bird up or, to make it tougher for opponents, pluck a few tail feathers to make the bird fly erratically.

Most passenger pigeons were gone by 1882. As the wild birds declined, the cost of trap-shooting rose. Tame pigeons were costly to raise and also were slow. Blackbirds were too easy to hit, purple martins too hard. Starlings, not yet present in the hordes of today, were too hard to trap in sufficient numbers. Bats were favored targets for a while. But the glass ball trap began to gain favor in 1870 and the Bogardus trap came along in 1877 and became the standard.

There were many trap ideas, including a reusable paper-ball target filled with powder that puffed when the ball was hit. It was good for about ten hits. Glass was a problem because of the debris it created. Ira Paine invented feather-filled balls to give the shooter the illusion of having hit a bird, but they cost $18 a thousand in 1878, compared to $5 a thousand for glass balls.

There also were exploding targets—in 1880, Woeber and Varwig, Cincinnati, offered a clay ball at $15 a thousand which exploded with a flash and a gust of smoke when hit, even with a single pellet.

The first clay bird came along in 1880. George Ligowsky, Cincinnati, patented the familiar domed saucer shape in that year. He said he got the idea from watching boys skipping clamshells on the water. At least he didn't have any dreams of being in a deluge of perfectly round clay targets.

So, trap and skeet using clay birds came into its own. Both can help a bird shooter develop certain skills, though I'm yet to be convinced that non-live target shooting in any way can capture the conditions and emotions of hunting. I know fine trap shooters who come completely unglued when something with feathers erupts before their gun.

GUNPOWDER

It doesn't much matter whether the Chinese discovered gunpowder or not; everyone thinks so and there are no antique Chinese around today to testify. About the earliest record of gunpowder being used in a belligerent way was at the seige of Constantinople in 668. While it may not have been black powder, it apparently made noise and fire.

But it took the monks, men of God, to foster something that could kill and maim their fellow man. Roger Bacon reported on gunpowder before he died in 1292. Berthold Schwartz, another monk, of Friburg, Germany, read Bacon and, in turn, described the explosive, thus introducing it to central Europe. For more than 600 years, black powder was the universal propellant used in guns. It's a mixture of saltpeter, charcoal and sulphur. Bat caves always have been a good source of saltpeter, which is extracted from the guano.

Early powder really was a pisser—literally. The mixture of charcoal, saltpeter and sulphur was combined while moistened. According to Robert Held's *Age of Firearms* (Cassell, 1959), human urine, preferably that of a wine drinker, was the preferred liquid.

Black powder is fairly irritable stuff, and early gunners, especially in the days of matchlocks, were not exactly low insurance risks. They ran about as much risk of serious injury from fooling with their own gun as being shot by someone else's.

The matchlock gunner carried coils of impregnated cord which glowed and sputtered like punk. Sparks often fell off the "match" or cord, and if one happened to land in the gunner's powder cache, it was so long back pocket, all the way to the bone. Shooting a matchlock in a rainstorm was by far the safest way to use the weapon. The rain usually put the match out and the gun then became a fairly good club.

The list of things that could go wrong with any muzzleloader from the matchlock through the caplock was enough to keep gunning a sport for the brave (or foolhardy). You could overcharge the barrel, which at best would purple your shoulder, at worst blow the gun up in your face. Or you could forget to half-cock the gun and shoot yourself while loading. Or you could forget to remove the ramrod and shoot it into splinters. Or you could forget to prime the pan and hear the disheartening "click" of a misfire as a charging enemy started a looping saber swing.

Another interesting little accident happened when the spring on the powder flask grew weak so that it didn't fully seal off the measured charge in the neck from the stored powder in the body of the flask. If a spark remained in the gun when the shooter recharged it, the new charge would ignite and, along with it, the flask would go off like a bomb. Not fun.

As I mentioned before, my boss, Jim Keefe, is a flintlock fan. He also has been hunting turkeys for twenty years without connecting, a record that he is not proud of. Twice in that time he has had a nice gobbler dead to rights only to have his flintlock let him down. Once his powder was damp and didn't ignite. The other time, he rolled over to shoot and spilled the pan powder.

Pioneer shooters had no local sporting-goods store where they could buy powder, no mail-order house from which to order the stuff. When they ran short, they either took a trip to the nearest powder mill or, if the materials were at hand, made their own.

Saltpeter is a naturally-occurring substance, but no one knows exactly how it's formed. It occurs in the earth of caves with alkaline soils, good air circulation, a temperature between 52 and 60 degrees and a humidity between 10 and 30 percent.

Saltpeter must be leached to extract the nitrate for mixture with sulphur and charcoal. The process often was done at the cave site, then the nitrate was taken to the munitions factory for processing.

Sulphur, the second of black powder's three major ingredients, is widely available. A bit taken internally is a fair mosquito repellant, but causes yellow sweat, which in turn is less than socially acceptable on the armpit area of a white T-shirt. Smouldering sulphur also will drive out unwanted bee colonies. I remember as a child my father trying to smoke some bees out of a wallspace in our home. Through some miscalculation, about as much smoke backed into the house as went into the walls and we found that humans also can be driven outside.

A mixture of sulphur and honey supposedly cures boils.

Light, soft woods such as willow are charcoaled to furnish the third major ingredient of black powder. The proportions are roughly 75 percent saltpeter, 15 percent charcoal and 10 percent sulphur. The three elements are ''incorporated'' or fused by several hours of grinding and the friction created by the grinding wheels fairly often led to explosions. Working in a black powder factory was not exactly a low-risk occupation.

There are several other procedures, including pressing the powder into cakes, then separating it into granules, polishing it by tumbling, finally baking it to free it of moisture. Any of these operations invited some neat fireworks.

If you're interested in making a little black powder at home (and also probably drawing the attention of several aggressive federal agencies) you can find adequate directions in *Foxfire Five* (Anchor Press, 1979). Make sure your insurance is both extensive and paid up.

It remained for nitro-cellulose gunpowder to end the era of black powder, an era that lasted at least 600 years. Now, black powder is confined to use by the many muzzleloading weapon enthusiasts.

Within a very short time after the final touches on the modern shotgun, about 1875, there were shotshell loaders similar to those of today that the home loader could use. The shotshell industry went through the same trauma that everything else did—the trial-and-error search for a good case, loading tools, a reliable primer. Metal and paper quickly emerged as the two materials best suited for cases, but it took a while to find the right combination of materials.

After its early history of being behind the rest of the world in adopting wing-shooting, the English stepped to the front as the innovators and refiners of shotguns and shotgun equipment. They developed primers for use with smokeless powder and by the mid-1880s, the era of black powder was nearly over. By the end of the 1800s, there were about 2,000 different factory shotgun loads available.

Home loading declined after that and didn't revive until the middle of the 20th century when trap and skeet shooters found it was far less expensive to load their own.

So we've come a long way from Hercules wingshooting science-fiction birds to the dawn of the modern shotgun, and it's time to take a look at the finest of the upland bird guns.

3

Upland Guns and Loads

When it comes to upland guns, I'll freely admit I'm prejudiced. The double-barrel is the only gun that deserves to be carted into the bird fields. There have been ultra-scientific studies showing third shots almost always are a waste of ammunition and even second shots frequently are ballistic cusswords, loud noises made by the frustrated gunner to make himself feel better for having missed the first shot. But I would not care if the studies showed that I could bulk my game bag by a third if I added a shell to my potential firepower. I'd still shoot a double.

A double-barrel generally is more carefully made than a pump or an automatic and far more esthetically pleasing, as well as lighter to carry and more reliable mechanically. The only repeating shotguns to deserve house room with the fine doubles are the Winchester Model 12 and the M31 Remington. The Model 12 is just about the most perfect shotgun ever made. Its track record does nothing to betray its lovely reputation. Model 12s have been used to stop everything from 9-ounce quail to 190-pound Jerries.

And, while I do prefer two shots for upland birds, if a line of Kaiser Bill's finest were advancing on my Argonne Forest trench with bayonets fixed, I'd prefer a fully-charged Model 12 to any double ever made. Its seven shots made it the most perfect ground swatter available in World War I. The thing was a short jump behind a machinegun and far more portable. Even today, sawed-off Model 12s adorn the inside of many a riot squad car.

My hunting pard, Foster Sadler, used to have a full-choke 20-gauge Model 12 which was a far cry from the ideal quail gun. But it's the gun he was handed when he started hunting, and kids, mostly being beggars, can't be choosers. So he became a fine quail shot. If he weren't dead-on the bird, he'd miss with its tight choke, and if he didn't take his time on his shot and let the bird get a little range, he'd shred it so thoroughly that what was left wouldn't be fit for the barnyard cat.

Foster's lovely old gun got burned up in a fire that cost him his wardrobe, photos, virtually everything he owned. But it was the gun he cried over.

Barring fires, the Model 12 is as ageless as the Pyramids. You can't really abuse one. It's stronger than you are. It is second cousin to a Missouri mule—you have to clout it twixt the eyes with a two-by to get its attention.

So, that's my only exception to the dictum that there is no upland gun save the double. I have an Ithaca Model 37 pump in 20 gauge that would serve as a quail gun (and a good one) if I could not take my Smith or my Daly. I'd use it. But I wouldn't feel good about it. A Pinto and a Mercedes both get you where you want to go. Which would you rather drive?

I learned to shoot with a Stevens single-shot that had been sawed off not far above the minimum legal length. It was not my choice of gun, but, like Foster's Model 12, it was the only one available. It taught me to flinch. It was a harsh master, for if the howitzer recoil didn't put a strawberry on my upper arm the size of Rhode Island, the locking lever deftly removed the webbing from between my thumb and forefinger.

I shed both blood and tears over that rotten old gun, and it's a tribute to my passion for tromping the fields of autumn that I continued to hunt, even though the result of each shot was like taking a left jab to the shoulder by Muhammud Ali. Only rarely did I tumble a quail and then only when one flushed suddenly and caught me by surprise and I fired instinctively. No one taught me to shoot properly, and so I learned gunning the same way I learned to play the guitar: by myself, half-assed, without instinctive talent, and the hard way.

Shooting is something that can be improved with practice, but there are those who were born to shoot, just as there were those who were born able to master operatic singing or understand tax laws. You can acquire a certain shooting proficiency without much talent just by practicing a good deal. But if you have that raw capability, you will shoot well without much practice, superbly with some.

Shooting styles have changed greatly over the years. The old upright style (which called for stocks with considerable drop) has given way to a tucked position, head down over the gun barrel, leaning into the shot. So today's guns have a much straighter stock, with little drop.

Upland gunners fall into two categories—quick guns and deliberate ones. The quick gunner, an instinctive shooter, can't tell you how much lead he took on a bird, shoots the instant the gun hits his cheek.

I'm a quick gun for two reasons: first, I grew up around grizzled old bird hunters who had a petulant rivulet of amber coursing down their stubbly chins, whose guns were silver-slick with use, and whose dogs were as bony as junkyard starvelings, but also as tough as whang leather. If you waited to take a deliberate shot on a covey rise with these leggy hillmen, there was nothing left to shoot. They all shot automatics and only rarely did three birds not rain down from a covey rise. They were exceptions to the dicta that a third shot almost always is wasted and that a second shot often is one too many.

The second reason I shoot quickly is that if I have to think about a shot, I might as well unload the gun, take the shell and throw it at the bird. An incoming duck or dove, seen at a distance, is almost as safe with me as a babe in its mother's arms. I begin to plot lead, to decide whether to shoot wide-eyed or squinch one eye. Chaotic thoughts pour through my head with the confusion of Chinese acrobats performing after a hot wine drunk. I wind up creating great noise and misdirection, like a political candidate asked to explain in detail his campaign financing.

Chances are, someone who cut his teeth either on waterfowl hunting or on a trap range will be a deliberate shooter, waiting till his birds get out thirty yards or so. I'd say thirty yards is almost too far for efficient upland bird shooting, even in uncluttered conditions. With field loads and a fairly open choke, a good birdshooter can kill his birds at twenty yards with few misses and few tattered birds.

George Markland, whose *The Art Of Shooting Flying,* published in 1727, was the first great treatise on wingshooting, had a bit of doggerel to explain his philosophy:

> Full forty Yards permit the Bird to go,
> The spreading Gun will surer Mischief sow;
> But when too near the flying Object is,
> You certainly will mangle it or miss.

However, the hunter who waits for his targets to get well out so he won't tear them up so badly may be doing both himself and the bird a disservice. The Missouri Conservation Department and the U.S. Fish and Wildlife Service conducted a waterfowl shooting study at Missouri's Schell-Osage Wildlife Area in 1979. Not pertinent to this discussion was the major thrust of the study—to determine crippling rates of lead and steel shot. But precisely to the point was the killing rate on ducks at different ranges. Under thirty yards, you can shoot rosary beads at ducks and kill them. The killing rate, regardless of shot type or load, drops off appreciably between thirty and forty yards. You'll kill not quite ten birds per hundred shots at more than forty yards (less than half what you kill under thirty yards).

The study involved 1,300 hunters who essentially came in off the streets—they were the day's randomly drawn hunters for each day of the season. They volunteered to shoot the 12-gauge test loads and no one, including area personnel, knew what load or shot was being fired. The hunters fired 11,000 shots, an extensive test by hunters ranging in skill from poor to superior.

So, I'd say fifteen to thirty yards is optimum killing range for shooting at any upland game bird. I suspect most woodcock and grouse are shot toward the lower end of that range. Likewise, brushland quail usually don't give you much time to shoot. Doves and prairie grouse may allow, sometimes even demand, long shots. Pheasants give you every damn shot in the book, bless their horny hides.

Obviously, if you center any of the birds at ten yards, even with a light load, what you'll pick up is an unattractive version of what used to go on a shingle in Army field kitchens. I've heard shooters brag about tipping birds with the edge of the pattern so as not to chew them up, and I suppose there are a lot of shooters good enough to do that. But I'm not one of them.

By the time the average shooter can react to a flushing bird, get the gun properly mounted, zero in on the bird, chances are it's beyond ten yards. If it isn't, then the shooter has the luxury of waiting that half-second until it does get on out a ways.

Most upland hunters shooting doubles go for an improved cylinder-modified combination. I know poor shots who buy skeet bored guns and shoot No. 9 shot at anything where that's appropriate, hoping that the more shot they shoot, the less their poor shooting will count against them. Maybe it works, but they never seem to shoot appreciably better. A single-barrel upland gun probably should be improved cylinder.

I think far more important than fooling around with different guns is to find one you feel comfortable with, then practice with it until you're as proficient as you're going to get. Have a professional stockmaker fit the gun to your shooting habits, good or bad, or else have a good shooter coach you into good habits—but find Your Gun and stick with it. Just as you wouldn't eternally buy and sell bird dogs, hoping for the once-in-a-lifetime animal, neither should you do the same with a gun. You have to learn to love your dog and your gun, to trust them, to adjust them to you and you to them.

LOADS FOR UPLAND BIRDS

You can effectively modify a full-choke gun for upland bird hunting without having to saw off the barrel or hang a multi-choke device on the muzzle. Shoot so-called "scatter" loads. The shot is divided into segments by spacers. The effect is to gain a pattern more like a modified or improved cylinder choke, rather than a full choke. Winchester calls them "Brush" loads and sells them only in 12 gauge. Remington termed them "Spreader" loads, while Federal had a "Scatter" load; however, all but Winchester have dropped the idea.

But it's possible to handload scatter loads. The idea is to force the shot string to flare as it leaves the gun. Don Zutz, well-known gun writer, is the guru of the home-loaded spreader load. He summed up the state of the art in a 1978 piece for *Handloader Magazine,* Box 30–30, Prescott, AZ 86302.

Winchester's factory load uses an "X" wad which separates the shot into four longitudinal segments. Zutz feels this weakens the center of the pattern—leaves a "blown" hole there. His loads use regular cardboard discs and, by dividing the shot into three or four segments (depending on the number of divider discs used), he controls how widely the pattern is dispersed—the more discs, the more spread.

Zutz used two loads. One was a Winchester AA case, Winchester 209 primer, 25 grains of WW 473AA powder, a trimmed RP-12 wad, 1¹/₈ ounces RXP No. 7½ shot. The second load involved a Remington RXP case, Remington 97 primer, 23 grains Unique powder, a trimmed RP-12 wad, 1¹/₈ ounces RXP No. 7½ shot.

Zutz cut his divider discs from 16-gauge nitro cards, feeling that the smaller diameter reduces friction through the choke constriction.

Zutz's spreader loads, depending on the number of dividers, spread a sixteen-inch pattern (at twenty-one yards) to nearly thirty inches. Two discs, which divided the shot column into three segments, would give a spread of twenty-two or twenty-three inches, with good shot distribution.

"What all this means, of course," Zutz wrote, "is that a hunter can manipulate pattern diameter by using specially developed scatter loads in his tight-shooting guns. For close-breaking game, he can chamber a four-layer reload and follow that with a two-layer or three-layer round to compensate for the gradually increased range."

What shot size for what game is one of those endless arguments that never will be solved. Personally, I shoot No. 8 shot at small birds, No. 6 at bigger birds, No. 4 at the biggest birds. I buy field loads with more regard to price; usually opt for the best ammo when it comes to turkeys. How much I spend on pheasant or grouse shot depends on how flush I am when I buy it. I've never loaded my own shells, nor do I intend to.

But if you're in need of a shot guide, try this one: No. 8 or 9 for snipe, quail, rail and woodcock; No. 7, 7½ or 8 for doves and pigeons; No. 5, 6 or 7 for chukar, grouses, Hungarian partridge, sage hen; No. 1, 2 or BB for turkey. That's not my guide—it's one I read. There is no substitute for Winchester's Super X Double X Magnum No. 4 in 12 gauge for turkeys. It's the hardest-shooting shell I know and you should use such a shell to give yourself the best chance of a clean kill.

Figure that 90 percent of the shot you shoot never hits anything. In an old *American Rifleman* article, Bert Popowski, who is especially noted for crowshooting expertise, recommends smaller shot sizes for most game than you usually see recommended.

Popowski's argument is that the total foot-pound of energy hitting a flying bird creates a shock that proves fatal. Impact energy in excess of sixteen foot-pounds will reliably drop duck-size birds. A table worked out by Popowski for various shot sizes at two different muzzle velocities (1330 feet per second and 1200 fps) gives some relative requirements for a killing hit from different shot sizes.

For example, given a rising pheasant, if you shoot a No. 8 field load at a bird twenty yards off, it'll take about ten pellets to drop the bird—ten shot from a load of 410 in a one-ounce load. If you're shooting No. 6 shot, it takes about five hits of a load of 225 pellets.

The point is that the heavier shot does not necessarily result in an easier kill. It is the *total* hit, not the individual shot, that brings the bird down (unless, of course, you hit the bird in the brain, in which case one No. 9 or smaller shot is enough on any bird).

Popowski further develops the theory that shocking power is exponential; that is, if one shot has a certain shocking capability, two shot do not have twice the shock but four times, three hits have nine times and so on.

The idea is worth trying. Popowski regularly used No. 9 shot on crows, including on long-range shots, and had better success than hunters using larger shot. He also heard from a man who'd shot No. 10 shot at crows with what he reported as sensational success.

So, it's worth trying smaller shot (not lighter loads) than you would normally shoot at upland birds, just to see how it affects your shooting. I consider myself an average gunner. I have days when I can't miss and other days when I couldn't hit the ground if I dropped my shotgun. So I never could be sure if my success on a limited test of smaller shot was being affected by the shot itself or one of my erratic and inexplicable shooting blackouts.

PATTERNING YOUR SHOTGUN

If you're interested in patterning your shotgun, there is a standard method of doing it. For all gauges except .410, the range is forty yards. It's twenty-five yards for the .410. Count the shot in five shells of the lot you're testing (or count the shot in five handloads) so you'll have an average of the number of shot in a given cartridge.

Put up large sheets of paper (at least forty inches square) at the required range, with an aiming mark in the center of the paper and fire at it the same way you fire at birds. Draw a thirty-inch-diameter circle around the thickest part of the pattern, then count the holes, marking each so you'll know which ones you've counted.

Multiply the total by 100 and divide by the average number of the shot in your five test shells. That will give you the pattern percentage. Fire at least ten patterns to eliminate any variability on a given round. A bird hunter, often shooting rising targets, would like a pattern slightly thicker above the center of the pattern so the bird will be flying into the heaviest part of the charge. Look also for holes in the pattern, the famed "blown" pattern.

The ideal is to get 70 to 80 percent pattern with full choke; 45 to 65 percent with modified; 35 to 45 percent with improved cylinder and 25 to 35 percent with cylinder bore.

At that same forty-yard range, the shot spread will range from forty inches with a full-choke gun to fifty-seven inches with cylinder. Most upland birds probably are shot at about twenty-five yards and, at that range, cylinder-bore patterns cover thirty-eight inches and full choke twenty inches—a mighty small spread. As a point of interest, the gunner who centers a bird at ten yards with a full-choke gun will put just about every one of those 300 or so pellets through the bird, meaning that the result will be something that looks as if it just spent thirty minutes in a Cuisinart.

The National Rifle Association's patterning method is complex and probably beyond the range of anyone other than a born tinkerer or someone with access both to a good gun-club range and to help from someone who is familiar with the method.

If all you are interested in is finding out where your gun patterns and how effectively, you can use a patterning plate, a steel sheet, coated with a nondrying paint (a mixture of zinc white in lard oil or ground white lead in linseed oil) that can be brushed between shots to cover strike marks. The plate can be any size, but should be large enough to contain the traditional 30-inch patterning circle, if you were to draw one.

Mark an aiming point at the center of the sheet. Test whatever load at whatever range is of interest. The patterning plate will give you an idea of pattern density at different ranges, of the center of impact in relation to the aiming point. Probably the biggest benefit to a quick patterning test on a patterning sheet is to tell you, once and for all, if it's you . . . or if it's the gun.

The more complex NRA patterning method is tricky and involved. You must count the pellets in at least five shells of whatever load you're testing to get an average number of pellets (since they vary somewhat from shell to shell). Be prepared to fire at least ten shots—the more, the more accurate the results.

Shotguns normally are patterned at forty yards. Skeet chokes and .410 guns are patterned at twenty-five yards.

Essentially, you fire each shot at a three-inch black square aiming point. Apply a clear-plastic circle template with a thirty-inch outer diameter and the center cut out to give a twenty-inch inner circle. Get the greatest possible number of pellet holes within the inner circle, then draw a twenty-inch and a thirty-inch circle with a pencil. Quarter the circles with two straight lines through the center. You'll find that the aiming point probably is offset—rarely, if ever, would the center of the circles coincide with the aiming point.

Now you can count pellet holes within eight fields or segments. You'll have a very accurate average of the number of pellets striking each segment. You'll know just where the pattern center is relative to the point of hold. You'll know what percentage of the total load strikes the pattern, how uniform the pattern is and how well each segment of the circle is covered.

				Pellets Per Load				
Weight (Oz)				**Shot Size**				
	#2	*#4*	*#5*	*#6*	*#7* ½	*#8*	*#8* ½	*#9*
½	45	67	85	112	175	205	242	292
¾	67	101	127	168	262	308	363	439
⅞	79	118	149	197	306	359	425	512
1	90	135	170	225	350	410	485	585
1⅛	101	152	191	253	393	461	545	658
1¼	112	169	213	281	437	513	605	731
1⅜	124	186	234	309	481	564	665	804
1½	135	202	255	337	525	615	730	877
1⅝	146	220	276	366	569	666	790	951
1⅞	169	253	319	422	656	769	850	1097
2	180	270	340	450	700	820	910	1170

The number of pellets is only approximate. It varies slightly with the shot's hardness and greatly from normal industry tolerances. Actual pellet count may vary as much as 10 or 11 per cent in spread and 3 to 6 per cent from the numbers listed above either plus or minus. *Source: National Rifle Association.*

The important difference between the NRA method and the traditional method of drawing a circle and shooting at it is that the circle isn't drawn until *after* you shoot. With a pre-drawn circle, there's no reference point to tell what your pattern looks like relative to what you shot at.

CHOOSING A SHOTGUN

Choice of a shotgun is an individual matter and far be it from me to impose my will on you (unless, of course, I get into the business of selling shotguns). I once knew a guy who was happy as a clam with a sawed-off Stevens single-shot 12 gauge, composed almost equally of rust and friction tape.

There are a lot of nice doubles floating around today, most of them over-and-under, but virtually all are foreign-made. The only American-made side-by-side doubles at this writing are the Stevens-Savage-Fox models and the Winchester Model 21 (which, unless you habitually drink wine from corked bottles, drive a German car that isn't a Volkswagen and have E.F. Hutton listen to *you,* you can't afford anyway). The Remington 3200 is the only American-made over-and-under.

The Winchester 101, the Brownings, Ithaca, most other well-known doubles, are Japanese-made. I wouldn't begin to endorse or condemn modern doubles. When you come right down to it, shotguns function pretty much the same, whether they're $1.98 clunkers or $10,000 gold-inlaid gems. Sort through enough cheap guns and you probably will find one that will pattern as nicely as a Purdey. Remember the swamp rat with the single-shot Stevens. The dog won't last as long, certainly won't be as pretty—but it'll do the job.

So, the only reason for carrying a classic to the field is that it means something more than straight shooting or fine-line checkering. The old doubles carry with them the dignity of their years, the veneration due something that has proven itself, reputation untarnished. These guns have not run to fat with age, nor have historians revealed youthful indiscretions that blacken their silvery history. They are of a time when even a production gun was somebody's baby, when you expected and got an honest day's work out of a factory worker.

Handwork and craftsmanship come so dearly today that no one can afford it. You couldn't afford to buy the classic doubles today, any more than society could afford to build the classic buildings that grace our cities. Quality has become too expensive. Rising prices (far beyond mere inflation) forced the doubles out of business, and there is no realistic chance that their time will come again.

I have a brand-new car, off an American assembly line, and the damned doors don't fit. They aren't sprung; there is no reason for them to hang the way they do— but they don't fit. They sound as if they're going to fall off when you close them. That's craftsmanship, 1980 style. What it implies to me is a lack of pride in the finished product. My L.C. Smith closes like a vault. It is fitted with jeweler's precision and the cheapest Smith of its vintage still would have had the same attention to quality and, assuming reasonable care over the years, would shoot as well today as it did when it left the factory.

My source for information on the classic doubles is Mike McIntosh, who loves these fine old guns with undimmed passion. Mike has owned them all at one time or another, trading them, shooting them, working on their innards, slowly assimilating as much and probably more information about them as any gun writer who's ever lived. His book, *The Best Shotguns Ever Made In America* (Scribner's, 1981), is the definitive book on the fine American doubles and I've stolen liberally from it and from Mike's extensive knowledge and opinions during long rambles through quail fields, endless nights on the road to this woodcock covert or that elusive partridge woods, interminable hours shivering in the gravelike chill of a goose pit.

Of course, there are many guns far more expensive to own than the ones I'm going to mention. But are they field guns? I think not. Only the very rich, the very perverse or the very stupid would take a fine English gun to the field these days. Every briar scratch is a $200 chip off the price tag. The gun newly bought for $5,000 is, to a collector, designed to remain the way he bought it. Put one round through it and you've shot its mint condition as well as the gun.

While the finest of the old doubles are too precious to get heavy field use (or use in vicious conditions), most of them still are what they were when they were made—guns to be shot. My Smith has nice engraving, a lovely stock. But it has been used and shows it. If I take good care of it, it should not get any worse; its value certainly will rise, and it will pleasure me, I hope, for many years. I will have my cake and will have eaten it, too.

I'd like to review briefly Mike's choice of the best American doubles, but if you want more information, far more than I could cram into these pages, see his book. It's the best.

There are two obvious types of double gun, two less obvious types of locks for them. There are over-and-under guns, and there are side-by-side guns. Some shooters, trained on single-barreled guns, like the over-under for that reason; others feel they shoot better with a side-by, sighting down the ramp between the barrels.

The two types of locks are box and side. Sidelocks are stronger in the frame, the metal part of the gun, but box locks permit a stronger stock. Shoot an old sidelock with modern high-power shell and you risk cracking the stock somewhere around the grip. I've shot my sidelock Smith often with high-powered shells and with no ill effects, but as it increases in value, my desire to risk it goes down and I stick pretty much with light field loads and use another gun for game that takes hotter shells.

Of the classic American doubles, only the Smith uses the sidelock; Fox, Ithaca, Parker, Lefever, Winchester and Remington all use boxlocks. However, most of the fine English guns—Boss, Purdey, Holland, and Westley Richards, for example—use sidelocks. Sidelocks have the advantage that they are detachable from the frame, so are easily cleaned or worked on. But the Westley Richards boxlock is even easier—there is a hinged lid that opens to reveal the two locks which can be pinched out with thumb and forefinger. Like a modern modular piece of electronic gear, the entire assembly can be replaced as simply as sliding it into the spot vacated by the defective one.

But few American bird hunters own fine English doubles and fewer still hunt with them—they have become art objects and shooting them is like doing touchup work yourself on your Rembrandts. Most of the classic English doubles are in bank vaults or home vaults secure enough to repel anything up to a medium-yield nuclear device, so talking about them as hunting guns is indulging in fantasy.

While the classic American doubles are also as gilt-edged an investment as you can make, they still retain their utilitarian role. People use them—almost every bird hunter I know has one and some have several. One of my friends, for example, has a Remington Model 32, two Ithacas, a Smith Grade Two and a Fox. Most are field guns, since they were bought by ordinary hunters for ordinary hunting. My Smith, a Grade Three, which is about the upper middle of the possible grades, started out as a skeet gun.

Those with shootable Parkers or Smiths or Foxes shoot them. The only exceptions would be the high-grade American guns, too elaborate to risk in the field. But there are far more of the field- and medium-grade guns than there are of Pigeon, Crown or whatever designation went to the king of the line.

The nice thing about the field-grade doubles from the classic era is that they were virtually as well-made as the top-of-the-line gun. It was a day of pride in craftsmanship and the field-grade gun worked as smoothly as the pigeon-grade one. It may have lacked the fine engraving, the rich burl walnut stock—but it shot as effectively and worked as smoothly. However, the pitfall is that the field-grade gun, because of its low initial cost, its common appearance, probably didn't get the care its uptown cousin did. So you run more risk of finding a gun with dings in the barrel, with a loose action, broken parts, cracked stock or any of the other ills that plague a mistreated gun. Before you buy an old gun, there are several ground rules for minimizing your risk.

1. Discard any gun with Damascus or other twist barrels. They are unsafe to shoot.
2. Check the tightness of the action. The top latch gradually moves toward the left as the action wears. The more offset to the right of center it is, the less wear on the locking system. Never slam a double shut—hold the top latch to the unlock position, ease the gun closed, ease the latch to lock.
3. Make sure it's chambered for 2¾-inch shells.
4. The ideal upland gun has barrels close to 26 or 28 inches. Don't buy one with 32-inch barrels, unless you're looking for a trap or goose gun.
5. Pattern the gun (assuming it's safe to shoot) so you know it shoots where you point it and throws a good pattern.

6. Using snap caps, check the safety and triggers. With the safety on, squeeze the triggers. Gently. Then, not touching the triggers, slide the safety off. The hammers should not fall. Snap each trigger (or hammer, if it's a single-trigger gun) to check for the crispness of the pull (or, if the pull is too light, for a worn sear).

7. Write up a contract or bill of sale and ask for any documentation about the gun—original bill of sale, any other information that's available. Agree in writing that you can return the gun if a serious defect shows up that existed unnoticed when you bought the gun.

8. If you're in doubt at any point, take the gun to a reputable (and knowledgeable) gunsmith and have it checked.

9. If it's one of the real collector's items, don't forget to insure it and beware of making any alterations that will destroy its value.

L.C. Smith

Let's start with my gun, the old L.C. Smith. I have to admit that I was ignorant enough about doubles that when I breathlessly held my newly bought, multibuck Smith to the light and found the barrels stamped "Hunter Arms," I thought I'd been taken.

But all was well. Of all the people connected with the L.C. Smith shotgun, L.C. Smith was the least influential. He gave his name and some money to the sleek, graceful gun that, in my mind, is the most artistic of all the fine American doubles.

William H. Baker founded what would become the Smith Company shortly before Smith bought out two of Baker's partners in 1877 and took controlling interest in the new firm. Baker guns became Smith guns, marked "L.C. Smith and Co., makers of the Baker Gun." They became simply L.C. Smiths in 1883. Baker jumped the Smith ship in 1880, leaving behind a gun rapidly becoming obsolete. It had external hammers, for one thing.

But Alexander T. Brown, who had joined the company in 1878, designed the classic Smith double, which included a patented sidelock (only true sidelock among the great American doubles), internal hammers and a unique cocking and bolting mechanism.

Brown went on to a mechanical career quite apart from guns. He and Smith turned over L.C. Smith Guns to the Hunter brothers in 1889, and Brown invented the first typewriter that could handle both upper and lower case letters (something that I often have a great deal of difficulty with). We know the machine today as the Smith-Corona typewriter and the company as Smith-Corona-Marchant, a leader in business machines.

It made little matter that Brown left—he had worked his magic on the Smith and very little new ever was added to it, right up to 1950 when L.C. Smith doubles joined the gleaming specters of the other great doubles.

The L.C. Smith double is the only true sidelock among the classic double barrels (the others are boxlock). Even this field grade Smith has the slim, elegant lines that characterize all Smiths.

Contrast three of the modern production guns with the old Smith at the bottom. At the top is the Remington 870, next the Winchester Super X and third the over-under Ithaca SKB.

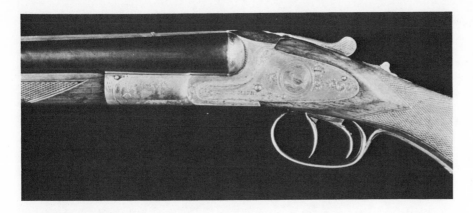

This closeup of an L.C. Smith Two Grade shows nice engraving, good checkering. All Smiths had fine workmanship (as did all the classic doubles, no matter the grade).

Mike McIntosh writes about the only real pitfall connected with the L.C. Smith shotgun—if you release the cocked hammers with the fore-end off the gun, you can't reassemble the gun until you recock the hammers. And that's a simple procedure, but one you have to know or you could damage the gun.

Marlin bought out Hunter Arms in 1945 and ended the line five years later. There was one final gasp for the Smith. Marlin redesigned the Smith, retaining most of its time-proven features, and reentered the market in the mid-1960s. The new Smith was offered only in two field grades and only in 12 gauge. It cost more than autoloaders and pumps, but not that much. But it, too, failed to sell and the L.C. Smith faded away in the early 1970s.

A.H. Fox

Ansley Fox produced the finest gun in the world. If you didn't believe that, you could have asked him—that's what he called it.

Although Fox was not noted for modesty, surprisingly little is known about him before he founded the A.H. Fox Gun Company in 1907. He owned the Baltimore Arms Company at the turn of the century, went bust there, did it again with his Philadelphia Arms Company in 1906 and yet again with the Fox Company in 1911. Fox faded from sight, but the shotgun lived on. The company survived an astonishing string of business reversals, mostly revolving around contracts to deliver arms to wars that ended after the company had invested in materials, but before it could sell the arms.

Fox went back into shotguns in 1918 and continued in production until World War II (a few were made after the war, but not many). Savage Arms owned Fox from 1930 on, but the guns were Ansley Fox's design. And his design was superb.

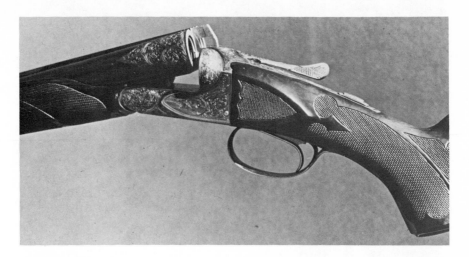

This A.H. Fox double barrel is one of the fine guns cherished by upland bird shooters. Ansley Fox designed one of the strongest, most trouble-free guns ever made.

There was little to go wrong with a Fox. It was designed for trouble-free use. There were only three parts in the Fox lock: the hammer, the sear and a spring. One thing that did go wrong was that the gun could doublefire and pop open.

It happened to Elmer Keith, famed gun writer, twice with the same gun. He sent the gun back to the factory, rubbed his bruised shoulder, and wrote that it was the only Fox which had treated him this way. Keith liked the Fox, despite its indignities to him. Keith, writing in *Shotguns by Keith* in 1950, mourned the death of the doubles.

"It looks as though we will have only the fine old L.C. Smith and the Fox and Stevens left of our best old double gun builders, and new double guns only from them, Winchester and the Marlin over-under Model 90," he said. He wasn't entirely right, but Lefever, Fox, Baker and Parker already had died. Ithaca ran out of doubles about the time Keith made his statement. L.C. Smith lasted until 1950.

Fox offered only three gauges: 12, 16 and 20. There were many options offered— ventilated rib, beavertail fore-end, extra barrels and the like.

The simplest Fox was the Sterlingworth, a utilitarian gun, stout as the farmers who favored it. You could buy your way up to a GE grade which cost a thousand dollars, even during the Great Depression. By the pit of the Depression, Fox was owned by Savage and its substantial assets, and so weathered that crisis, only to fall victim to World War II, in common with almost all its fellow doubles. Savage has revived a Savage Fox side-by-side that sells for under $300.

Lefever

Dan Lefever had not one, but two careers as a successful gunmaker.

Three, if you count his partnership with John Nichols. Lefever opened a gunsmithing shop in Auburn, New York, in the 1850s, but to build rifles, not shotguns. A good many of his accurate rifles, carried by New York State bluecoats, unhorsed surprised Johnny Rebs in the Civil War.

Uncle Dan's locking system for his breechloaders was designed both to be foolproof and to mollify those shooters who were spooked by a gun that came apart in the middle. After all, the breechloader was trying to overturn several hundred years of faith in muzzleloaders. And that juncture between hammers and chambers was uncomfortably close to the shooter's face. It was bad enough to worry about touch-holes blowing out the side of the gun or shrapnel from caps, without wondering if the locking system was going to hold when you touched one off.

But Lefever's locking system was hard to argue with, an underlug and a top fastener as well. He formed a partnership with Nichols in 1876. Two years later, Lefever designed and built the first American hammerless, breechloading shotgun. W.W. Greener and the team of William Anson and John Deeley had built slightly less sophisticated hammerless breechloader in England a few years earlier.

Lefever started his second career by founding the Lefever Arms Company at Syracuse in 1884. The average hourly wage was twenty cents, so his $300 top-of-the-line price tag was a whopper. By the mid-1890s, Lefever had designed as trouble-free a gun as could be had. Every vital adjustment was by a screw. The wear-prone mechanisms had adjustable parts so a perfectly tight gun was possible virtually forever, given reasonable care. In 1893, you could buy Uncle Dan's top factory-grade gun, the Optimus, for $400.

Unbelievably, given the superiority of the gun, Lefever Arms got into financial trouble and Lefever sold out in 1901.

In 1902, he and his five sons founded D.M. Lefever and Sons, first in Syracuse, then in Bowling Green, Ohio. Now there was the strange twist of two companies, in direct competition, building Lefever shotguns. Lefever Arms, the old company, continued selling the original gun, while Dan Lefever designed a new double with even more innovations. Nearly 30,000 guns were built under Uncle Dan at the old company.

Dan Lefever died four years later, in 1906, and the Bowling Green guns, marked either "D.M. Lefever, Sons & Co.," or "D.M. Lefever Co." are the real collector's items of all the Lefevers. Most also were stamped "Not Connected With Lefever Arms Co." The Bowling Green company folded after Dan's death, but Lefever Arms continued until Ithaca bought it in 1915.

Compared to the other fine shotgun makers, Lefever was unproductive. Not counting the Nitro Special, a low-cost Lefever introduced by Ithaca in 1921, there

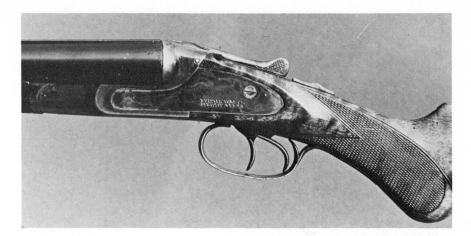

Lefever Arms was the second of three major companies founded by Dan Lefever. Later, he wound up competing with himself—after he sold Lefever Arms out in 1902, he founded D.M. Lefever and Sons and produced guns in competition with his former company.

This is a D.M. Lefever gun, Dan Lefever's second classic double. Not a copy of his earlier Lefever Arms design, it contained innovations not found in the earlier gun—but D.M. Lefever folded before Lefever Arms and these guns are the real collector's items.

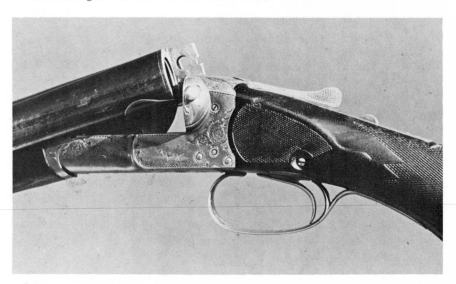

The workhorse of the Lefever line is the Nitro Special. A well-made, simple, plain gun that still shoots and wears well and is as available as any of the old doubles.

were 73,000 Lefevers made, compared to 242,000 Parkers and 203,000 A.H. Fox shotguns.

The highest grade Lefever ever made was the Uncle Dan. It cost $1,000, the most expensive shotgun sold in 1913. Today, an Uncle Dan Grade Lefever, from the Bowling Green factory, easily would be worth $7,000 to $9,000, or more.

Ithaca

Gun companies and makers have crossbred and intertwined like a hutch of unattended rabbits until it's hard to tell who did what to whom and with what.

William Baker, founder of L.C. Smith's company, left Smith and teamed up with L.H. Smith, L.C.'s brother, L.H.'s son and George Livermore—who was L.H.'s brother-in-law—and founded Ithaca.

Eventually (in 1915), Ithaca would buy Lefever. Over the years, Stevens bought Fox, Savage bought Stevens, Parker sold out to Remington. . .if there was some sex involved, it would make a hell of a soap opera.

Meanwhile, Baker and his partners brought out the first Ithaca shotgun in 1883, manufactured, appropriately enough, at Ithaca, New York. Baker designed an external-hammer gun that was exceptionally strong and was advertised as "the strongest, simplest and best American gun manufactured."

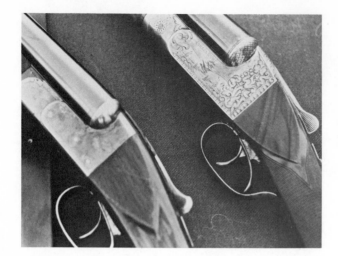

Recently defunct Ithaca is another of the old-time double-barrel companies. Here are two of the good old guns, a field grade at left and a No. 4, with nice engraving at right.

Ithaca had a long history and more than a quarter-million of the best of them, the Flues Model and the New Ithaca, were produced. This is a No. 2 grade Ithaca (on a scale of 1–7).

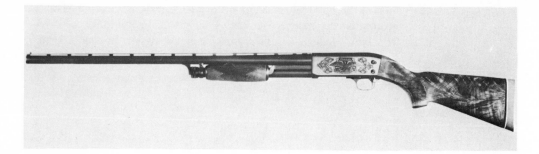

Ithaca Model 37

Baker died in 1889. In 1893, what now was called the Ithaca shotgun became hammerless with its Crass Model, named after the designer. Some 77,000 guns later, in 1903, another model was introduced. There were several more, but the longest-lived was the Flues Model (1908–1926). There were 223,365 produced.

The New Ithaca came along in 1926 and before the double faded from the Ithaca line in 1948, there were 47,000 of them produced. Ithaca graded from 1 through 7—and a No. 7 grade Ithaca was a fine piece of machinery, today worth perhaps $5,000 to $8,000, depending on extras and condition.

The New Ithaca looked much the same as the older models, but had a stronger frame and a different locking system. The rotary bolt system had some early flaws in that some of the guns tended to pop open on the first shot, as did some of the Foxes. But McIntosh rates the New Ithaca as the finest of all the Ithacas.

Ithaca as a company became a dinosaur in December, 1978, but the doubles had gone long before that—in that sad time after World War II when the sporting world went nuts over three-shooters and when rising costs made two-shoot guns much more expensive to produce.

The American philosophy usually is ''more is better,'' so it's not surprising that autoloaders and pumps superceded the doubles. And now, when some of the bloom has faded from the hot passion for the mechanical marvels, the good old double has gotten too expensive for the common folk.

Hardly a day goes by in hunting season that some hardware store isn't advertising a sale on Remington 870s or 1100s, They're probably the most common shotguns available today and, of course, can be used for upland bird hunting quite satisfactorily.

The Ithaca Model 37 pump is a fine little bird gun in 20-gauge and, even though Ithaca is out of business, the gun still is available in good numbers at a reasonable price. More expensive is the Browning automatic, a long-time favorite of the three-shot school of hunters.

There's a ton of foreign doubles and don't overlook deals at good gun shops on used shotguns (but have someone who knows his guns help you look).

Winchester's little Model 23, a nice gun, but not a classic, is nearly $1,000, while the Model 101 which started out as a $250 gun now is nearing the thousand dollar mark.

Parker

Everyone knows the name Stradivarius when it comes to fiddles. Talk about baseball bats and the Louisville Slugger springs to mind. Coca Cola gets grouchy if you call Double Coia a "Coke," but a lot of people do.

Some brand names are almost synonymous with the product. Thus it is with Parker when it comes to fine American doubles. Never mind that Smith or Fox turned out a gun every bit as good—Parker is the standard by which fine doubles are known.

Charles Parker founded the Meriden, Connecticut, company in 1832. . .to produce coffee mills. By the time of the Civil War, the plant produced many items, but not guns. However, Parker went into gun production with two models, 1860 and 1864, of some 10,000 repeating rifles so deadly in the hands of Union troops that the Confederate government called them inhumane and asked President Lincoln to pull them from the battlefield.

The first Parker shotgun came out in 1868, a breechloading 14 gauge with twenty-nine-inch barrels. No thing of beauty, it was hell for stout and its locking system prevailed for thirty years.

Parker's firm hold on the fine shotgun affections of the shooting public began to slip a bit in the 1880s and Charles Parker, by now seventy-one years old, worked with Charles King, who had joined the company in 1874, to redesign the Parker shotgun.

What evolved was a gun that probably deserves to be called the perfect double-barreled shotgun. I don't think Parkers are as *beautiful* as some of the other doubles, but that's both immaterial and irrelevant.

The gun that began to evolve in 1889 and finally achieved perfection in 1910 used a doll's head extension from the top rib and a tapered wedge set into the vertical lug, locked by a sliding bolt which was operated by the top lever. The system was tight and was designed to stay that way virtually forever.

A Parker designer, James Hayes, reduced the eighteen parts of King's cocking system to four—which reduced the chance of malfunction to nearly zero. After 1910, the only changes were the introduction of a single trigger in 1922 and a vent rib in 1926.

Parker offered a number of grades, culminating in the A-1 Special (which sold for $796 in 1930 and today would be worth at least $75,000). The grades were V.H., G.H., D.H., C.H., B.H., A.H., A.A.H. and the A-1 Special. The "H"

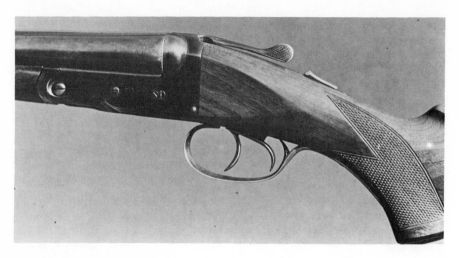

Parker's V-grade gun was the workhorse of the line, simple and without engraving—but, like all Parkers, it was enormously reliable and strong.

denotes hammerless, though there were no external-hammered Parkers after about 1920. An "E" after the grade denotes automatic ejectors.

Parker, unlike some of the other double makers, made a wide variety of gauges and gun types. There was nothing available for a shotgun that a Parker buyer couldn't get, except maybe Joseph Manton's musical locks. Parker designed and built the first 28-gauge guns ever offered (in 1903).

Many of the early Parkers were made with Damascus barrels (imported from Belgium, but finished in the United States). Those guns today often are in eminently shootable condition, as far as the mechanical parts are concerned, but, to repeat an earlier warning, no Damacus barrels are safe to shoot with any load or any powder.

The ultimate Parker perhaps exists somewhere, waiting to make some lucky finder wealthy. In the late 1920s, Parker decided to celebrate its 200,000th gun by building a super-shotgun, called The Invincible. There were two produced. The one with the Serial Number 230,329 is worth at least $100,000 today—probably a lot more; the other, No. 200,000, has vanished. No one knows where it is. But there were two produced and the location of only one is known. Where is the other? It's hard to believe it was bought by an average gun owner and stuck in a closet somewhere. But almost all the gunmakers until relatively recent times kept unbelievably sketchy records.

Parker sold out to Remington in 1934, victim of the Depression, having built 235,100 guns. Remington built another 7,285 before ending the Parker gun in 1947.

The Megacorporations—Winchester and Remington

Where most of the other fine double manufacturers concentrated on shotguns, Winchester and Remington, probably the biggest names in guns over the last hundred years, made double-barreled shotguns almost as an afterthought.

On the other hand, both companies still make doubles where all the others are out of business, save Fox which is only a Fox in name now.

Both companies had sold doubles early, in the days of external hammers, but neither pursued the market. Winchester imported high-quality guns made in England in 1880. Remington made doubles even earlier—the first came out in 1874.

You can argue that Winchester never really was an American double manufacturer until the Model 21 since the guns were English-made. Remington's doubles were American guns, and there were a lot of them built. The company produced nearly 134,000 of its Model 1889, last of its external hammer guns. Its first hammerless double was the Model 1894. It ranged in price from the simple Model K at $35 to the top of the line, the Remington Special, at $750. One problem with these early Remingtons for today's shooter is that they had Damascus barrels as standard; steel barrels were special order (though at no extra cost), so many of the Remingtons would be unshootable today because of their twist-barrel construction.

The early Remington side-bys offered a hunter a good choice of gauges (10, 12, 16) and barrel lengths, from twenty-six through thirty-two inches. A Remington Model 1900 in 16 gauge, with ''Ordnance'' steel barrels, had an English walnut stock, weighed a mere 6^{1}/2 pounds, could be had with a variety of extras such as engraving, vent rib and automatic ejectors—and cost a whopping $230 to $300 depending on how fancy you wanted it.

Remington's side-by guns faded and died at the start of World War I because of the increase in popularity of its pump and automatic shotgun line. But the day of the Remington double was not done.

In 1930, fired with enthusiasm by the acceptance of John Browning's Belgian Superposed gun, Remington designed the Model 32, an over-and-under shotgun with an ingenious breech-cover locking system that not only locks the gun, but protects the shooter from any possible blowback from escaping gases. The barrels are separated, one of the few over/under guns ever made this way. The resulting heat dissipation makes them especially fine for trap or skeet shooting where rapid firing can cause heat distortion to confuse the shooter's eye.

There were only a few more than 5,000 Model 32s made and today they are collector's items, as well as superb shooting guns.

But the Model 3200 is the spiritual descendant of the Model 32. Though no copy of the Model 32, it has many of the same features and is a well-made gun. It was first marketed in 1972, sells for about $1,000.

Winchester's Model 21 was born in the Depression, from a depressed company. If ever there was a shoot-the-moon gamble, the 21 was it. It appeared in 1930, the year Winchester declared bankruptcy. Yes, mighty Winchester went bust. The

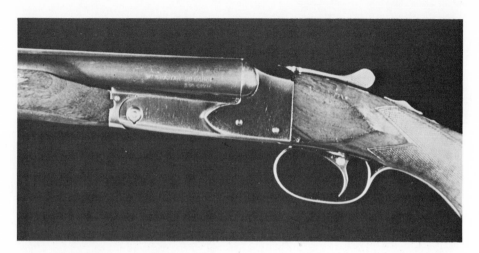

Winchester's Model 21 still is available—if you've got the scratch. It may be the strongest, most reliable double gun ever made. In 1932, the Model 21 sold for an incredible $59.50. Now, the chances are excellent you don't have enough spare cash to buy one.

Remington's Model 32 still is a classic trap gun because the separated barrels dissipate heat generated in rapid firing. Just over 5,000 of these classic guns were made. They're enormously strong and reliable.

Unless something happens to rescue Winchester's gun-making operation, this contemporary Model XTR Field Gun may join the classic doubles—Winchester has announced it will cease making guns. The XTR, at $1,400, was due out in the spring of 1981.

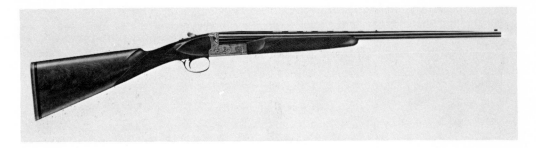

Winchester's Model 23, made in Japan, is lightweight and attractive—and costs $1,175. No one ever said shooting a double is cheap.

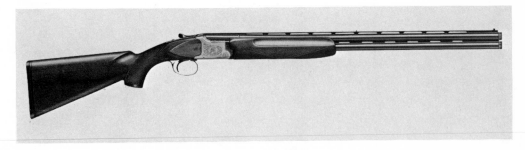

One of the modern classic double guns is the Winchester Model 101. You still can pick up used 101s for $400–$500, but the new XTR lightweight gun sells for a whopping $1,150.

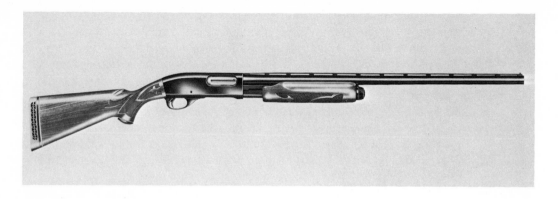

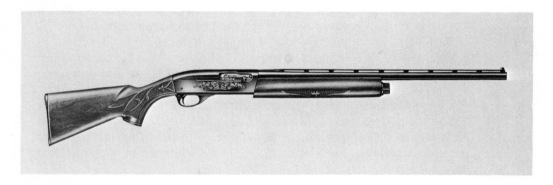

Remington 1100 and 870

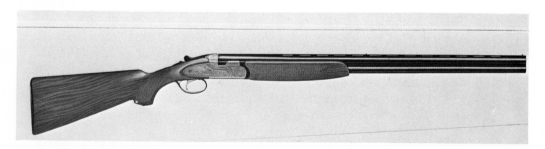

Beretta is one of the many foreign double-barrel makers. This is an over-under model.

company—and the Model 21—was rescued by the Olin family's Western Cartridge Company. John Olin, who became Winchester's boss, saw in the Model 21 a wonder gun, a thing of beauty and perhaps the salvation of the company.

He was, and is, its champion. Olin visited his new company in 1932 and fell in love with the Model 21 which, to that time, hadn't sold very well. It will break the heart of anyone who has bought one in the last twenty years to know that the gun's basic selling price in 1931 was $59.50. By the mid-1960s, that became $1,000 and the cost now escalates so rapidly that you have to ask for a factory quote. Depending on your options, a Model 21 probably would cost you between $6,000 and $14,000. Winchester watchers are pretty sure that when John Olin goes, the Model 21 will not be long in following. Olin was eighty-seven in 1980.

What makes the Model 21 so cherished? Well, it's almost indestructible. The frame is machined from heat-treated alloy steel and the barrels are of chrome molybdenum steel. The barrels are dovetailed for the strongest possible junction. The single trigger was one of the most reliable ever on an American shotgun.

The Model 21 may be a luxury to own—but it was a luxury for Winchester to produce, too. In 1959, Winchester accountants discovered that the gun never had sold for a profit (there had been 28,840 built). Since 1959, the guns have been custom-built.

You can't talk about the Model 21, nor most of Winchester's great guns, nor Winchester itself without mentioning T.C. Johnson, who led the design team that invented, if that's the right word, both the Model 12 (Perfect Repeater) pump and the Model 21. Johnson was born in 1862 and joined Winchester in 1885. He stayed with the company until his death in 1934. During his career, he took out 124 patents, which he assigned to Winchester.

While Winchester and Remington produced the finest of the fine shotguns by the supergiant companies, there are three other big gunmakers who all have taken a turn at producing doubles. Savage's Fox Model B sells, in 1981, for between $300 and $350, lowest priced of the three remaining American doubles.

And both Savage and Marlin offered medium priced, but stout over/unders which will crop up in the used-gun market. Savage's faded in 1942. Marlin's Model 90 made it until 1957. Savage also makes an over/under rifle/shotgun, usually with a .22 caliber rifle barrel atop a 20-gauge or .410 shotgun barrel.

The gun also can be had with a .30-.30 top barrel over either a 20-gauge or .410 shotgun barrel. The idea of a rifle/shotgun is not new. The founder of what became the L.C. Smith Company, William Baker, made drillings, double-barreled shotguns with a rifle barrel nestled underneath. The Germans, always advocates of massed firepower, made drillings as well. As Elmer Keith said in his shotgun book, ". . .one never knows when he may be out for a mess of guinea fowl and suddenly come face to face with a lion or a leopard." He was talking about Africa, but to judge from the black panther reports that all conservation agencies get, maybe all us birdshooters should be carrying drillings.

4

Is There a Universal Dog?

Is there a Universal Dog? I say yes and I own two of them.

The Brittany was created by a beneficent God to make me happy. Owners of other bird-dog species will rise as an angry mob, thinking burbling thoughts of tar, guano-stained feathers, and a bumpy ride out of town on a splinter-split length of red oak, but they gotta catch me first and under the impetus of terror, I run quite briskly.

First of all, Brittanies are beautiful animals. Oh, I know all about criticism of their portliness. And there are those who carp at stub tails and red noses. But they're beautiful to me. Granted, an Irish setter is dog beauty carried to its ultimate, but leprechauns have invaded the brains of far too many Celtic curs and turned them into creatures whose intelligence is as feathery as their tails. A tail on a bird dog is useless. Briar-stung bird-dog tails bleed copiously; they'll bloodstain everything you own, including your clothing, car, shotgun, as well as the minister's wife if you stop by the manse on Sunday morning to explain why you weren't at church between November 10 and the end of the bird season.

Brittanies don't have tails.

I have known and loved pointers, but also have hunted behind some with the physical charm of large, angular rocks. I swear, some of them descended from dogs whose brains atrophied in the time of Christ and succeeding generations spent the next nineteen centuries building muscles the better to gallop out of earshot with.

Just as there is no such thing as bad loving, only encounters less wonderful than others, so there is no such thing as a bad Brittany. I do not lie when I say that I never have met a Brittany owner who has badmouthed a Brittany.

Nicholas Cox wrote *The Gentleman's Recreation* in 1686 and, oh! doth it warm the heart of a Brittany owner to hear him say, "It is now the mode to shoot flying, as being by experience found the best and surest way, for when your game is on the wing it is more exposed to danger; for if but one shot hits any part of its wings so expanded, it will occasion its fall, although not to kill it, so that your spaniel will soon be its victor.'' Note that bit about the spaniel, precursor of all of them. Spaniels were doing things right long before the first pointer or setter gawped dumbly at his master and mumbled, ''Where's duh boids?''

Brits used to take a rap as dogs that can't range, that hunt in your hip pocket and cover as much ground as your handkerchief. But standard-issue Brittanies these days include versions that work close for grouse/woodcock hunters, all the way to field trialers you need the long glass at Mt. Palomar to locate. My male, Chip, hunts close-by, and is death on woodcock, good on pheasants and grouse. My bitch, Ginger, is all leg, weighs about as much as a hefty jackrabbit and is autumn smoke in the russet stubblefields.

I know of no other bird-dog species that smells as sweet (often Chip's hair carries a hint of woodsmoke, perhaps from the internal fire that flames so hot when he hunts), keeps as clean, nor is as affectionate. Aside from an unfortunate and almost universal tendency to eat road apples with unholy relish, most Brittany faults carry a certain elfin charm.

Brittanies and most other bird dogs came originally from spaniels. Dogs as identifiable creatures go back perhaps forty million years. They've been involved in hunting since about 7000 B.C. and by the time fowling became a gunsport, dogs already were a big part of it. Dr. Johannes Caius, University of Cambridge, writing about 1517, said, ''Another sort of dog there be serviceable for fowling, making no noise with foot or tongue whilst they follow the game. These attend diligently upon their masters and frame their conditions to such becks and motions and gestures as it shall please him to exhibit and make, either going forward, drawing backward, inclining the right hand or yielding to the left. In making mention of fowl, my meaning here is of partridge and quail. When he hath found the bird, he keepeth a sure and fast silence and stayeth his steps and will proceed no further and with close covered, watching eye layeth his belly to the ground and so creepeth forward like a worm.''

We have here a quail dog, staunch to point, trained to hand signals . . . and in 1500. There are a whole lot of bird dogs today not that dependable.

A few years later, around 1600, Richard Surflet wrote about the progenitor of my Brits. ''There is another sort of land spannyels which are called setters and they differ nothing from the former [the springer spaniel] but in instruction and obedience, for these must neither hunt, range, nor retain, more or less, than as the master appointeth, taking the whole limit of whatsoever they do from the eye or hand of their instructor. They must never quest at any time, what occasion so ever may happen, but as being dogs without voices, so they must hunt close and mute and when they come upon the haunt of that which they hunt, they shall suddenly stop and fall down upon their bellies and so leisurely creep by degrees to the game till they come within two or three yards thereof or so near that they cannot press nearer without danger of retrieving. Then shall your setters stick and by no persuasion go further till yourself come in and use your pleasure.

The noblest sight a man is privileged to see, akin to the first cracking of the Gates of Paradise—Brittanies locked solidly on point.

"Now the dogs which are to be made for this pleasure should be the most principal, best and lustiest spannyels you can get, both of good scent and good courage, yet young and as little as may be acquainted with hunting."

Aside from setting a style of English that has carried over into the present-day instructions for filling out your income tax, Surflet could have been describing today's upland bird dog. Note, though, that he talks of "spannyels." They came first, not setters, nor pointers.

Sir Isaac Newton's water spaniel knocked over a candle and burned his priceless manuscripts. Mine have both vomited and defecated on manuscripts which, while not priceless, are worth better treatment.

One theory holds that Brittanies and other land spaniels originated from Pyrennean mountain dogs. The French word for Spanish (*espagnol*) is supposed to have been corrupted to "spaniel." Pointers also supposedly come from Spanish stock. The Spanish pointer was described as a "coarse, slow dog, sadly inefficient in the matter of speed and range." To correct this deficiency, they bred pointers with foxhounds, so today's pointer has hound blood in him.

Some authorities believe English setters, the most popular of today's setters, also had Spanish forebears—probably Spanish pointers ("coarse, slow" dogs) and (here it comes) some sort of spaniel.

Spaniels were in there pointing and otherwise acting just like bird dogs should a long time before upstart setters and pointers came loping over the hill, busting coveys, peeing on their master's lunch and otherwise acting normal. At least a thousand years ago, the French had pointing spaniels. Today's Brittany dates only to about 1850 when a tailless male dog was born of a union in the Breton town of Pontou between a local spaniel bitch and a field dog of unknown breed (possibly a setter).

Most Brittanies today are born without tails; however, my male, Chip, fathered a litter of five tailed pups. The standard is tails four inches or less.

Why a Brittany as the Universal Dog?

Because he is a pointing dog, the only pointing spaniel; is a natural retriever; is incredibly easy to train; will hunt dead with great zest; is the best all-around dog for grouse and woodcock, but will hunt every common game bird (and even will retrieve waterfowl, though his short coat is insufficient for very cold water); is affectionate, intelligent, wonderful with children, playful and, best of all, is a good listener.

To be a successful Brittany owner, you must learn to love the dog for his faults as well as for his virtues. There are those who consider a bird dog nothing more than a hairy hammer, a canine crescent wrench, whose sole function is to find targets for the master to shoot. Such dogs spend their strictured lives in kennels and dog boxes. There is no more of a bond between such dogs and their master than there is between the master and his hunting boots. Sure, he takes care of the boots—but he isn't in love with them.

Mark me down as a hopeless romantic, an unashamed boob when it comes to bird dogs, but I have loved my Brittanies unreservedly, egg-suckers and champs alike. I consider them not just dogs, but good friends.

I hear about dog trainers who will, unemotionally, put down an unpromising pup. No second chances, no patient wait for maturity, no settling for mediocre or even average. If the dogs don't cut it and cut it quickly, kill them. I have hunted with men whose dogs were automatons. Were I in the business of selling dogs, these men couldn't pay me enough to get one of mine.

Contrarily, some of the best dog trainers (or at least the owners of some of the best dogs I know) babytalk their puppies like some fatuous dowager sugarmouthing a yappy Peke. And, while listening to such treacle can be nauseating enough to gag a Pulaski County sow, yet there is an obvious bond of love between man and dog that's a damned sight more attractive to me than watching some upland *Sturmfuehrer* bark glacial commands to a four-legged trooper.

Most of this material about dogs has been written with one or more dogs draped across my boot tops. I take my dogs for rides in the car because they enjoy riding in the car. They sit up front, not crouched miserably in a drafty dog box. And if, when Chip sometimes leans against me somewhere on the long road from here to there so he can slurp my ear, he deposits a sprinkle of cast-off Brittany hair on my Navy chamois shirt, then so be it.

With that in mind, accept that anything I say about dogs in general and Brits specifically is richly colored by my blind fondness for them. Understand, though, that I am not all sugar when it comes to my puppies. I don't dismiss their transgressions, nor live comfortably with their faults. When I think it's time for an object lesson, I am not averse to using the proverbial two-by-four to get the mule-headed dog's attention, but I try to balance out the whippings with a liberal dose of hugs and ear scratchings. So far, at least, this treatment has not soured any of my mutts on their daddy.

Dog discipline takes different forms, from a frown to punishment far more severe. I think anyone who shoots a dog, no matter what the dog is doing, should himself be given a ten-yard running start before you let him know how it feels. On the other hand, I've been known to run Chip several hundred yards through thick brush to thrash his mangy hide for running rabbits. He considers the whippings well worth the fun he gets out of chasing bunnies and, so far, has not showed any inclination to mend his ways.

I once watched a friend, taken by a fit of pique when his Labrador willfully misbehaved, grab a double handful of her, raise her, sideways, about waist high and bounce her off the ground hard enough to trip the seismograph at St. Louis University (we were on Chesapeake Bay at the time). It's a wonder he didn't snap a couple of the dog's ribs, but he didn't, and after the dog got her wind back, she was far more in tune with the process of crime and punishment. And, when it came time to pass out plaudits, she got a double handful of those, too. While I don't advocate slam dunking your dog (for one thing, you have to know how resilient the dog is so you don't break something important), I do believe in firmness, even when it results in substantial knuckle bumps.

As we've seen, all sporting dogs are brews of hunting dog blood. There is no such thing as a "pure" hunting dog, for, through the centuries, pointers have been seasoned with hound blood, setters with spaniel blood, spaniels with setter blood and so on.

Yet John Krider, a gunmaker and noted outdoor enthusiast of the mid-1800s, wrote in 1853, "The nearer the dog approaches to purity in stock, the nobler is his character and the less he is addicted to evil ways. We have never heard the clean-bred pointer accused of sheep killing; the setter is not so free from taint. Indeed, he has been known, in one instance, at least, to forsake his professional business and assail a flock of sheep, which has come his way in the course of a day's sport.

"This dog, said to have been an imported English stock, unaccountably left his master, in the stubbles, and a few minutes afterwards was actually seen, by the proprietor of the land, throttling sheep in an adjoining field."

Krider obviously was a pointer man. Another noted early outdoor writer, George Bird Grinnell, would have had no patience with my Chip, nor with any cautious dog, prone to point too much rather than not enough.

"A dog which habitually false points is next to worthless for field work," Grinnell said. "The fault is displayed by some dogs under unfavorable weather conditions which affect the scent. The majority of dogs will false point when fagged out or when stale from overwork day after day. There is no cure for habitual false pointing. It probably is the result of a faulty brain or nose or both combined or it may be of over-caution.''

One of the finest pointing dogs I've ever seen is no master of style and would be laughed out of even puppy stakes on a field trial. Her name is Dolly and she belongs to Andy Ammann, woodcock guru now retired from the Michigan Department of Natural Resources.

Ammann has trained several dogs to find woodcock broods. It takes a very careful dog. ''Not all dogs are amenable to this kind of work,'' Ammann says. ''They have to be low-key and careful. Most good grouse dogs have a chance because they're relatively easy-going and can slow down before they bump the bird.''

Dolly finds broods in the spring so Ammann and other woodcock researchers with whom he works can band the birds and find other information about them. But she also works both grouse and woodcock in the fall.

She is a slow, careful worker and I'd rather hunt with her than with all the wide-ranging dogs ever bred. For one thing, hunting upland birds today tends more and more toward the brush. I would say that well over half my hunting is done in heavy cover, no matter the game bird. And that means to me that more than half the time I'd be wondering where in the flaming hell my running dog had got to.

While an afterburnered dog may be fine for some big-field hunting situation—probably either pheasants or quail—he's less than useless on woodcock, on grouse, even on prairie birds, which tend not to hold for a point anyway. What's more, most pointers are not good dead-bird hunters, nor retrievers. Many setters are the same way. My feeling is that a running dog is a single-minded dog. He runs to hunt; he is impatient with pause and loath to prowl about for downed birds.

Yet, in today's dog, there is such a thing as too careful. The traditional bird dog quartered—hunted in a zig-zag perpendicular to the hunter's path. It may have been a viable hunting method once, but now that system is a waste of time, for most of the ground a hunter surveys does not hold birds. Far better a dog, slow or fast, which instinctively or through training heads for likely cover and, having coursed it, goes to the next promising patch.

There are people who train dogs and there are those who have dogs that they train. Let's take you, standing there waiting to see what I'll say next. You look a lot like me (handsome, lucky devil) and I'll bet you are a dog owner like me—you don't make a living breaking dogs to hunt and you don't have the time it takes to hone a razor-keen bird dog. But you also don't want to drag an eggsucker into the field if for no other reason than you dislike being laughed at by your hunting pards.

Your choices are two: (1) you can pay a professional to sculpt your dog for you or, (2) you can do it yourself, less than perfect, but adequate.

There are some fine books available that can tell you far more than I ever could about dog training. My personal favorite is Richard Wolters' *Gun Dog*. Wolters is the Dr. Spock of Dogdom and offers commonsense training methods. Wolters' book is specifically written for the dog owner with limited training time.

Certainly as respected and helpful is Bill Tarrant, whose several dog training books all will do the job. Probably the best-known is *Best Way to Train Your Gun Dog,* with Tarrant as the writer and Delmar Smith, a noted dog handler, as the expert. There are many other dog training books and I think the best source, both for dog books and dog supplies, is Dunn's Supply, Grand Junction, Tennessee 38039.

As I said, I'm not a dog trainer, nor a single-minded hunter. I'm merely a hunting enthusiast who owns a couple of dogs. My dogs are not steady to shot—holding staunch on point after the flush and shot until commanded to retrieve—and I guess that puts me in the same boat as the French.

Charles Apperley, who wrote under the name Nimrod, the mythological synonym for a hunting enthusiast, considered the French the absolute pits as far as bird shooting goes. Be advised that Apperley was considered a conceited snob. Son of a scholarly country gentleman who read Greek before breakfast, Apperley rode to the hounds and began to write on foxhunting for *The Sporting Magazine* in 1822. But, in 1830, hit by financial woes, he moved to Calais, France, where he picked up some really mean prejudices against French gunners. "Very few French pointers or setters are taught to back," [to honor another dog's point] Nimrod wrote.

"Here I am compelled to observe that the French *chasseur* violates the first principles of dog management by running up to his game when it falls and encouraging the chase of wounded hares."

Nimrod has a point when he stresses that dogs should be steady to shot (and chews out the French for not teaching it): "It would be by no means agreeable should a wrangle take place between two (dogs) to see Sancho coming with a leg and Bumber with a wing of your bird. The Frenchman shoots and having dropped his game immediately advances with his discharged gun to assist his dog in finding what he has dropped.

"The English shooter and his dogs never stir from the spot until he has reloaded when, if his game be wounded, he commences pursuit."

Well and good—except that if I wing-tipped an Iowa cock pheasant and Chip and I stood patiently while I recharged the gun, that pheasant, born of a union between the avian equivalent of Wilma Rudolph and Frank Shorter, would be nearing the Minnesota border, picking up steam.

On the other hand, I heard a true horror story about a hunter who fired at a crippled bird that was flying low and killed his dog, who leaped at the bird just as the hunter touched the trigger.

So, training methods, levels of dog competence, breeds—nearly everything connected with upland bird-dog phenomena has pros and cons, with supporters all equally vehement. Even now there are pointer men looking at my choice of the Brittany as The Universal Dog with a yallered eye and thinking seriously of decorating my thick skull with welts.

5

Dog Training

Although I spent the first twenty years of my upland-bird hunting acting as my own bird dog, I was but half a hunter. It doesn't matter whether the hunter stomps the brush alone, hoping to kick something up, or whether he hunts with dog-owning buddies, he is not a fulfilled bird hunter until he has his own dog to hug and cuss.

Dog owning is a mixed blessing. I know hunters who really shouldn't own bird dogs. They just don't have the feel for it. Either they expect too much of the dog or not enough. They simply don't operate on the same wave length as the dog. Consequently, they have ill-trained dogs and there grows to be an antipathy, at least on the part of the hunter toward the dog. The dog is ''stupid'' or ''crazy'' and comes to be regarded as a liability rather than an asset.

Certainly there are bird dogs who are hopeless. Even the most patient, most talented trainer is forced to chuck in the terrycloth. Foster Sadler, my hunting pard, has made bird dogs out of several raw vegetables—but he once gave a temporary home to a setter bitch named Dolly who has to be the stupidest animal ever bred. Dolly was placid in the way that oxen are placid, but she had the brain of a rock and bumbled through countless covies without giving any indication she regarded the event as other than a bewildering interruption to an otherwise serene day. Foster finally found her a home with a nice family that doesn't hunt, where she could do what she did best—curl up on the rug and sleep.

But I think those dogs are rare. Most bird dogs have it bred into them to hunt; it's up to the trainer to shape them.

My dogs have eaten everything from expensive running shoes to an empty wineskin (later thrown up on the rec room rug). They have fouled my carpets with vomit and diarrheal deposits, have miscued in every conceivable way, but there was not a moment of the most trying time that I considered getting rid of them. Even at the peak of black rage, when some very thin shred of sanity kept me from knocking their goddam heads off, I would not have let anyone else have them, for love nor money.

For they have balanced their delinquencies with moments of poetic magic. They have nurtured my soul with crystalline vignettes of vibrant points, quiet memories of proud retrieves, of trusting eyes and warm bodies nestled close to me on the long, dark drive home.

The initial cost of a puppy (which ranges from none to a whole lot, but probably averages $50 to $100 for a papered, but non-champion-lineage pup) is only the start. The full complement of shots for rabies, distemper, lepto is expensive enough, but now you should have a parvo virus shot as well and in most of the country, daily doses of heartworm preventive are highly recommended. Needless to say, veterinarians do not give all these health aids away as a public service.

Bird dogs have a digestive system as simple as that of an amoeba. Virtually a straight gut, it requires enormous amounts of raw foodstuffs from which the dog extracts a minimum of nourishment before discharging waste material in amounts greater than what he ingested—a bit of dietary magic unmatched anywhere else in nature.

Dog food is expensive. Even shoveling the cheapest stuff into the animals will result in an annual bill of $50 to $75 for my two Brittanies. Actually, it's more, for I carry expensive dog food on hunting trips when the dog is using his afterburners and needs high-octane fuel. I carry several dog food packets in my hunting vest and feed the dogs at noon.

A hungry dog is not averse to snacking on birds carelessly left in a hunting vest while its owner wolfs down a greasy cheeseburger in a country store. I've witnessed this trespass twice. Once, I did not own the dog and that was an occasion for jollity at the expense of the poor sucker who owned the malefic mutt.

The other time, I was the poor sucker.

LOST DOGS

Dogs, being only slightly more level-headed than the average hunter, occasionally get lost. It's a traumatic situation for both hunter and dog, especially if the hunter is far from home and has to leave his four-legged pard. The dog, of course, is in unfamiliar surroundings and has no more idea which way to go than you or I would have (I don't know about you, but no mountain man am I; I can get lost going home for lunch).

Chip, inflamed by doglust for a tarty bitch, once wandered off for two days, his eyes glazed, his groin aflame, while Ginger went along for the ride, being too young to do more than gaze with wide-eyed interest at the scandalous goings-on.

I'd almost given them up for good when a kindly lady called to say they'd corralled the pair. I careened over to the house, leaped from the car and found the family in the back yard feeding my errant hounds. You never heard such howling, sobbing, whimpering, begging for forgiveness, promises never to do it again (don't ever believe a dog; they lie). I thanked my benefactors and went back to the car—

only to find it gone. In my anxious haste I hadn't gotten the car completely in gear; it had jumped into neutral, rolled across the street and into someone's front yard, nearly wiping out an elderly lady driver in an oncoming car.

The woman was standing in the middle of the street, wringing her hands and telling throngs of gawping neighbors about her narrow escape when I hove on the scene, a yowling Brittany clutched in each hand, trying to thank the gentleman who'd found them and who also wanted to share with me his life since 1917, trying to apologize to the woman and explain to her that I am terminally stupid, trying to ignore the neighbors who'd never seen the Keystone Kops perform on their street before.

If your dog is lost, what do you do?

Driving the streets in a city is almost futile. Unless you know what direction Dog headed, so is driving country roads. A dog in a county is a needle in a haystack, so prepare the dog for his Odyssey with a good collar (I like flat, not rolled or round ones) on which is engraved the dog's name, your name, address and telephone number (including area code—remember, you may be a long way from home). Shot tags should be firmly fixed with something that won't come loose. The little S-hooks veterinarians usually provide usually don't last long on a brush-hunting dog. The shot tag lets people know the dog has had rabies vaccinations and might defer them from shooting your friend as a stray. Don't bank on it—Chip right now is recovering from a gunshot wound and he was wearing his collar and tags.

Don't put on a choke collar. It's dangerous. I keep the collars loose enough that if they snag, the dog can pull it over his head. At least the dog is free and not trapped far from help, doomed to starve. Ginger finally came home without a collar, so she'd slipped hers somewhere.

I carve my name, address and telephone number in the leather of the collar. It isn't artistic, but it's helpful information to finders. Check the legibility of the information periodically. Everything but our telephone number had eroded from Chip's collar.

Assuming you have a faint idea which way the dog went, start asking at farmhouses, passing the word around that you have a missing dog. It may get you back your dog. It may also temper with caution or a second thought the first inclination of some irascible type to shoot any dog he sees, especially one he sees or suspects is harassing his livestock. Leave a card or note with instructions on how you can be reached and a description of the dog.

There's quite a bit of willing (usually) help routinely patrolling country roads. Call the post office and ask if the rural mail carriers will be on the lookout for Dog. Contact the sheriff's office, ask for help from deputies. Be sure, if Dog is found, to cancel the alert. That's common courtesy.

Whether the dog will approach humans depends on the dog's personality. If he's gregarious, chances are he'll seek out a farmhouse and thus be found. In Ginger's case, she went to a country kennel (oddly, the one where we stable our dogs occasionally except she'd not been there yet so they didn't recognize her). Chip first went to somebody who shot him, then dragged himself to the home of a kindly man who, again oddly enough, lives across the road from our veterinarian.

If the dog is stand-offish, your problem is more severe. Dogs, being twenty-four-hour creatures, are as adept at night as they are in the daytime and a suspicious dog easily could go feral, foraging at night, only rarely being seen by anyone. Chances are, he's a permanently "lost" dog (he knows where he is; you don't).

Of course, you advertise in the newspaper. A simple ad probably will run a dollar a day. Give the dog's breed, description, name, vicinity where he was lost and your telephone number. Call all the radio stations and ask to have an announcement made. You'll have to call them every day to renew the notice. There's a day or two lag time before an ad will appear in the newspaper.

Make sure you call the dog pound every day—don't rely on them to call you if your dog comes in. Remember, they destroy unclaimed dogs after three days or so.

Most supermarkets have bulletin boards. Post a card with the pertinent details.

Finally, call every veterinarian in the area. If the dog has a shot tag, it will have the vet's name and address on it and the finder may call the vet. But also, vets tend to get a lot of information from their customers and, at least the ones I know, are more than willing to help any way they can.

DOG RUNS

Keeping an active dog confined is a feat of sorcery easier contemplated than done, which leads to the next great expense, the dog run. You can and should let your dogs in your house. It makes them part of the family, gives them a feeling of security, a sense of importance, and the reward of occasional comfort that comes with being a good dog.

The dog looks at it this way: why bother to do wonderful things when all it gets you is a stinking, cold doghouse at the end of the day? Of course, they really don't reason that way and would hunt the same regardless, but I still think you get a better class of dog if you treat him as family some of the time.

But not all the time. As marvelous as a bird dog is—sensational working tool, esthetically pleasing, sympathetic companion in time of stress—he can be a throbbing pain in the ass in your house. He has no sense of modesty (one of my puppies once peed on a friend's television set, which showed excellent taste but a lack of rudimentary decorum), suffers from falling hair winter and summer, carries (and sheds) ticks and fleas, and invariably does whatever you consider the most disgraceful possible thing.

So, build a good dog run and a tidy house where the dog(s) can dwell in relative comfort. Let them out as much as possible to run, exercise and train, let them in the house to see folks, curl up before the fire or otherwise be a part of De Shootinest Gent'man at rest—but when bedtime comes, his bed should be out in the pen and no arguments.

If anyone in the family suffers from asthma or other respiratory trouble, all bets are off and consider visiting the dog in *his* home, rather than the reverse. You can't imagine how much potentially harmful hair floats around the house with a fulltime resident dog.

There probably are a thousand and one designs for a dog run, but it needs one thing above all. It needs to be as strong as a pillbox on the Maginot line. It needs to be able to turn a Tiger tank upside down. It needs to be strong enough to withstand a medium-yield nuclear weapon.

It needs to be designed to hold a bird dog in, and a bird dog confined is a bird dog with escape ingenuity that Willie Sutton couldn't imagine the best day he ever had. I've seen a dog, which does not have opposable thumbs, grab a doorknob and turn it as if the feat were child's play. In fact, I have children of school age who couldn't figure out how to escape from pens that wouldn't baffle the densest bird dog.

If they can't dig out, they'll leap over. If they can't leap over, they'll chew through. Dogs confined are dogs unhappy and an unhappy dog has massive persistence when it comes to seeking an exit. The bird dog who wouldn't hold a point longer than a millisecond will spend days gnawing at a piece of wire that, eventually, he will part from its supposedly indestructible weld, creating a tiny opening which, in due time, will be a big opening. The dog then will wander the neighborhood, creating the kind of havoc that lies in the wake of a particularly spritely tornado.

I used welded wire on my pen and, since it was low budget, cut cedar posts off my own land. Ginger has managed to chew through one four-inch cedar post as if she were the offspring of a beaver and a chain saw. Because Chip can climb like a Polynesian coconut chopper, I had to roof the pen with yet more wire. For the moment it's secure, but I know those two are plotting, at this very instant, ingenious schemes to get out.

The run should be long enough to let the dog at least pace back and forth. Ideally, the floor should be concrete for ease of cleaning, lack of mess (dirt turns to mud in wet weather) and sanitation. The house should be large enough to be comfortable, yet small enough to retain dogheat in winter. Cedar wood shavings make a better bed than straw and make the dog smell nice. Both my dogs shove whatever I put in the house out of it anyway, so it doesn't matter. I insulated the floor underneath and the house is waterproof.

My pen is no thing of beauty. It will not be mistaken for the Taj Mahal. It is as ugly as a wave on a slop bucket, but it does have some things going for it. First of all, since there is wire everywhere, it serves as a trellis for a pair of grape vines on one side. These grapes, fertilized by dog runoff, have threatened to take over Cole County. You never saw grapes like these. They have muscles. There also is a small garden plot immediately downhill, so Chip and Ginger not only help me put quail on toast, they help me put nutrients on the garden. Who could ask for more from man's faithful companion?

BASIC TRAINING

You can train your dog to whatever degree you want, but there are basics. I know a man who has a Lab who will climb a ladder and retrieve beer cans tossed on the roof of the house, but the practical value of tricks like that in the field is questionable.

At a minimum, the dog needs to know "come," "sit," "stay," and "heel." Making the dog lie down on command is nice, but I don't see it as an imperative. Likewise "kennel" is impressive when the dog eagerly jumps into the car, but most bird dogs are so wild to go along that "get your ass in there" usually works just as well.

You can whistle-train your dog by calling "come!" and blowing the whistle, then gradually eliminating the voice command. I've never whistle-trained my dogs, but the Acme Thunderer is the best-known dog whistle.

The multi-purpose dog needs to learn some command to slow him down when you're hunting in close cover—maybe his name, followed by "back!" or "easy!" I think hand signals are important and use them to make a dog quarter in woodcock cover or to direct him into the brush. You may look like the village idiot while you're training the dog to hand signals, but it takes forceful thrusts of your arm, accompanied by a dramatic lunge in the direction you want the dog to go.

Summertime is the sagging gut of the hunting year. It's easy to forget you own a bird dog in the summertime, but remember that Ace may forget some of what he knew last season. If he's a pup, you're wasting valuable training time before the upcoming season.

The heat of the day is good only for training mad dogs (and Englishmen, assuming they're trainable), so confine your workouts to early morning or late evening and keep them short. No point in wearing out or overheating either you or Ace.

One of the first things I try to teach a pup after the basics is to freeze at a distance from me when I shout "stay!" I want that dog to stop instantly and wait for further instructions. The reason I teach this is that one of my dogs once trotted in front of a car, his eyes fixed on me, because I didn't have any way to stop him. The dog survived, fortunately, but it was a hell of a shock to both of us.

Since then, I've stopped dogs on the opposite side of the road several times until traffic passed by. My experience is that bird dogs have little traffic sense and if you let them run free around busy roads, sooner or later they'll get hit. Summer also is a good time to work on "heel," which again can serve as a command to save the dog's life. If he's at heel, the only way a reckless driver can kill him is by getting you, too.

Summertime also is good for retriever work, if nothing more strenuous than a few tosses of a tennis ball and subsequent fetches. Ideally, the dog should chase the ball, bring it to you, sit and deliver it to hand. The toughest lesson to learn is sit and deliver. Some dogs want to spit the ball out at your feet; others want to play keep away.

If you can pursuade your wife to let you store some bird wings in a plastic bag in the freezer, they make great training aids for New Pup. The theory is Pup chases the wing until he wears out or reasons that he isn't going to catch it and pointing it would be more fun.

Don't condemn the dog for being playful, but don't let him get away with it either. If he's too full of romp to retrieve, forget retrieving and wrestle with him until you iron out the kinks, then work on his schooling. Even kids get recess once in a while.

Water retrieving isn't common for bird dogs, but there are times and summer is a good season to teach the dog water retrieves. It cools him off, teaches him to enjoy swimming and adds another dimension to his training. Several breeds can be used as waterfowl retrievers, at least in mild weather, so water training is vital if you plan to use your dog that way.

You also can work on hunting dead by breaking out the bird wings you so carefully saved last season for just this moment. You did put a bunch of wings in the freezer, didn't you? Well, maybe next year.

The theory of the wing-on-the-string is one that works . . . sometimes. You tie a bird wing on the end of a fishing line and let the dog chase it. Keep flipping the wing ahead of the dog until, finally exhausted and frustrated, he points. Then you good-dog him and a little light bulb pops on over his head and he knows forevermore that pointing, not chasing, is what you do with bird-smelling objects.

This technique worked on my first two Brittanies, but Ginger ran the wing until she foamed at the mouth and never did point it. She finally just flopped down and said the hell with it. Yet she pointed real birds instinctively the first time she ran into them.

Using live birds for training is, I think, a far more valuable technique.

For example, a call-back box or trap for quail is a super training aid. You buy a dozen or so game farm quail, plant them in suitable habitat for your dog to work, then let the bird or two you left in the trap call the scatters in.

The call-back box is made of hardware cloth, available at any hardware store. Buy the two-foot width, which runs $1.50 or less per running foot, and get the kind that runs four squares per inch of mesh. You'll need twelve feet of cloth and enough rubber from an old innertube to make the strip seal on top. Make an entrance funnel of the leftovers and trim the inner (smaller) end of the funnel to leave sharp spurs, which discourage the quail from trying to get out.

The advantage of this type of call-back box is that you can reach in through the overlapped strips of rubber and extract birds for training, without a lot of fuss and feathers. The possible drawback is that a weasel or other small predator could go up the entrance spout and wipe out your birds.

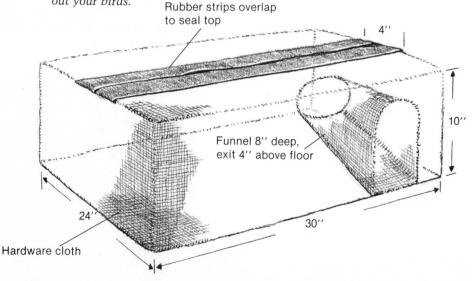

Rubber strips overlap to seal top

4″

Funnel 8″ deep, exit 4″ above floor

10″

24″

30″

Hardware cloth

You can fasten the box together with wire or use spurs from the hardware cloth itself to crimp the pieces. Make sure you crimp all projecting wires or you'll draw blood every time you move the thing.

Use young birds, from three to nine months old, since they're more oriented to coveying up and responding to an assembly call than are older birds. Release the birds in the evening (the urge to reassemble will be strongest then). An hour's dog work and two hours for the birds to be lured back to the trap means that, in late summer, you should be in the field ready to go no later than 4 p.m. The weather in most of the country is still plenty hot in September/October, so don't put the box in the direct sun or the birds might die. In my home, Missouri, you must have a $5 wildlife hobby permit and must band the quail. Other states undoubtedly have more or less restrictive regulations.

Don't work the birds the first several times they're planted so they become accustomed to reassembling at the box. You'll inevitably lose some quail, but you may pick up wild ones. While it may be tempting to replace your strays with wild birds, it's illegal, and I certainly wouldn't recommend it (especially since I work for a conservation agency). For damn sure you shouldn't go home packing more birds than you started with. Conservation agents can count.

If you're on a tight budget, you can do what a couple of my friends did. Buy a quail or two (two is better because they keep each other company—really) and hobble them so they aren't able to fly very well. You can tie a small fishing sinker to a leg or a piece of bright-colored engineer's tape with a small weight. After a couple of labored flights, the birds are easy to pick up. It may not be the ideal way to work a dog on live birds, but it's cheaper than the other methods.

You can dizzy a bird by tucking its head under a wing and whirling it around a couple of times. The fuddled bird won't fly off when you plant it. Some experts shun anything that makes the bird less than fully equipped, and I certainly wouldn't argue with this ideal approach—but weighting birds or dizzying them works well enough. I doubt dogs make the distinction between a fully charged bird and one that's been tampered with. At least not the dogs I hang around with.

You can catch pigeons if you have access to a barn, silo or can find a flock of the birds. The pigeon trap is exactly like the call-back trap for quail except that the entrance is built differently. Bait the trap with food and water and tie the "bobs," the hanging wire stops that form the door, up for a while until pigeons get used to using the trap. Then drop the bobs. Pigeons can push the bobs up and back to enter, but when they try to get out, the bobs are checked by the sill of the door.

The advantages of using pigeons for training are that they are free and you can shoot them over the dog, where game farm quail, at least in Missouri, can't be shot without an expensive permit. Pigeons are hardier birds than quail also. But quail are what you hunt.

Timing in dog training is crucial. My childhood dog, Chaps, was prone to chase

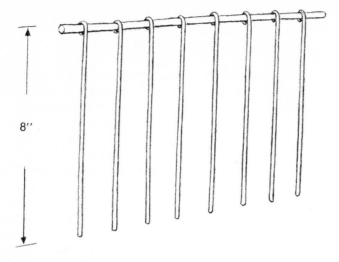

8″

Gate on a pigeon trap will swing in as the birds push against it from the outside, but a stop along the bottom of the row of prongs prevents the birds from pushing them back the other way, thus trapping them inside the trap box.

cars. It didn't even slow her when I screeched at her in my pre-adolescent voice. She just knew she was going to catch my uncle's Model A and do it grievous harm. Then one day my grandfather picked up a road rock and, with an overhand delivery that Nolan Ryan couldn't have matched, busted Chaps right in the butt, at the same time shouting "No!"

She yiped and scooted back to him with her stub tail tucked between her legs. From that day on, she considered him God and, by inference, me as God's disciple. It made discipline a lot more simple. You can't always depend on a well-aimed rock to make your point—even Ryan occasionally walked batters.

It's all well and good to read good dog-training books for ideas, but you have to put the ideas into practice. and that means a lot of work. Richard Wolters and Bill Tarrant/Delmar Smith differ fairly widely both in method and in their ideas of a finished dog. Smith trains dogs to poop on command; Wolters is far less of a perfectionist than that. So read either or both, adapt or adopt . . . and then work seriously and steadily at perfecting it.

Probably the most frustrating thing in dog training is having an animal that won't come. I call it "selective deafness." The dog hears you when he wants to, but becomes dead-eared when he's doing something he doesn't want to abandon.

Chip is a good example. He chases rabbits. He hears me calling him to quit, but he doesn't quit. He has decided that whatever punishment I deal out is worth the fun he gets out of running the bunnies. Chances are had I drilled him more thoroughly as a young dog, I could have exorcised his bad habits and today had a more perfect dog. But dog work takes a lot of time and I know few bird hunters who take enough. So we accept dogs that do things pretty well. And we envy the occasional man with the perfect dog.

I believe you can start training a pup at weaning, from six to eight weeks old. But don't expect much. You can work on "No" and "Come" and "Sit" with some expectations. "No" by its very sound is an attention-getter, and when you swat the pup on the rear, he'd have to be pretty dense not to realize the word's general meaning.

"Come" is the usual command to bring the dog in, but Delmar Smith claims "Here" is better. Take your pick. Try the reward approach—show the dog food and call the command at the same time. With patience, this should be enough. But if the dog is hard-headed (selectively deaf), put him on a check cord and let him go. As he hits the end of the rope, call "Come" and jerk him on his butt. It doesn't take much of that to encourage him to respond quickly. Be sure to praise him.

"Sit" is easy enough. As the dog faces you, give the command and push down on his hindquarters. Keep the pressure up until he sits, then praise him. It shouldn't take long until he sits on command. Once you can make him sit without using your hand to force him to do it, stand in front of him, hold your hand toward him, like a traffic cop, and make him sit.

Pretty soon, you'll have a dog who will sit when you hold your hand toward him. You don't have to command it. Next step is "Sit-stay!" Make the dog sit and command "Stay," pushing your hand toward him, palm up. Back off, watching the dog. If he starts to get up, forcefully push your palm toward him, step toward him and command "Stay" again. He should stop, probably in confusion, but it's what you want him to do. If he comes to you, tell him "No," take him back where he was, make him sit and start over.

Patience pays off. It's a tough thing for a dog to understand. But sooner or later he'll sit and stay until you command him to come. Gradually lengthen the time you make him sit and stay. When you're sure he'll stay until told to come, get out of sight to test him further.

Finally, call him and, when he's still some distance away, forcefully command "Stay!" with the hand signal. Probably he'll shamble to a halt, completely confused. If not, do it over until he gets it in his head that he comes or stays no matter where you are and where he is. This is the command that could save his life someday.

Training sessions shouldn't be more than fifteen to twenty minutes, though you can squeeze in a couple a day, and when either you or the dog or both get unhappy, quit. Take a few minutes to talk things over with the dog. Literally. Sit down and give him a hug and pet him some and tell him what you think about life, love and good hunting techniques. It restores the mutual affection and respect that should be part of the overall relationship between you and erases the anxiety of the master-pupil situation.

It's a bit of force-training, but it works. Let the puppy get going pretty good, call "Come!" sharply and, if he doesn't, jerk him on his fanny. Don't use a choke collar. And don't use more force than is needed to make the point that "Come" means come.

Sit is easy to teach. As you command "Sit!" push down on the dog's hindquarters until he sits. Praise him. It shouldn't take more than one or two short lessons to teach a smart puppy.

After you teach "Sit!" then work into "Stay!" Make the pup sit, command "Stay!" and reinforce it with an upraised palm. Don't back off too far. If (when) the puppy breaks, firmly re-sit him, command "Stay!" again. Sooner or later, he'll get the idea. Then work on making him stay for extended periods.

Once you're out in real field conditions, you can begin to hone the dog's hunting techniques. Some dogs instinctively head for brush clumps, gullies, places where birds might be, but others need to be guided. Train the dog to hunt where you want him to, not where he wants to. It's a lot of work for both of you, but make the dog respond to your hand signals when you're crossing a field or walking down a road. Call him back to you occasionally and make him sit. Heel him for a little while when he's hopped-up with energy. It reestablishes who is boss.

You'll also have to work to make your dog hunt in the brush. You'll have to get in there with him at first, show him where you want him to go. Some dogs like to stop and smell every rose they pass. Most of those bucolic sashays have no bearing on what you're out there for—they're coyote squirts or field mice or something equally irrelevant.

I command "Go on" when I want the dog to move on and reinforce it by stepping on his heels if he doesn't move smartly. Chip is prone to false point, and if I'm not sure whether he means it or not, I tell him softly to "Go on" and if he does, I know it's a practice point. But if he stays locked on, I get ready, for there are birds close by.

Brush hunting is tough with a dog. It takes a close-working animal, and the toughest thing on earth (next to making kids mind) is hobbling an eager dog. Yet, a dog, even one firmly locked on point, is no good if you can't find him. I prefer a dog that works perhaps too close, but who can be goosed into ranging farther out than one whose natural range is the curve of the earth.

I use the command "Back" to turn my dogs. Ideally, a brace of Brittanies will interweave their casts in front of you, covering everything. But it's asking a lot of the average dog to expect him to hunt ceaselessly and keep track of his master at the same time, especially if the master changes direction. So I work the dogs with the command "Back," which they come to understand means to change direction. Sometimes, if they're too far out, they'll move back toward me. If they're too far out on a wing, they'll range back in front of me. Either way, it's what I want.

One way to train a dog to heed the command "Back" is to begin by calling the dog's name, followed by the command "Back." When the dog turns to see what you want, give him a hand signal. Gradually you can eliminate the use of the dog's name (or of a whistle signal) and even the hand signal as the dog comes to associate the command with a change of direction. As is true with most dog work, back-yard training is the best. Don't wait to get into the field to give obedience training.

I've never had a problem with a gun-shy dog. Popping caps or making loud noises as you feed and sooth the dog is one accepted way to accustom them to noise.

Another method is to take the pup to a trap range—but all the noise may be too much. Better to have a friend shoot trap while you sooth and calm the dog. The best way to treat gun-shyness is never to let it develop. As a general rule, I think, males are less prone to it than females.

But all dog training depends on the amount of time you put into it. You wouldn't be a good CPA or first baseman or rum runner, or whatever you do to earn a living if you didn't practice. Look at lawyers—they practice all the time . . . and maybe someday they'll get it right.

So, what you get out of a dog is what you put into it.

You have to have a place to work. It can be the back yard, but only to a point. Unless you have a house covey, you can carry the dog only so far on the back lawn and then you need real birds for the final touches.

Don't overlook public hunting or refuge areas for dog training. Some refuge areas, which often have a very high game-bird population, may be open for dog work. You even may be able to fire a blank pistol to simulate hunting conditions. Of course, you must check with area officials to make sure you follow the rules. Also remember that the month or more before the hunting season usually is cool enough to work dogs in public hunting areas which also will have their peak population of game birds at that time.

Another possibility is to work dogs on fee hunting areas which are open year-round. If you don't want to pay the sometimes stiff fees for planted birds, perhaps they'll let you work your dogs at a reduced rate on resident birds, as long as you don't shoot any.

Many gun clubs have substantial grounds which may not be open to hunting, but which contain game birds and which can be used for dog training. Investigate the local facilities and, if it looks good, join the club.

6

Other Dog Breeds

Sure, I'm partial to Brittanies. But that's a matter of recent conditioning. I grew up with a springer/cocker spaniel crossbreed who seduced my father one day as he passed a Chicago pet store and carelessly looked in the window.

Chaps survived a few years as a city dog before we moved to a Missouri backwater town so small that it would have fit comfortably into my old South Side neighborhood. Chaps readily adapted to country life and became a superlative squirrel dog. She lived to be fifteen years old and died quietly in her sleep, no doubt dreaming gradually fading dreams of long-resolved chases.

We had a setter once when I was in high school, payment on a bad debt. My father thought he had come out ahead. He was wrong.

I hunted behind and loved Foster Sadler's iron-muscled pointer Mickey. Mickey had a superlative nose, but liked to see the pretty birdies fly, so was prone to bust points, especially when you weren't within rock-throwing range. Mickey was the world's boniest lap dog and I thought him indomitable, but a burly truck proved just a bit more muscular than he was one sad day.

Spence Turner's diminutive setter bitch Patty flows through the memories of quite a few seasons. A still-graceful but aging lady, she hunts yet. Not quite as hell-for-leather, not quite as tireless—but still a fine and dedicated seeker of quail.

Let's look at other possible upland dogs.

POINTER

The traditional pointer is muscled like a Cape buffalo and all those muscles are visible, since he's short-haired, an advantage in burr country. The best pointer is probably better than the best of any other breed at finding birds, especially quail.

Pointers have developed from a mix of unknown breeds in Spain, as far back as the 13th century. There's a good probability our pointer has a sluice of hound blood in him as far back as the Spanish dog and it's certain today's English pointer does.

The pointer is the ultimate quail dog and in the South especially if you're talking bird dog, you're talking pointer. Pointers have a bit more hound blood in their history than other bird dogs which probably accounts for their almost invariable good nose.

The English, looking for a faster dog, fed in greyhound blood, as well as blood-hound and foxhound crosses—giving them a dog with the ability to run far, wide and with endurance, plus a superb nose. First records of English pointers date to about 1650.

In the 1700s, pointers were crossed with setters (which had originated from ''setting spaniels'') to keen up the nose of the setter. A century later, setters, a more pleasant dog, were crossed back with pointers to calm the pointer's sometimes irascible nature.

So you can see that no bird dog is without his bar sinister in the family heraldry. God did not create pointers and setters—people did, sometimes by accident, mostly by design.

Pointers are most widely used in the South—and that means on quail. I grew up on pointers, almost never saw setters and never did see a Brittany or any other pointing dogs until relatively recently. Missouri was pointer country.

While pointers have the most highly developed pointing instinct of all bird dogs, you can discount the oft-heard stories about lost pointers holding a point until they starved to death, later were found in skeleton form still staunch on point. People who believe stories like that also believe in elves, filling inside straights and income tax refunds.

Frankly, I don't find the pointer a good-looking dog. A pointer on point is lovely, but there is something about the flat, baleful Mongolian stare of a broad-headed pointer that does not make me want to snuggle up with him.

Pointers develop early. You can hunt with a young pointer far earlier than you can with other young dogs (and, again, this is a generalization, for I know of six-month-old Brittanies who performed almost flawlessly).

Indeed, before setter blood was re-mixed with pointers to gentle them, one dog writer commented, "They have a ferocity of temper which will not submit to correction or discipline, unless taken in hand very young."

Not all pointers are wide-rangers, just as not all Brittanies work slowly and close-in. But as a general tendency, the pointer works quickly and covers a lot of ground. He's at his best working coveys in large fields, covering the perimeter of the field. The typical pointer would be nearly worthless on woodcock or grouse, which makes it mandatory that you know what kind of hunting you're planning before you indulge in a dog.

If, like me, you live where you have a variety of bird shooting and also plan trips to hunt an even wider array of birds, you should consider a more versatile dog, able to do a lot of things well, even if he does none of them as superbly as the pointer finds and points quail or pheasants.

SETTER

"The setter" is a misnomer, for there are several setters, prominent among which are the English, Irish and Gordon. But most people are thinking of the English setter when they talk of setters.

Setters are the dogs you think of in connection with grouse and woodcock. Where the short hair of the pointer is an advantage in the warm South, the setter's longer hair is a help in the colder North, and also is a protection when the dog is hunting in woodcock and grouse thickets.

Most dog history is insufficient, filled with probable error, a whole lot of supposition, and that of the English setter is no exception. One theory says that setters evolved from land spaniels, but Hans Bols in a 1582 book indicates that setters and spaniels were two distinct breeds even then and that the spaniels had docked tails.

Earlier yet, writers give us clues that setters may be the result of crosses among Spanish pointers, water spaniels and springer spaniels.

The American Kennel Club, in an official history of sporting dogs, dates the modern English setter to 1825 when Edward Laverack began breeding setters from a pair of dogs named "Ponto" and "Old Moll." Laverack's dogs, in time, were crossed by R.L. Purcell Llewellin with some setters from northern England to produce the famed Llewellin strain—not a distinct breed, but a strain of English setter. Most of today's finest setters can trace their ancestry at least partly back to one of those two historic kennels.

There are several setters, but the English is the most common. It's the traditional grouse/woodcock dog of New England and, as a general rule, works closer, is a bit easier to train than the pointer.

Setters are superb all-around dogs for bird hunting. They're good family dogs, and they have all the hunting instincts you'd want in a bird dog, including a retrieving instinct and the temperament to be agreeable to hunting dead. You can find running setters or close-working ones. As a breed, English setters have no faults. They'll work any upland game. The breed's only inconveniences are that the long hair is unsuitable for warm-weather hunting and also creates a maintenance problem in burr country.

GORDON SETTER

Gordon setters have to be treated as a breed separate from English setters because, first of all, they are. But more important, their general traits are so different as to make them as distinct from their English cousins as the Scots are different from the Britishers.

English setters are vital, balls of nervous energy. Few I've shared a car with are good travelers. They tend to drool, vomit and prance around the car, all of which tends to make me want to do some of those same things.

The black-and-tan Gordon setter has a bum rap as a slow worker, hard to see. But they're kind, sweet dogs and easy to train. With a belled Gordon, hunting dense cover where you don't want a ranging dog, you have a winner.

Now I realize that's an unreasonable prejudice, that the English setter still is the standard bird dog in most of North America. But if I had to choose a setter, it would be a Gordon.

For these reasons: (1) The Gordon is a placid dog, close-working and thorough. (2) It is a one-person dog and a good family dog. (3) It is a fine brush-country dog, which is where I hunt most of the time. (4) It is a thorough hunter and points strongly.

Those who knock Gordons do so on two counts—its alleged slowness and its color, which makes it hard to see. On the first count, my first two Brittanies both have been slow workers and they still find as much game as some of the rocket-assed dogs they've hunted with. And as far as color goes, in the jungles I hunt you couldn't see a dog that was red, white and blue with silver spangles. Put a bell on 'im.

Gordons got their name from the fourth Duke of Gordon, a Scot who juiced up a local hunting line that already had bloodhound and probably setting spaniel blood in it with collie blood from a bitch, Maddy. Maddy was supposed to be a fine bird dog who "watched" game she found, rather than pointing it. I used to have collies and they were the most stone-nosed dogs on earth, but I'm sure had any of them ever seen any game, they would have watched it with great interest.

Anyway, Maddy allegedly produced the black and tan pattern of the modern Gordon and, for a time, a lovely collie tail as well.

Gordons are exceptionally handsome dogs, but when you stack up their plusses against those of other dogs, you'd surely have to go with something else—unless you could find the exceptional Gordon who could compete all-around with a Brittany, vizsla, German shorthair or one of the other utility infielder breeds.

GERMAN SHORTHAIR

The German shorthaired pointer is a long way from the English pointer in looks and, in the same way the Brittany spaniel compares to other spaniels, the only thing the German shorthair really shares with his long-tailed cousin is the name "pointer."

German shorthairs probably are descended from the Spanish pointer, bloodhound and German retriever, so share common ancestry with most other bird dogs.

About the only drawback to a German shorthair is its availability. They're all-purpose dogs, destined to become more popular as more people discover them. They're strong, big dogs, bigger than Brittanies, with all the same qualities—pointing, strong retrieving instinct, keen hunters, powerful, attractive.

One of the "new" breeds is the German shorthair pointer, a very agreeable dog that looks like a bobtailed pointer. Shorthairs are intelligent and versatile, but not too available.

They haven't been in the United States long, since the 1920s, but they'll do anything. They'll hunt all upland game and retrieve waterfowl as well. They are highly intelligent and make good pets. They will hunt at night and have been used as deer hounds, or on raccoons.

The males weigh up to seventy pounds, females to sixty, so it's a big dog, in a class with English pointers. They're leggy and deep-chested.

Any hunter limited to one dog for a variety of game should consider the German shorthair. A hell of a fine dog.

VIZSLA

I can only think of vizslas as ''her'' and consider them the Gabors of the dog world, Hungarian lovelies as trim and pretty to look at as to hunt behind.

That's because a fine little vizsla bitch named Sandy pointed and retrieved my first pheasant and I had the pleasure of hunting behind her for a couple of seasons.

I suspect the only reason you don't see more vizslas is because no one can spell the name and few can pronounce it. God knows, the dog has been around almost as long as people.

It, like Mama, Eva, Zsa Zsa and however many others there are, came from Hungary. The vizsla is a nobleman's dog and always has been a bird dog. Sandy was almost Irish-setter red, typical of the breed, long-legged, shorthaired, stub-tailed and graceful as a greyhound.

The vizsla, like the German shorthair, is an all-purpose dog whose popularity is limited by its lack of availability. Vizslas have a long history, originating in Hungary as bird dogs for the nobility.

Jeff Griffen, in his fine book *The Hunting Dogs of America* (Winchester, 1964), theorizes that vizslas originated partially from red hounds, but any other forebears are speculative. The dog resembles the Weimaraner, though it's smaller and a different color. It, the Weimaraner and the German shorthair possibly had the same kinfolk 'way back.

Whatever its origin, the vizsla today is an all-around hunting dog and well worth consideration by any hunter who needs a dog that will hunt anything pretty well. I suspect that if I were to get out of the Brittany business and get a vizsla, tomorrow I'd be writing encomiums about the joys of vizsla owning. It almost happened— my first Brittany died under the wheels of a car that didn't bother to stop and Stub Taylor, Sandy's owner, called as soon as he heard about it to offer me Sandy.

"I don't get to hunt her enough," he said. "I'd like her to go to someone who'll treat her right and work her." It was hard to say no. It was hard, in fact, to say anything around the big lump in my throat, but I had my heart set on another Brittany and so Sandy stayed with Stub, sharing his Rock Port, Missouri, feed store office, curled up by the stove listening to outrageous lies, vulgar stories and windy brags. Sometimes a visiting hunter would be dogless and Stub would loan Sandy to him. She'd hunt for anyone. So, the visitors would tramp the big Missouri River bottom fields behind a flowing red dog and they'd put up pheasants and quail and the little Hungarian lady would bring the dead birds in. Sadly, she's gone now, too, just another bittersweet memory in my yellowing album of dogs that used to be.

Like some of the less-popular breeds, the big drawback to the vizsla is availability. The first dogs came to this country as recently as 1950 and the breed never has become widespread.

But it should—it will do everything you want a bird dog to do. It's affectionate, intelligent, kind, protective and ideal for a solitary hunter since it hunts close, but thoroughly. Size is a maximum of sixty pounds.

SPANIELS

While today, the Brittany joins with pointers and setters to form the "Big Three" among sporting dogs, it has happened only recently. The traditional spaniels were, especially, the springer and the cocker.

Both are flushing dogs—close-working, zig-zagging dogs that harass pheasants or grouse into flight within gun range of the master. Both are retrievers and good dead bird hunters.

There is no substitute for a flushing dog on pheasants which, after a day or two of gun pressure, seldom hold still for a pointing dog. Flushing spaniels are such quick, energetic little dogs that they confuse and panic the usually cool old cock pheasant into doing something he'd never dream of doing without the dog—fly.

Brittanies are almost a breed apart and most nearly resemble setters. As far as I am concerned, dog-men can drop the "spaniel" designation and merely call them Brittanies.

My two Brittanies at this moment are yowling for their supper. They're my chosen breed and have come on as the No. 3 breed in popularity behind setters and pointers. Brittanies can do it all and do it well.

Clumber spaniels are so rare as to rate only a mention. I doubt any hunter will buy and train a clumber as his only hunting dog. Clumbers are popular in England and their heavy bodies show the influence of the basset hound with which they were crossed early in their history.

They're slow workers, suited for estate-type hunting where there is much game, small fields and no need for a wider-ranging dog.

Cocker spaniels are familiar to most people as the wimpy little yipes that pee on the rug if you glance at them. Not so the traditional cocker, a feisty dog with the heart of a lion. Cockers are great family dogs and if you can find one with a hunting instinct, some leg to get him around and the guts of his forebears, you'll have a hell of a fine bird dog.

The cocker's name comes from its use as a woodcock dog. Although at one time the cocker was among the top few dogs of all breeds in popularity, it was at the same time being turned into a house mouse, as worthless in the field as a Mexican hairless.

The historic cocker was unparalleled at flushing woodcock and snipe, as well as pheasant, and would today (if you could find a good one) be as good an all-around flushing dog as any. Cockers were trained to squat at the flush and wait for a command to retrieve. Cockers weren't recognized as a breed until 1892, and a dog named Obo, whelped in 1879, generally is recognized as the founder of the Canadian, then United States line of cockers.

The clumber spaniel is about like he sounds—heavy and slow. They're an English dog, not widely known nor available on this continent and aren't likely to become so.

Cocker spaniels can be superb hunting dogs if you can find one bred to hunt, not for show or somebody's lap. They're a flushing dog, not a pointer. Frankly, I've never seen one in the field.

The cocker's larger cousin is the springer spaniel, also a flushing dog and fairly common. They're superb on pheasants, useful on grouse, and they'll retrieve anything and find dead birds too.

Cocker enthusiasts generally hunt the dogs in pairs (as do many Brittany owners). They're small and it's hard work to bust brush, so they don't have the lasting power of larger, more powerful dogs.

If you're interested in hunting cockers, stay way away from show stock. Find a field trial line and stick with that. Show stock pees on the rug.

Springer spaniels are the other most-common type. A springer is the quintessential pheasant dog, big enough to bust brush and hunt all day, keen-nosed, intelligent, able to beat a pheasant at his own run-hide game.

They retrieve and hunt dead well and can be used on waterfowl for retrieving. They're not good quail dogs, nor are they much good when hunted with pointing breeds, for they tend to stay with the other dogs and flush birds out of range—a trait that screws up the pointers and is likely to lose you some friends if you own the springer and the friends own the pointers.

Springers and cockers sprang from the same ancestry; indeed from the same litters, for the larger dogs in a spaniel litter were called springers, the runts cockers. In England today the springer and cocker look much alike except for size. Most springer hunters live in the northern United States.

Again, though springers are used on other game, it is on pheasants that they are in their element. It's a limited breed, but can be used on rabbits as well as game birds. Springers are exceptionally friendly and make superb pets and family dogs. They're bright and peppy and are a joy to be around.

RETRIEVERS

Upland hunters who also go after waterfowl should give a lot of thought to getting a good Labrador or golden retriever, instead of a bird dog.

Either dog will work pheasants and grouse as a flushing dog and, if you keep them close in, will flush woodcock and quail close enough for some shots. The dogs, with good noses, will ''make game''—give an indication that they're smelling the sweet scent of something—most of the time and give you a chance to be ready to shoot before the flush. It may be a rabbit or other animal, but it also may be a covey of quail. And it goes without saying that retrievers retrieve and hunt dead birds exceptionally well. The only drawback is that if you enjoy watching a pointing dog work, you lose that with a retriever.

Golden retrievers always have reminded me of what a friend calls ''the basic farm dog.'' Sort of shaggy, soulful eyes, looks like the kind of dog small children hug and wool around. And he is—a superb family dog, easy to train, absolutely as fine a dog friend as you can have.

It's a relatively new breed and its history is fascinating. The original story was that Sir Dudley Marjoribanks (visions of the Khyber Pass!) bought a troupe of eight Russian tracker dogs from a circus in 1860. The exceptionally intelligent dogs were heavy of body and coat and were used to herd sheep. Allegedly, Sir Dudley crossed these Russian superdogs with bloodhounds and got the present golden. It makes a great story.

A golden retriever puppy would make Scrooge baby-talk. Goldens make incomparable pets, as well as fine retrievers. They have keen noses for dead birds and will act birdy on live ones to give you a chance to get ready for a shot.

But it isn't true. Sir Dudley, apparently one of those British types who enjoy a good, if obscure joke, and who have a P.T. Barnum sense of comic promotion, was having us on.

He did found the breed—but he did it with a gold-colored pup from a litter of flat-coated retrievers, a well-known retrieving breed. He crossed this dog with a tea-colored Tweed water spaniel, a local breed of retriever. This happened in 1868 and the pups were called Ada, Crocus, Primrose and Cowslip. (Try giving dogs with those names orders in a duck blind and see how long you'll keep your rough-hewn hunting buddies.)

Sir Dudley continued to line breed the yellow dogs, occasionally mixing in some more Tweed water spaniel or wavy-coated retriever blood, and finally had a true-breeding dog. There is a bit of yellow Labrador in the golden today, since some of the pioneer kennels would stir in some of that blood occasionally. The breed was recognized by the AKC in 1932.

Goldens are used frequently as combined water/upland dogs and probably are the most suited for that double duty of all the retrievers.

LABRADOR RETRIEVER

Labs come in black and yellow packaging, which means something only to Lab owners, not to the dogs. Labs outnumber all other retrievers and for good reason—they have all the virtues and none of the faults of any of the other dogs.

While I might prefer a golden, a field trialer will tell you a golden is too sensitive and a north-country duck freak might say the golden is not hardy enough in icy water. Hell, the Lab can swim in icy water and accept the proverbial two-by-four across the brow to get his attention and come back for more. Labs are super dogs.

They're extremely intelligent, superb family dogs, can do everything but iron and clean house and probably would do that if you suggested it. The average Lab ranks higher than the average anything else, at least the average retriever of any other breed. I feel you can take run of the litter on Brittanies, probably on pointers or English setters and get a competent bird dog, just as you can take an average Lab and get a competent retriever.

But that's not true of any other breed.

Labs come from the St. John's Newfoundland, a variation of the huge Newfoundland (and we're talking about an enormous dog, big enough to pull a pony cart). But the St. John's was close to what today we call the Labrador. It was bulkier of head, but had the thick, slick-oily coat of the Lab and great swimming ability.

As early as 1800, hunters were buying St. John's Newfoundlands for duck retrieving. The St. John's became extinct in Newfoundland when a law prohibited a family from owning more than one dog. It's hard to produce a litter of puppies without also producing a litter of families under such a law and within ten years the island ceased to be a source of this fine water dog.

Labrador retrievers are the quintessential waterfowl dog, but they're also good flushing dogs, hunt dead fairly well and retrieve superbly. Besides, they're among the most intelligent, lovable dogs.

But its blood, already called the Labrador by Col. Peter Hawker, who owned some, was at work in shaping today's Lab. Some claim St. John's Labs were crossed with setters, especially Gordon setters and Irish setters, but that's only a theory. Almost surely some flat and curly-coated retriever blood was stirred in.

Gradually the modern Lab evolved. There still are some genetic peculiarities. Yellow Labs may pop up in a litter whose parents both are black. There is no guarantee that yellow will breed true, since the color is recessive. Labs also can be chocolate and have brown, black or yellow eyes.

Retrieving is so natural it doesn't need to be taught—but sometimes it needs to be channeled. Recently I watched a friend shoot a dove which his Lab dutifully fetched . . . to about ten feet away where she crouched, tail wagging happily, wanting only a good, romping game of Keep Away. They were far enough away that I could only hear the faint stern tones of the master as he commanded ''Wendy! Fetch!'' and Wendy, a tiny toy dog at that range, pranced with great joy in a circle around him until finally, in frustration, he took off his hat and threw it at her and shook his fist. Consumed with contrition, she apologetically brought the dove to him, undamaged. After all, what's a dove hunt without a little fun?

For upland gunners, the Lab is as good as any dog at pheasant chasing. It is fine for dove work, but hot weather is tough on heavy-coated Labs so always be conscious of the dog's comfort. Plenty of water, both to drink and to cool off in, is imperative.

Labs will work as flushing dogs for any birds and have a good enough nose to find dead birds and, of course, retrieve them.

Labs are one of the three or four breeds of dog I would give house room. They're exceptionally fine companions and I'm proud to be friends with several of them. I hope they feel the same about me.

WEIMARANER AND IRISH SETTER

Of course I know there are Weimaraners and Irish setters who can do everything with a game bird but casserole it for you—but I have yet to see a good hunter of either breed.

They are not at all prevalent as bird dogs and neither shows signs of being a blossoming breed. So, I'm lumping them together as ''other dogs.'' Unless you have a fatal attraction for either breed, the chances are you should consider any one of the other breeds we've talked about as your bird dog.

Irish setters are lovely dogs but, like cocker spaniels, have been bred so long for show purposes that their gutsy field qualities have been lost. It's hard to find a hunting Irisher, at least in my part of the world.

Aside from the prevalence of show dogs, rather than hunters, bird men don't like the Irish because of his color. But, like the Gordon, he can be belled. The long coat is a problem in burr country.

Irish setters are big dogs, though the field dogs are smaller than the show monsters. But a big one still could hit ninety pounds. That's something to think about when

Weimaraners are showy dogs, but every one I've ever been around was as squirrelly as Moe, Shemp and Larry and I wouldn't have one, even as a gift. However, I'll guarantee there are superb hunting Weimaraners.

feeding time comes. And sometimes big, rangy dogs wear out more quickly than tight, close-working dogs, so you may wind up with a half-day dog.

As is true with any breed of dog, you can find a superb one that transcends all the criticism, all the flaws—but as a general rule, you will come closer getting a good hunter with many other breeds.

And I think the same is true of the weimaraner (a dog a childhood friend of mine persisted in calling a ''weisenheimer''). It's a beautiful dog, a natural pointer, but functions more as a retriever. Sort of a pointing Labrador.

Weimaraners used to cost an arm and a leg and few were worth the powder it would take to blow them to hell. They were lousy hunters. Today's weimaraner is a better hunter, but still not exactly sweeping the field.

Like the Irish setter, the weimaraner is a big dog, powerful enough to knock down tall trees. It looks like a great big vizsla with a stub tail, silvered brown color.

Again, it's one of those dogs that, if you have a throbbing urge to own one, you should choose—but if you're a babe in the dogwoods, there are breeds far more easy to train and to keep.

Dog owning is a matter of personal preference. Any dog, including one whose pedigree dates back to the last alley encounter of its mongrel bitch mama, can turn into or possibly be turned into the best bird dog in the world. But certain breeds give the neophyte dog owner a better chance of coming up with a decent field dog.

You can go wrong with any of them. But you'll stand less chance of developing an egg-sucker with a pointer, English setter, Lab, Brittany. Popularity generally

There is no more beautiful, graceful dog than the Irish setter, but they tend to be less than superbrains. Find a good one and you'll love him. The secret is in the search.

is deserved and the various breeds have been around long enough now to establish themselves.

The Brittany started slowly, picked up steam and now threatens the superiority of the English setter in overall popularity. Contrarily, there never was a more overblown publicity campaign than that showered on the weimaraner, and once everyone got over the heady optimism created by that and saw what the dog really does, quite a lot of the glamour faded.

Also, dogs from proven parents produce good working offspring more often than those from questionable ancestry. Blood tells. Maybe not all the time, but taken overall—and you're trying to maximize your chances of getting a good dog.

The breeds I'm partial to are those that thrive on a dog-man relationship. I want a dog that is a friend as well as a tool. I want ones I can talk to and who would if they could talk in return.

Yet I know there is a vast body of owners to whom a dog remains a dog, an inferior creature treated with affection and care, but not with love. There are breeds that respond to that kind of treatment—pointers, for example.

So it depends on who you are and what you want from your dog. Somewhere there is a dog for you . . . unless, of course, you're one of the two greenhorn duck hunters who were sitting in their blind one day talking about the poor luck they were having.

"Not doin' too good, are we?" said one.

"Nah," said the second. "Maybe we're not throwin' the dog high enough. . . ."

7

Boss of the Ridgetops

The whippoorwill has been perched on the same log for half a dozen years. Maybe it's not the same bird. Maybe it's a series of birds on the same log. Maybe, like a grouse drumming log, this flaking old log has whippoorwillish attractions invisible to my increasingly rheumy and jaundiced eye. So, if a whippoorwill, darting through the night after bugfood, occasionally does what he always seems to be threatening to do (flies up his own rear end and disappears), another whippoorwill moves right in.

The firelight capered, tickled to animation by its own giddy thermals. My stewpot simmered quietly and I leaned against my backpack and read a book in the rapidly dimming light. A bank of thunderheads swallowed the drooping sun to the west and I wondered if a sudden, heavy spring rain would mire my pickup out on the dirt road where I'd left it.

But it would take more than the threat of being stranded in the turkey woods to upset me. There are far worse things than to be forced to live in adversity with wild turkeys, deer, morel mushrooms, the perennial colony of buzzards, blooming blue-bells and pink flowering crabapples.

The campfire died to a dull glow and I stirred it with a stick, fed the stick into the revived fire. Just as the sun set, I heard a rattling gobble down in the woods behind me, a quick burst of defiance from one of the old ridgetop bosses whose insistent gonads were keeping him up late these days.

The moon rose, drifting toward a collision with the approaching thunderheads. I shivered in the chill of the spring night and slid into my sleeping bag.

Sometime in the night, I woke. It was that still time when the life forces have wandered quietly into deep, dark, silent pools. It was a grim moment when I knew that man is mortal, holding his ultimate fate at uneasy arm's length. I realized with a dry mouth that I am not the very big boy I thought I was and I was afraid and alone.

Then the strident whippoorwill, his voice throbbing with life itself, let me know that I was not alone in the night and I slipped back into the warm comfort of sleep.

There are moments in a hunter's life when he wonders what devils move him, what malevolent humours surge through his aghast system and impel him to irrational actions. One of those times is when he squats in a duck blind that would have to warm up to be termed arctic, cold squeezing his very soul, watching ducks not fly. Another time is when he blows sweat drops off the end of his nose and peers with burning eyes at what either is a hovering cloud of gnats or black spots signalling the onset of heatstroke, as doves fail to fly.

But perhaps the darkest moment of all, literally and figuratively, is when he wakes in the pit of night and his luminous dial watch tells him it is time to slide out of a down-filled sleeping bag, its embrace as warm and loving as the arms of a good woman, onto the frigid floor of a tent no more comfortable to the thinly clad butt than the floor of a hockey rink.

God! It was cold! Try not to think . . . turkey season is worth the discomfort. Never mind the fact that no sane person would be up at such an hour. Struggle into longjohns, muttering curses. Humming tunelessly . . . sleepin' with my gun, like life in a slimy foxhole on the fringe of No Man's Land . . . chaotic thoughts.

It's tough trying to remember everything in the confused blackness. There's no coming back. It's a long haul down the ridge, into the steep-sided valley, across the sandy creek, up the other ridge. Try not to think about it. Depressing. Gun, shells, call. Call. Shine flashlight briefly on billfold, get little mouth caller out, stick it in mouth to soak. Tastes like billfold. Not good. Deep breath. Try to clear head. Rub eyes. Check pockets. Got gloves. Got breakfast bars. Especially breakfast bars. Hunger is great enemy of turkey hunter. Camouflage headnet.

Rub eyes again. Okay, time to go.

A barred owl gargled his strangled report on the mouse population status and, from somewhere on down Mussel Fork, a fellow nightbird agreed. Barred owls aren't just content to prowl the mousefields; they have to tell each other about it.

There are few turkey-hunting precepts left unscarred, but one that is decrees that the hunter first in the woods has the advantage over the late arrival. It almost always helps to be up before the turkey—though I've scared more than a few birds off the roost stumbling through the woods to my hide. So, it's a mixed blessing.

Roosting a bird is the ideal way to eliminate the problem of spooking birds off the roost. You can hear turkeys fly up to roost if you're in the woods at sunset. From about fifteen minutes before sunset to fifteen minutes after, you can hear birds flying to roost for perhaps 200 yards on a still evening. Listen for five minutes. If you hear nothing, run, don't walk, to another vantage point (obviously, high, open spots give you the greatest listening range) and listen again. It's fine exercise and, if you can locate a bird within a few yards, it'll save you a lot of time the next morning.

It's almost always black-dark when I start for the far ridge. This time was no exception. There was a sliver of moon and some starlight, enough to see the big things such as trees, but not enough to see sprouts or holes in the ground. Consequently, my passage was slow, noisy and halting, punctuated by muffled curses.

A pair of gobblers come warily to the call. The bird on the right already is aware that something isn't right. Absolute immobility is the hallmark of the good turkey hunter. Turkeys will come to a poor call—but not to a moving hunter.

No matter. I wasn't likely to alarm any turkeys that early unless I walked directly under the roost tree (which I have done several times). One year, I spooked a deer (and vice-versa when it flushed in the night just beside me). The deer ran off a few yards, stopped and proceeded to eat me out in deer-ese—foot stomping and noisy blowing.

But this time it was quiet. I camp on one ridge, hunt the next. Actually there have been turkeys shot on the same ridge where I camp, but human nature being what it is, the grass is greener and the turkeys more numerous on the next ridge over.

The two ridges are separated by a deep creek valley where bluebells invariably are in bloom during turkey season, as are Dutchman's breeches. Some hunters don't take time to notice the flowers, or the way the creek curls cheerfully through little gravel beds and over small ledges. That's their problem.

There always are turkey tracks in the wet sand and heart-shaped Valentines left by the dainty hooves of deer. My hunting ridge has several Indian mounds on it. It would be a nice place to spend eternity, looking over the Mussel Fork valley, cooled in hot summer by the big trees and the ever-present breeze, warmed in winter by a snug blanket of fallen oak leaves.

There was a faint glow in the east by the time I slithered down the camp slope into the creek valley. The first day birds peeped sleepily. The whippoorwills called incessantly, trying to get said what they had to say before the imminent rise of the sun. Off down in the valley, where it still was night, the barred owl gargled again.

I heard the first turkey of the morning, a long way up on the ridge and to my right. He was about as close as early turkey hunting theory said you should begin working—300 yards. Now, most successful turkey hunters try to get much closer. And they don't worry too much about making noise en route.

Prevailing theory now is that you get as close as you can as quickly as you can, running like an amok islander, leaping logs, falling over boulders, tumbling into deep ravines. There are at least two reasons for this mad dash. One is that you probably will be competing with hens for the gobbler and if you call first, he may come to you before servicing his established harem. The second reason is that you are competing for the gobbler with other hunters and it's wise to get in the first bid.

Calling patterns are as varied as the hunters who use them, but a proven method is this: For the first three hours of the day, use the mating call or a lost hen call or a cackle (or a combination) every five minutes.

The next three hours, start with a low mating call, wait fifteen to twenty seconds, then give a louder one. If there's no answer, give a lost call and clucks. Then wait fifteen seconds and give another, louder lost call. Wait ten minutes and repeat the pattern. Once a gobbler is within a hundred yards, use only clucks and whines. If the gobbler stops gobbling, don't think you've lost him. He may be coming quietly. For more about calls and calling, see Chapter 9.

And don't ever assume that because you have not heard a gobbler there are no male birds around. Young gobblers are especially prone to come pussyfooting in without making a sound. The first sound you'll hear is the percussive spit of alarm and then a massive crashing and thrashing of wings as the bird spooks when you scratch your butt, yawn noisily, sigh heavily, curse crawling ticks and otherwise drop your drawers in front of the Queen.

I found a downed treetop, nestled into it, my back against a growing tree. It was an ideal hide—good concealment, but with a field of fire. You can get too hidden, to the point where you'll never be seen by a lured bird, but if he can't see you, you can't see him either.

A natural blind is best—a downed tree, low bushes—because anything artificial looks artificial. LeRoy Braungardt, my turkey-hunting mentor, carries a portable blind made of camouflage material and lightweight aluminum supports, but he hunts with a bow and must be able to pull the bow without the inevitable motion spooking

The alarmed turkey is running; his running mate, visible under the hunter's arm, is thinking seriously about it. The only thing on earth faster than a running turkey is a flying one. The hunter will be lucky to kill this bird.

his birds. The gun hunter usually doesn't have to make extensive movements to bring his weapon to bear.

I cogitated on the origin of the name of the bird I was hunting, shifting slightly to lessen the bunburn from a piece of chert as sharp as a mother-in-law's tongue. George Bird Grinnell said, ''Precisely why it should have been called 'turkey' by the English is hard to say, except that as Turkey is a part of the Far East, it may have been supposed to have some relation to India. It has been suggested that the name by which we know the bird is a corruption of a Hebrew word 'pukki' said to mean 'peacock.' ''

Henry Davis looked at the supposed origins of the name, finally went along with Grinnell's Hebrew theory, then went on to make fun of the scientists who'd christened the bird *Meleagris gallapavo,* which translates to guinea peafowl, neither of which the turkey is.

Davis goes on to quote Ben Franklin, who opted for the turkey as the national bird, in preference to the bald eagle, saying the turkey ''would not hesitate to attack a grenadier of the British guards who should presume to invade his farmyard with a red coat on.'' Which, of course, is a crock, for few if any wild turkeys are dumb enough to attack any man, much less an armed soldier.

A.W. Schorger researched some 6,000 references to write *The Wild Turkey* and concluded that the word antedated the discovery of the American bird: ''During the reign of Edward III (1312–77), William Yoo of the county of Devon had on his coat-of-arms 'three Turkeycocks in their pride proper.' '' So our bird got called turkey because he looked like a European bird already called turkey.

And then, on the ridge 200 yards to my right, I heard the rattling challenge of a gobbler—perhaps the distant bird coming to my call, perhaps a bird fresh off the roost. Almost before the last note of his declamation died away, there was a counter challenge from a gobbler about the same distance from me, to the left, along the same ridge.

A cold finger skittered up my back and the little hairs stood up. *Someone walking over my grave.* There is no thrill in hunting, at least in my experience, comparable to the adrenal fix offered by a meeting with a choice gobbler. This was the stuff of dreams—two turkeys converging on each other, so inflamed with the sour acid of jealousy that they were blind to danger. And me in the middle.

Softly and very carefully, I kelped three times, my heart thumping, palms sweaty despite the chill morning. Now, with a bit more experience in the turkey woods, I'd only cluck. Anytime a turkey is coming, you're better off either clucking softly or not calling at all.

But instantly on my yelps, the right-hand gobbler thundered back at me. Gobblers don't just declaim. They thunder. They orate. They throb. A close-in gobbler sounds like a bull drum carrying an entire orchestra on its brawny shoulders.

The second gobbler, farther away, sneered at the first one. I was taking little breaths, the way you did when you were a little kid in the dark and you woke up and the house was death-still and you *knew* there was something in the room with you.

A redbird whickered, became abruptly silent, perhaps sensing the drama playing itself out on the long ridge. A car whined on the distant highway and a sough of wind sprinted up the bluff and through the treetops, then was gone, leaving the woods silent save for the sodden, heavy thumping of my heart.

Then the nearest bird gobbled again and he was closer, far closer. Now I had to make a choice. I necessarily had to face one way or the other, for the birds surely would converge almost on my trembling body. Since the bird to the right was considerably closer, I scooted my butt carefully around until I was facing him, the tree at my back. There was about fifteen yards of fairly open space, then underbrush, an ideal situation. I had seven hot loads, Winchester Double X Super X Magnum No. Four Shot in the old Model 12. By God, I'd keep shooting until he quit kicking!

There was no point in me calling again. The second bird gobbled, perhaps a trifle closer than he had been, but it didn't matter, for the first bird was so much nearer that I almost could smell him cooking for the Thanksgiving table. He rattled the trees again, his cavernous chest rumbling beneath the high-pitched gobble. It

Occasionally even a blind pig finds an acorn. Here Joel Vance hoists a young gobbler that came to his call on a north Missouri turkey hunt. Usually 30–40 percent of birds taken in a spring season are young gobblers.

sounded like a distant, ominous storm and my hands shook as I carefully balanced the slide handle on my knee and pressed the safety button off. The old gun nestled to my cheek as I eased forward and sighted down the long slope of the barrel.

The turkey was close enough that I heard his careful footfalls crunching in the dried leaves, close enough to kill . . . except that I couldn't see the damn bird. His toes left only tiny noise-dents in the smooth still of the early morning woods. Turkeys and deer, damn their ornery hides, can be the noisiest—or the most wraith-like—of all the wild critters.

They can hide behind a new oak leaf no bigger than a mouse's ear, they can walk over a dumptruck-load of popcorn, broken glass and crumpled wrapping paper as if it were foam rubber. But turn a turkey loose on a chunk of oak forest floor when he's hungry and satisfied there are no predators around and his scratching will sound like an alley cat orgy on a tin shed roof.

The gobbler paraded tantalizingly just out of eyesight in the underbrush. But even had I seen a feather, a piece of what I thought was turkey, I would not have shot until I could identify the entire bird. The memory of Denny Ballard's experience was all too fresh in my mind.

Ballard, a friend and fellow outdoor writer, was bowhunting turkeys one spring. He and a fellow hunter moved on a gobbler from opposite directions. As Ballard stood in a forest road, turkey-fletched arrow held across his chest, his fellow hunter spied the feather through the screen of underbrush and blasted Denny, knocking him a dozen feet with the close-in charge of turkey shot. It's a miracle it didn't kill him.

The soft footsteps eased off to my left. The woods hushed as if in anticipation. I felt my heart thumping heavily, blood surging turgidly in my ears. I barely breathed, jaws clenched so tightly they would have hurt had I thought about it.

There was a gentle crunching in the brush ahead of me. He was there, only feet away. My finger sneaked around the trigger. My eyes burned and I blinked rapidly to clear them. Then I had to swallow and did so, spasmodically, the sound incredibly loud to me, like a refrigerator falling down an elevator shaft.

Surely the bird could hear it. Maybe he had, for there was no sound. Suddenly, startlingly, the second bird gobbled and *he* was close behind me, the son of a bitch! He'd come in after all. Couldn't be more than fifty yards directly behind me. Well, if he wanted to get in on this, he'd better hurry.

But what had seemed such a cut-and-dried drama suddenly began to ravel. For, the right-hand bird moved again, no doubt strutting, dragging his wings and parading in cocksure defiance. Only trouble was, I still couldn't see him. But I could hear him and it was obvious he had moved just over the brow of the ridge and now was moving parallel to me.

Simply damned unbelievable! There was no way this could happen . . . but it was happening.

If I'd been an inch taller, I'd have seen his head. I'm sure of it. I measured each crunching footstep as he walked past me, just over the dropoff, no more than ten yards away. Not once did I see a feather. Incredibly, he was bypassing me, the lustshot hen he'd heard calling so sluttishly, and was joining with the second gobbler—directly behind me, 180 degrees in the wrong goddam direction.

I heard them close with each other, their feet scuffling the dry leaves.

Few times in his hunting life is a hunter faced with such an agonizing decision. What to do?

Sit tight? Hope the birds came back past me? Let them putter off and either try to call them back or try to outflank them? Ease around the tree trunk for a shot? Spring up as quickly as possible, hoping for a shot at a running or flying bird?

Eons passed. Planets collided. Galaxies collapsed. Black holes came and went. I made my decision.

I tensed every muscle, praying that if levitation ever has worked, it would work now. I lurched awkwardly to my knees, scuffling for purchase, one hand frantically pushing down on the damp moss, the other pulling the gun up and around. I came to my knees, then my feet. It seemed to take forever, but was only a second or two. Still, that's a long time in a turkey's life.

There was a moment of time suspended, a scene I shall never forget. The two birds were directly in line, the near bird no more than a dozen steps away, the other perhaps fifteen feet farther on. Both already were reared back as if they'd suddenly run into a brick wall.

They stared at me for a millisecond, eyes as big as marbles. And then, in perfect unison, they sprang into the air, straight up, and peeled over, as smooth an exhibition of formation flying as could be imagined. It was a scene that burned itself on my mind, those two huge gobblers, tassels of their virility dangling from their breasts, great wings, bronzes and blacks shimmering in the spears of sunlight that punctured the thin spring leaf canopy.

With the agony of futility I threw the old gun to my shoulder, knowing it was far too late.

The birds were airborne thirty yards away, side by side, great wings thrashing through low limbs. Maybe I could have knocked one down. Maybe a lucky shot would have broken a wing or hit one of the birds in the head.

And maybe not. . .

So I lowered the gun and stood there as silence came back to the woods. Anger and frustration and awe and giddy delight chased through me, a bouillabaisse of strong emotions.

It all was too much for me. I pushed the safety back on, laid the old Model 12 on the moss and slumped back down against the tree, my mind empty.

The sunlight crept across the clearing. A gray squirrel flicked a tail at me, skittered across to another tree. A redbird whickered brassily.

Gradually, my bleak mood lightened and I felt a smile tease the corner of my mouth. It would make a hell of a story around bacon and eggs and brawny camp coffee. After all, how many guys call up a pair of bull gobblers and, but for a freak of fortune, have them with their peckers exposed at ten yards?

My stomach growled and I thought about hickory smoked bacon strips trembling in their own juice, a couple of farm eggs simmering in butter, some wild plum jelly globbed on hot biscuits. . . .

Tomorrow I'd nail my turkey. I hefted the gun and started the long walk back to camp.

8

Bringing Back the Wild Turkey

There is no woods like the spring turkey woods. For one thing, there is no other upland bird hunted in the spring. It's a different woods then, not the golden woods of the early autumn woodcock, nor the stark, leafless woods of the late season grouse.

No, it's a woods where the hot spring sun dazes a turkey hunter operating on too little sleep and not nearly enough gritty camp coffee. It is a woods where baby squirrels frolic on your boot-tops, where the trees and bushes wear a green gauze veil as their leaves sprout. Nothing is dead in the spring woods; all is alive. Yet the nights are cold, a thermal rap on the knuckles, reminding you that Ma Nature still is in charge.

We're damned lucky to have the wild turkey around today. We almost lost it. Only fifty years after the first white settlers hit the Atlantic coast, in 1671, it was rare to find a wild turkey in the Maine woods.

Dwight Huntington, writing in 1903, bemoaned the decline of the wild turkey in my Ozark hills. He hunted there "with a local sportsman who knew the woods." Though he spent several days, he didn't see a bird, but when he and the hillman got back to town, someone told them "a boy had killed one with a stone, from a small flock which appeared in the village."

Well, there are far more turkeys now than there were in 1903, but you aren't going to kill them with a rock. The bird of today, hunted by today's methods, is far tougher to take than he was when the Pilgrim fathers splashed ashore. It didn't take long for them to set the standards of cut-and-get-out that would be followed by gunners for the next 300 years—if it moves, kill it.

The widespread extermination of game in this country is a shady chapter every bit as shameful as our treatment of the Indians, though Russell Means and some of the more intransigent Indian activists may not agree. But I'm a bird hunter, not a champion of Indian rights, especially when those modern-day rights, in a typical bureaucratic and weaseling attempt to atone for century-old wrongs, result in modern-day exploitation of our wildlife resources. Game laws are made to protect the resource, not to harass the Indian, and I don't see any reason to penalize our wildlife as an apology for Wounded Knee.

Even allowing for the dime novel exaggeration of our pioneer chroniclers, the abundance of wild turkeys must have been staggering. Buffalo Bill, who rode the range well after the beginning of the near-end for turkeys, said, "While at this camp, we had a lively turkey hunt. The trees along the banks of the stream were literally alive with wild turkeys and, after unsaddling the horses, between two and three hundred soldiers surrounded a grove of timber and had a grand turkey roundup, killing four or five hundred of the birds with guns, clubs and stones."

Capt. A. H. Bogardus, one of history's great exhibition shooters, also was a famed hunter. In 1866, he and two others killed more than fifty wild turkeys over a three-week span on Shoal Creek in Clinton County, Missouri. The area is almost all open land. Despite Missouri's remarkable renaissance in turkey restoration, Clinton County today (and probably then, too) is such marginal turkey habitat that it remains closed to hunting.

All my life I've read about the decimation of wildlife, but only rarely does it have an impact, or a feeling of immediacy. Most of the time I gloss through the pages of history, numbly accepting the drab accounts of what was and is no more. I know the passenger pigeon was exterminated but I can't really conceive of the vast flocks that existed.

I have an old book, *Birds of Kansas,* published in 1886 and apparently stolen from the Sante Fe reading room in Dodge City sometime about the turn of the century. The book is a curiosity and I thumbed through it, mostly with idle interest, until I ran across the fact that ruffed grouse had been native to Kansas. They were gone by the time the book appeared, but the author, N.S. Goss, said, "In the early settlement of the state [the grouse was] a resident in eastern Kansas."

And, Goss says, wild turkeys were abundant in the early settlement days "but are rapidly diminishing and will soon be exterminated."

How sad—to see it going, know it's going. Goss's dry little book is a voice from the grave, a sepulchral telling of grim facts. And just for an instant, I glimpsed grouse in the wooded creek bottoms of eastern Kansas, woodcock swirling up from spring seeps, turkeys rattling the ridgetops above a waving blanket of big bluestem as tall as a horse's shoulders. Just for an instant . . . and then the vision faded and once more there was in my mind the belching blat of a diesel tractor pulling a six-bottom plow through what once was tough, untamed prairie sod.

By the 1930s, the wild turkey was only a faint memory in most of its former range. It was as close to extinction as it ever will come. The last turkey faded from Massachusetts in 1851, a little over 200 years after William Bradford, governor of the Massachusetts Colony, and his Indian friends celebrated the bounty of the woods. It's doubtful that any of the attending Indians realized they were eating their destiny as they eagerly crunched wild turkey bones. Although the Indians had tried to domesticate the turkey, they weren't very good at it . . . and the settlers weren't about to waste good farmland on heathens anyway.

On the other hand, the Indians leaped right in on the exploitive merry-go-round. A.W. Schorger reported that in 1816 Indians around Prairie du Chien, Wisconsin, commonly sledded in for sale twenty to thirty dead wild turkeys at a time. By 1860, the bird was nearly extinct in the state and by 1881, it was. Commercial and unrestricted private use hunting, plus habitat destruction was a one-two punch that turkeys could no more resist than could any of the other wildlife species sent reeling by our forefathers' ignorance.

In the case of some species—for example, the passenger pigeon—it was a fatal blow. In the case of others—the buffalo or the prairie chicken—it was so near as to make no difference today. But turkeys are a different story, a biological Pearl White, snatched from sure death at the last possible moment.

Missouri's experience with turkey restoration is a model one nationally, a classic example of what has gone on (and, to a great extent, still is going on) nationwide. In 1934, Rudolf Bennitt and Werner Nagel did a study of game species abundance in Missouri. They estimated a maximum of 3,585 turkeys in the state and felt the population still was declining. To get a grasp on how successful the restoration has been since then, consider that Missouri hunters registered a combined 1979 spring-fall kill of more than 23,000 and a 1981 spring kill of 22,191 without in any way affecting the flock health. Something dramatic happened over those forty-five years.

Remember that in the 1930s, wildlife management was a science scarcely out of a class with alchemy and astrology. So, it's not surprising that the first idea was to restock with hybrid birds, a blood mix of wild and tame turkeys. It was a damn sight easier to raise turkeys in a game farm than to try to trap the wiliest of the wily wild turkeys—the few who'd survived 300 years of plunder and pillage. The common domestic turkey originated from Mexican turkeys which went to Spain with early explorers, ultimately made their way back to this continent as barnyard fowl.

Starker Leopold, son of Aldo Leopold (whose *Sand County Almanac* is the Bible of conservationists and should be in *every* sportsman's library), studied wildness in turkeys in the mid-1940s and concluded, "Something inherent in the bird, derived either from its southern ancestry or more probably from its long tenure in the barnyard, appears to prohibit its establishment as a member of our wild fauna."

Leopold was writing after the fact—from 1936 through 1943, Missouri dumped some 14,000 hybrid and domestic turkeys into the Ozarks, hoping for some genetic lightning strike that would restore the turkey to its historic range. It was an experiment that looks, in retrospect, naive, but it was honestly motivated.

We all like to laugh at people with egg on their face, but the egg got there because they were willing to try something, even if it was dumb. Back in 1894, George Bird Grinnell reported on efforts to increase quail numbers: "Sportsmen at large discussed with much earnestness the question of what should be done to restock the game covers. The first efforts took the direction of importing bobwhite quail from the south and turning them loose in covers that had been shot out. This was done, but the birds were soon shot off, for no one seemed to think of stopping shooting."

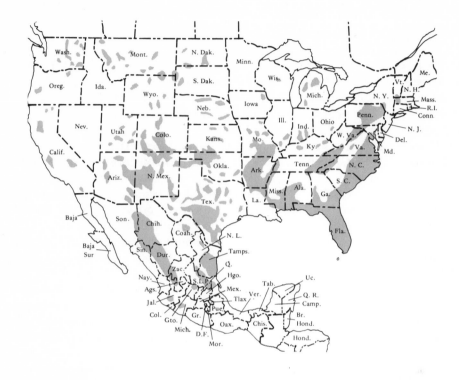

The wild turkey today has a wider range, if not a larger population, than it did in historic times. The restoration was a long time coming—turkey trappers netted wild birds and restocked them in suitable habitat.

Hybrid turkey stocking was just about that successful. The birds wandered into farmyards and quickly became easy meat for countless Sunday suppers. Or predators descended on them with cries of gusto. Hybrid stocking lasted until 1943 when the estimated wild turkey population in Missouri was 4,340. It was no triumph of wildlife management, even though the population showed a modest rise over 1934. More, it was a combination of the Depression and World War II taking gunners off the land. Breeding turkeys simply got a breather at a time when that was vital.

In the 1940s, Missouri had turkeys in thirty-one counties, but only seventeen had more than six flocks each. Wild turkeys were exterminated on 83 percent of the historic Missouri range. Paul Dalke, in a 1946 study for the Missouri Conservation Commission, blamed overgrazing, especially of woodlands; wildfires (Missouri for several years led the nation in the number, if not the acreage, of forest fires); and the illegal kill: "Turkey shooting is a tradition as deeply ingrained in the Ozark people as burning the woods," Dalke said.

THE BREAKTHROUGH

The season had been closed in 1936, not to reopen until 1960. Over that twenty-four-year span, turkey managers worked patiently (after they got the hybrid craze out of their systems), using a method first successful with whitetail deer, that of live-trapping wild animals and moving them quickly into suitable habitat.

Their weapon was the cannon net.

If there's a wildlife management Hall of Fame, Howard Thornsberry and Herb Dill should go in it. Thornsberry was an assistant at Swan Lake National Wildlife Refuge back in 1950. Herb Dill, refuge manager, was faced with the need to catch a lot of Canada geese for banding. Somebody—it really doesn't matter which one because the two will go down in wildlife history as co-inventors of the cannon net—thought up the idea of propelling a net over baited birds.

The two found an item about Peter Scott, a British ornithologist, who had tried firing a net over birds with rockets, an experiment about as successful as some of the 1950s rocket shots at Cape Canaveral.

But Thornsberry modified the rocket idea to mortar-like tubes that fired weights to which was attached the leading edge of a net. The rest is history. Instead of patiently waiting for dubious, smart geese to decide to walk into a baited trap (or, more likely, deciding not to), Dill and Thornsberry found themselves capturing half a hundred unsuspecting geese at a shot.

It didn't take a very bright wildlife manager to figure out that what worked for geese also would work for turkeys (or deer, Bengal tigers and woolly mammoths). It was the ultima Thule of restoration, the breakthrough. In order to restock, you need things to restock, as many as possible.

Florida turkey trappers used doped corn, starting the birds on the road to an anticipated sexual frenzy with a drug binge. Sounds almost depraved.

As far as I know, none of the modern turkey trappers used Johnny Audubon's method. I can't imagine why not—the pioneer ornithologist said he caught seventy-six turkeys over a two-month winter trapping period, up to seven at a time. He built a log structure twelve feet by ten feet, roofed over. Then he dug a trench eighteen inches deep and wide, sloping sharply up into the inside of his log trap. The trench was baited and a string of corn led out into the woods. The turkeys would follow the bait line, squeeze through the trench to get at the corn inside, then be unable to figure out how to get back out (a feeding turkey follows its appetite, not its power of reason). Audubon said he knew of eighteen turkeys at a baiting being taken, which is comparable to the best you can hope for with a cannon net and baited trap site.

Wildlife populations build slowly, from a near-zero base, but once you get a substantial enough base (barring some catastrophic factor such as epidemic disease), the population can explode. It has happened with both deer and turkeys.

There is no genetic reason why wild turkeys cannot be as productive and prevalent as pheasants or quail, given good habitat. They are every bit as prolific and more hardy and more catholic in their food preferences to boot.

A grouse will lay a dozen eggs, raise perhaps eight young. A quail hen may drop fourteen eggs and raise ten young. A pheasant hen will realize perhaps eight offspring from her dozen eggs. And a turkey hen easily may lay fifteen eggs. While she may raise only six or seven poults, that still adds up to a bunch of turkeys annually, a very attractive net profit—especially considering that hunting success is far more meager with wild turkeys than with any other game bird.

Why, then, aren't we submerged in wild turkeys? Perhaps we are on the brink of it. Missouri already has heavy populations of turkeys that hunters as yet have not stabilized. John Lewis, longtime Department of Conservation turkey biologist, flew over one north Missouri county in the winter of 1979-80 and counted a flock of 200 turkeys. I've seen flocks of a hundred. There were several reports of 300-bird flocks in the 1980–81 winter.

Turkey restoration has been like The Little Train That Could. It took a while to huff and puff to the top of the hill, but the downhill run has been a piece of cake.

SWAPPING WILDLIFE

Trapping and relocating native birds is the best way, since the birds are acclimated, but some states didn't have a seed stock, so there arose a fascinating sidelight to wildlife management—the swap.

Somebody had the idea of trading critter for critter. Somehow it doesn't (and didn't) seem right to pay for wild animals. But swapping is deeply ingrained in the American, all the way back to the Pilgrims bartering trinkets for Indian goods. Wildlife swaps have been a boon to biologists trying to bring some order back into the biological chaos our ancestors created.

States have swapped everything from fish to alligators, but the wild turkey has become the universal coin of the swappers. Missouri, hog rich in turkeys, has worked swaps with several states for ruffed grouse, pheasants, striped bass and even prairie plant seed. Minnesota, Iowa, Kansas and Wisconsin all have substantial flocks of former Missouri turkeys. Missouri's trap/relocate program started in 1953 and the cannon netters had caught nearly 4,000 birds through 1979-80. More than half went to about 150 release sites in nearly every Missouri county—certainly every county with even marginal turkey habitat. Others went in swaps.

California has traded everything but the Los Angeles Dodgers for turkeys—chukars, mountain quail and pheasants to Texas; Afghan white-winged pheasants, mountain quail and chukars to Arizona; mountain quail to Utah; white-tailed ptarmigan, mountain quail, chukars and those sly old Afghan pheasants to Colorado; and chukars to Wyoming. The birds have been wild-trapped in most cases, then shipped quickly to their new homes by commercial air. California, in its typical shoot-the-moon excess, also has gone international with its trades. It has swapped quail for such exotics as French red-legged partridge, Greek chukars, Spanish red-leg partridges, and Afghan see-see partridge.

New York swapped varying hares back in the late 1950s for Pennsylvania game-farm turkeys—Pennsylvania has a policy against trapping wild birds. The New York flock has prospered . . . but predictably enough not from the game-farm birds; rather from natural migration into the state by Pennsylvania's wild birds, plus New York's own trap/transplant program. In fact, New York's success has been such that it, in turn, sent birds to Vermont and Massachusetts where they have burgeoned.

I find the whole wildlife swapping story a fascinating, even heartwarming one. It's a case where some visionaries recognized the obvious (the hardest thing on earth to do) and, for very little money, everyone got what he wanted.

Figuring out ratios is the toughest part. There are no charts detailing how many pheasants make up one turkey, so it takes some doodling to come up with a ratio everyone is happy to support. As I write this, Missouri is trying to figure out how many turkeys make up a river otter or vice-versa, so it can work a trade with Arkansas.

The long-established dollar figure for one turkey is $350, but that figure was set long before the days of rampant inflation, and manpower and material costs both have skyrocketed since, so God knows what a wild-trapped turkey costs in real money today.

Thus, the wild turkey has made a dramatic comeback. In fact, it now exceeds its historic range, though not its historic population. Perhaps that day will come. I try not to be pessimistic. Habitat loss, not hunting, is what will limit the turkey flock. Hunters can't begin to constrict the modern turkey flock, but bulldozers can—and they can do it in a day.

In the spring of 1980, there were thirty-nine states open for turkey hunting. All the Deep South states, where the turkey never really left the ball game, should continue to have fine hunting. The Midwest and eastern states with good habitat will continue to see increasing flocks. Winters are a factor in the northernmost parts of the most northern states, but it takes a hell of a lot of winter to kill a turkey.

Western hunting should increase as flocks of Rio Grande and Merriam's turkeys expand. Nowhere do I know of pessimism about the immediate future of the modern turkey. So, for at least the next few years, we should see a steadily increasing hunter opportunity.

9

Hunting Wild Turkeys

If I have learned anything about turkey hunting over the years, it is that nearly all I've learned either is wrong or obsolete.

Case in point: When I started hunting turkeys in the mid-1960s, you were advised to spend as much time scouting for turkeys as hunting them. You looked carefully for tracks, droppings, scratchings, dusting areas and the like (and, more often than not, didn't find any signs since turkeys were thinly spread in those days).

But now, at least in Missouri, turkeys are just about everywhere and you can be within earshot of a gobbler just by going into the woods. Scouting still serves to confirm the presence of turkeys and if you're packing in to get away from the hunter herd (I can't recommend this too highly), scouting will close you in on birds.

Unless they're harassed, turkeys have a fairly small range and tend to follow a pattern of feed-water-roost. An old gobbler, for example, may come to the same little clearing every morning, call up his harem, then drift off in the same direction. I once spent three days in Arkansas figuring out the pattern of just such a bird, had myself stationed in ambush—only to have some thunderfooted hunter shamble into the middle of my little drama, calling like a little green heron with one leg caught in a cornsheller.

That's why I recommend backpacking deep, deep into the turkey woods. I once sent a neophyte Iowa hunter into the Current River country, told him to pack in as far as he could, set up a base camp and hunt out of it. He later wrote to say he'd killed a trophy gobbler . . . after calling up more than twenty birds.

There really is nothing to killing a turkey and I'll tell you concisely how to do it: Get to where there are no other hunters to mess up your act. Be reasonably proficient with the mating yelp and the cluck and maybe a whine. You shouldn't need anything else. Don't call too loudly. Don't call too often. Be fairly well-hidden (if you are completely hidden, you can't see to shoot, either), and *completely* motionless. Be prepared to stay as long as it takes to call in and kill a bird. That's really all there is to it. No big secrets, no gadgets. But every damn one of those precepts is harder than you think, especially keeping still.

There's a multiplicity of turkey calls, all designed to "yelp" like a hen. Wayne Bailey, nationally-recognized turkey biologist from North Carolina, uses one of his box calls. The Lynch Box Call, best-known of them all, is below his hands. To the left of that is a slate-and-peg call, then a mouth call, and, at upper left, two lipped box type calls.

There is no other hunting sport so fraught with rules as turkey hunting. Don't do this! Be sure and do that! The ponderous load of helpful hints is enough to make the average hunter start thinking fond thoughts about the instruction booklet for Form 1040.

Of course, helpful hints can be helpful—but don't let them rule you. It takes a lot of the joy out of turkey hunting if you go to the woods scared half to death you'll screw up if you don't follow the Manual of *Meleagris* as if it had been slipped to Moses along with that other stuff chiseled in stone.

CALLING

Turkey hens make every noise ever created, most of them less like what the experts say turkeys sound like than the howl of a castrated transmission. Turkey hens forever are coming up with squawks and squeaks that sound as if the hen had her bosom caught in a wringer. Gobblers respond to that, so why not to your horrible calls?

I think it is that the hen sounds natural. She has confidence. After all, she doesn't know she yawped when she should have yelped. There's no embarrassed silence, punctuated by muffled curses, no strained follow-up attempt to atone for the clinker. So, be natural. If you mess up a call, relax and continue. It'll be hard to do—if you haven't been there, you'll be disconcerted by the silence of the early-morning woods. You get the feeling countless ears are listening to you and you'll get stage fright.

So practice at home and do it outdoors where it will sound the way it will in the woods. Don't practice in huntable woods—you easily can make gobblers call-shy, if not for you, then for someone else. Work in areas closed to hunting.

The easiest call for a beginner to work is either a box or a slate-and-peg. I think the slate-and-peg sounds most like a hen turkey. I'd steer away from any of the sucking-type calls, such as a wingbone or a manufactured horn. They're too hard to work.

Best of all, but also the hardest to learn, is the mouth caller. I'd suggest you buy either a box or slate-and-peg, and a mouth caller. Use the former while you learn the latter. The disadvantage to the hand-held callers is that you have to move to use them and that motion can spook an incoming turkey (you'd be amazed how many times turkeys sneak in within a few feet of you without making a sound). They also react in wet weather and, if they get wet, can become useless. Hold such calls close to your body and brace your elbows when calling.

Slate and box calls like this one, and slate and peg calls, are faithful in tone, but take two hands to operate, as does the box call or lipped box.

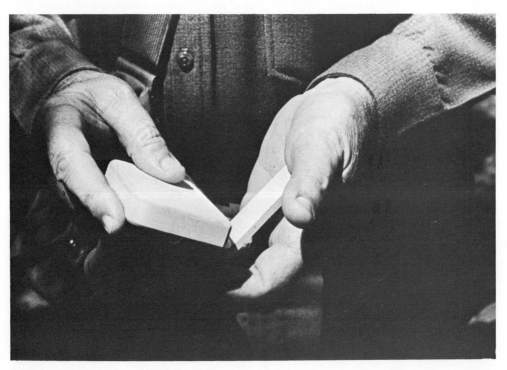

Real hens have little pattern to their yelping. When I learned to call, "they" said you gave three yelps and shut up. Nolan Hutcheson, an Ozark turkey hunter friend of mine, never has failed to kill a gobbler of more than twenty pounds over twenty years of hunting. He calls frequently, using a lipped-box caller, an oddity in an age of mouth callers. He varies the number of yelps each time—perhaps three this time, eight the next, even ten. "That's what hens do," he says.

There's little point in calling before shooting hours. You run the risk of calling up a bird you can't shoot (you'd better not, anyway, if you want to call yourself a sportsman and mean it). If you yelp to a gobbler on the roost, he might just stay up there longer, shouting back challenges (and probably attracting other hunters).

You can roost a gobbler, if you're lucky, by getting to the highest possible spot in your woods an hour before sunset. Stay there until the sun is completely gone. Often, an old gobbler will shout a few times from the roost and you'll know exactly where he is come next morning.

You also may make him gobble from the roost early the next morning, before he flies down, by using an owl hooter. Gobblers often will respond to any loud noise, even the slamming of a car door, but I wouldn't recommend that. Try to imitate the local owl (barred or great horned in my part of the country).

LeRoy Braungardt is the best turkey caller I know or ever have heard. When I first met him, he looked as if he should be playing steel guitar in Ferlin Huskey's country band. LeRoy had a slicked standing wave in his coal-black hair that looked like a Waikiki comber and a face on which was firmly etched the map of the Back Forty. Calling in and killing turkeys is so easy for LeRoy that he's forsaken the gun—gone to a bow and arrow.

Both he and Nolan Hutcheson call up gobblers almost at will, but their methods are vastly different. LeRoy will use cackles, clucks, a repertoire of turkey language beyond the scope of most experts, much less the shambling amateurs like me who do well to mimic the lustful moans of lorn hens well enough to fool barnyard jakes.

LeRoy believes in ultimate concealment. He is completely camouflaged, including a headnet with eyeholes built around an old pair of sunglass frames. He wears gloves, heaps leaves over his legs. When he's bowhunting, he carries a portable blind behind which he can draw his bow without telegraphing motion to incoming birds.

Hutcheson, on the other hand, depends on finding a downed treetop to break up his outline, wears old, drab clothing, but not camouflage, does not cover his face—but can duck under the brim of an old hat.

But both call quite softly. Both are entirely motionless when a bird is coming. And both have patience, patience to stay in the woods until they score. Remember those basics.

I don't plug products unless I think they deserve it and LeRoy's forty-one-minute record on hunting and calling turkeys deserves it. It's available for $10 for the LP album, or $11 for tape cassette or eight-track from LeRoy Braungardt, Box 160, Moscow Mills, Missouri 63362.

The well-dressed turkey hunter—complete camouflage. Even the shotgun barrel is covered. But, with the numerous turkey hunting accidents, most because either one hunter mistook another for a turkey or because one didn't see another one, hunter safety officials are beginning to question the need or desirability of complete camouflage.

ONE-SHOT HUNTING

Turkey hunting should be one-shot hunting. The object is to kill the bird instantly with one well-placed, close-in head shot with a shotgun. Far too many turkeys are crippled by hunters who take the first shot too far away and follow it up with several more as the turkey cripples off. Some birds undoubtedly die of the wounds. A turkey is a tough bird, though. I know a hunter who shot a bird that had been shot previously the same week by another hunter. The wounds were fresh, yet the bird responded to my friend's call. A dose of heavy-duty bird shot hadn't even taken a short reef in that horny old bird's blue-diamond erection.

But just because turkeys are hardy and probably will recover from a wounding is no reason to take shots that are doubtful. It's human nature to try marginal shots where shots are few and far between and to be more selective when there are a lot of shots to select from. But, human nature or no, a hunter has an obligation to the sport he should cherish to pass up shots that have little chance of success.

You should know your gun and the best way to do it is to pattern it with the shells you'll be using in the woods. I think the ultimate turkey gun is a full-choke Model 12 Winchester. It holds seven shots, and I remember one gobbler that was shot four times before it finally quit trying to run off. The first two shots were from a fellow hunter, the last two were mine. All were theoretically close enough to kill the bird, but the bird refused to be convinced.

Draw a turkey head on a sheet of paper and pace off a distance of twenty to thirty yards. See where the gun shoots, how many pellets you can put in the head. I think the ultimate shotshell for turkeys is Winchester's Super X Double X Magnum, available in both No. 4 and No. 6 shot. Stay away from No. 2—too few pellets.

When you choose a spot from which to call, take a moment to pace off the range to a few reference points so you'll have some idea of how close a turkey really is if one shows up. Hunters are notoriously poor at estimating distance. Waterfowl hunters almost invariably put birds ten yards closer than they really are. *Know* how close that bird is.

Some states, especially in the West, allow rifles for turkeys. I've never hunted them with a rifle, so I can't speak from personal experience, but James Brady in *Modern Turkey Hunting* (Crown, 1973) says a .22 caliber, 45-grain soft-point bullet at a velocity of 2,400 to 2,600 feet per second is ideal for shots up to 150 yards. Longer shots take the same bullet at higher velocities.

But with rifles as with nearly everything else about turkey hunting, the experts disagree. Henry Davis preferred a .22 Hornet for turkeys, but Edward McIlhenny, one of the early turkey writers, preferred a bullet that didn't mushroom.

Roger Latham, in his *Complete Book of the Wild Turkey* (Stackpole, 1976), said, "If expanding bullets are used, flesh destruction (and also shocking power) can be reduced by lowering the velocity. This can be accomplished by reducing the powder charge or by using a heavier bullet. On the other hand, if a non-expanding bullet is used, the shocking power can be increased by raising the velocity or by reducing the weight of the bullet."

The best aiming point with a rifle is the wing butt on a broadside shot and the base of the neck on frontal shots. Where you'd shoot for the head with a shotgun, you would not with a rifle—the target is too small. No one recommends shooting a turkey facing away, but if you have to, the aiming point is the middle of the back. Since a good many turkeys are taken under poor light conditions, a good scope of about four power with light-gathering capability will help the shot.

CAMOUFLAGE

Now, as to the matter of camouflage. I hate to be heretical, especially when there's a good chance I don't know any more about the subject than a hog knows about Sunday, but I'll take the plunge. Turkey hunters almost foam at the mouth when you suggest they wear some form of visible clothing—either hunter orange or, at the minimum, a red/black camouflage outfit. Most will swear on their dying mother's apple pie that turkeys see colors and that a fluorescent hunter will send birds into hysterical flight.

I keep harking back to Denny Ballard, tumbled ass over appetite by a charge of birdshot. I keep writing news releases about the prevalence of turkey-hunting gun accidents—far more prevalent than deer-gun accidents.

Whether turkeys do see colors or not is at least arguable. They almost certainly do see intensity of color and probably are spooked by unnaturally bright objects. On the other hand, is a turkey sent fleeing in terror by the sight of a flowering crabapple or a bright redbud in full bloom?

Authorities feel turkeys should have color vision because of the composition of rods and cones in their eyeballs, but of course it's impossible to ask the birds. Chickens see blue and violet poorly, which conjures up the ghastly vision of a turkey hunter forced by regulation to wear a lavender jump suit to the woods.

John Lewis, longtime turkey biologist for the Missouri Conservation Department, has trapped turkeys from a red pop tent and says the birds paid no attention to it. But a tent is not a hunter.

LeRoy Braungardt has called birds close in while wearing safety-color clothing. But then I feel he could call birds in if he were wearing a suit of armor and playing a five-string banjo.

Red is no sure protection from gun accidents. I know of an instance where a turkey hunter wearing a red and black plaid shirt was wounded by another hunter who thought the red was the wattles of a gobbler. A conservation agent friend tells about a father who mistook his son for a turkey and peppered him, fortunately not seriously. "It was another case of failing to identify the target before pulling the trigger," the agent said. "Both the father and son were graduates of a hunter safety course and the father is a National Rifle Association firearms safety instructor."

In fairness to hunter safety trainees and instructors, the incident definitely is the exception and not the rule and in no way taints either the desirability nor the necessity for hunter safety training.

It just goes to prove that no one is perfect.

States try to set their spring gobbler season when the birds are at the peak of sexual frustration. It should be at that short time when most hens are nesting and not listening to the longpecker brags of yon gobbler, but before the old boy shuts off his libido for another season. Catch him with a hard-on and nothing to blunt it on and it doesn't take a very good caller to bring one in.

HUNTING STRATEGY

Within a given hunting day, turkeys have a general pattern that will help you find them. Obviously, they roost at night, high in a tree, and you haven't lived until you've walked in on a roost and had three or four turkeys go flapping out over your

head just before dawn when it's so still you can hear your heart beat. *That* gets the old ganglions stirring!

Your gobbler probably will shoot a few challenges off into the dawn at first light, still from the roost. If you're close, you'll talk back with clucks only—one or two, no more. He knows you're there, then. You'll hear him fly down. Nature programmed hens to go to peremptory gobblers, so there's a built-in resistance to the gobbler coming to your mating call. That's why so many gobblers "hang up," refuse to come on in. One trick you might try is to turn your caller away from the gobbler or muffle it so it sounds as if the hen is moving away from him.

If two hunters are together, let the caller quietly move away and call while the shooting hunter is between caller and bird. The ruse may pull the gobbler close enough to be shot by the gunner.

As a general rule, a turkey is more likely to move uphill to a call and you should be on the same ridge with the bird. You should face into an open area since the birds like to move into such an opening and strut their stuff.

If real hens beat you out of the opening round, don't give up for the day. Virtually all the day's gobbling is done the first hour or two of sunrise, but gobblers in mating season are almost incessantly horny, so once the gobbler gets his wind, an hour or two after having his way with his real harem, he may come looking for a piece of strange (you) that he heard talking earlier. This is where patience comes in. You know there was a gobbler there at first light. He hasn't gone up in a puff of smoke. He's just busy with other stuff.

But you're going to get hungry and tired and impatient. Hungry is your fault. You should have packed some breakfast bars. Quit thinking about bacon and eggs back at camp, dammit! Do you want a turkey or not? The well-equipped hunter should have food, a compass (and don't forget to take readings on the way in so you can back azimuth to get out), extra callers, and a cushion to sit on. The slickest trick is to build a cushion hinged at the back of your jacket that can be fastened up around your shoulders for walking, released to flop down under your butt for sitting. Cushions keep you both dry and comfortable. Your camouflage outfit, whatever form it takes, should include gloves and paint, tape or a sleeve to camouflage your gun barrel. Be careful that whatever you use doesn't gimp up the gun's action.

The ideal turkey is the one that comes boppin' in to your calls, strutting and gobbling and ripe for the plucking. But there are those birds that long-time turkey hunter Charlie Elliott calls "shutmouth gobblers." Those are the birds that suddenly materialize thirty feet away from you when you have a breakfast bar halfway to your mouth. Jakes, young turkeys, are especially prone to do this because they don't gobble very well and they're shy about their voice cracking, like an adolescent boy. The answer is to be ready for such unannounced visitors.

Patience . . . remember that basic tenet. The hunter who sticks with it is likely to be the successful hunter. Patience is a virtue that few are blessed with. Sitting still for long periods is almost impossible for me and for most everyone I know. Everything intervenes—bodily discomfort, hunger, boredom, thirst, you name it.

Some hunters think, an avocation indulged in all too seldom by turkey hunters and candidates for public office. One I know thinks incessantly of sex. No, it isn't me—I only do that about 75 percent of the time. I've heard hunters caution against getting too comfortable because you might fall asleep. Well, that seems a bit of cautionary overkill. If you're that worried about falling asleep and missing the trophy of a lifetime, how about going to bed earlier the night before?

I've reformed a bit recently and find that Christian living isn't as bad as I thought it would be. This is not a Billy Graham conversion. I'm not likely to appear on the PTL, except as a bad example, but I have cut back on the pre-hunt libations and have taken to going to bed with the turkeys and getting up slightly before them. It does me no harm and I stay awake in the turkey woods with a whole lot less effort.

I used to sit around the campfire with the rest of the tale-tellers and sip from the warming cup and imagine fantasies of the hunt that soared and spun like the very firelight. Mornings hurt. Inevitably I would fall asleep in the woods; however, the last turkey I shot stood virtually astride my numbed body when I woke. Even inadvertently, I'd done everything right. I had called, then drifted off to sleep during which time I didn't call any, and I didn't make noise.

Getting a good night's sleep lets you be in the woods an hour before daybreak (first light, not the official sunrise). Chance are you will hear gobblers on the roost.

The instant you hear a first gobble (close enough to be a viable bird), *get moving!* Go to the bird. Try to get on the same ridge with him, at least on the same level or higher. Move as briskly as you can without making too much noise. Find your hide within 200 yards (no closer than 100) and get completely settled before making the first call. Your gun should be positioned so you have to make the slightest possible motion to bring it on the bird if he comes from the anticipated direction (if he doesn't, you're screwed anyway). If you have to move the gun, do it when the bird's head is behind a tree.

It could be a hen, you know, so know how to tell a gobbler from a hen. Obviously, a bird strutting and gobbling is a gobbler. But a sleeked-down bird could be either. The beard is the most obvious symbol. This tassel-like sprout comes out of the bird's breast and can be more than eleven inches in length. Gobblers generally have red heads, hens blue or blue-white. Gobblers, even jakes, are much larger than hens. If you're not sure, don't shoot. Identify your birds alive, not lying dead in a welter of blood and feathers.

If you shoot a turkey, be prepared to shoot it again. Turkeys take a lot of killing and I know of several cases where hunters knocked a bird down, left their guns laying and rushed to the bird, only to have it throw off the shock of the shot, leap up and run or fly off.

Remember—90 percent of the gobbling will be done in the first two or three hours of the morning. But just because they quit gobbling doesn't mean they quit responding. Until mid-morning, turkeys will be feeding and if you've located fresh scratching, that's a good area to try.

When the sun is straight overhead, turkeys will find a dusting and loafing area. Since this behavior is fairly random, it would be tough to predict. But if you've found a dusting spot, a depression with a bed of dust, a lot of turkey tracks, then the birds might come back to it in mid-day.

Feeding picks up in late afternoon, if you're in a state that permits afternoon hunting. Random forest feeding would be hard to pinpoint, but some game management areas have food plots that are an obvious place to hunt in mid- to late-afternoon. Charlie Elliott talks about hunting your backtrail—calling as you head back out of the woods and sometimes inducing a "shutmouth gobbler" that has come to an earlier call to answer you, often from very close by.

FALL HUNTING

So far, we've talked only about spring gobbler hunting; however, fall hunting is equally popular and calls for quite different methods. Chances are, you won't kill an old gobbler in the fall, except by ambush, and your chances of calling one up are almost as good as they are of having the courts rule you are Howard Hughes' heir.

Fall birds are taken usually by one of two methods: (1) by ambush, often by deer hunters on a stand who also have a turkey permit; (2) by breaking up a flock, usually a family group, then calling back one of the young birds or a hen.

Fall hunters depend on the *kee kee run,* a call given by young birds which starts out as a peeping whistle, ends up as a series of yelps. It's impossible, as are all turkey calls, to describe in print, but there are any number of calling records and tapes. One of the best is by Rob Keck, who works for the National Wild Turkey Federation, Wild Turkey Building, Edgefield, SC 29824. It's worth the $10 it'll cost to join the group—the magazine, *Turkey Call,* alone is worth the price with its many ads for callers, tapes, etc., and its many stories on how to work turkeys.

Keck, like LeRoy Braungardt, is totally dedicated to the ethical pursuit of the wild turkey. I've met a lot of turkey experts, and these two impress me more than any. They'll do to hunt with.

Keck specializes in fall turkey hunting. "Calling in old bearded gobblers in the fall is one of the most difficult things to do," he says. "I haven't met anyone yet who can call single old gobblers consistently in the fall. They're bachelors. They have no real reason to associate with other birds. The best results I've had is by getting into a bunch of litter mates, two- or three-year-old birds who never had broken up." Scattering a flock is easier said than done.

As in the spring, you look for feeding areas, scratched-up places that indicate a flock is around. Listen for the clucks and pitts and purrs and other fairly quiet, but regular sounds turkeys make as they putter along through the woods. A still day is best for scouting, since wind plays hell with your hearing and also makes turkeys more skittery. Feeding turkeys make a lot of noise scratching. Listen for it.

If you locate a flock, your objective is to send the birds off in a jillion different directions. If they flush in the same direction, you haven't accomplished anything. They'll land together and there will be no need to regroup. The more you can startle them, the better you are. If you locate a flock and can determine its feeding direction, make a wide circle and set up an ambush. Maybe you won't have to scatter them— you can pick one off as they feed within range.

Scatter them by yelling, making as much noise as you can, running into the flock. Some recommend shooting into the air (not into the flock), but I'm leery of running and shooting, and damned sure wouldn't recommend it to anyone else.

Once they're scattered, position yourself in the middle of the scatter site and try to call a bird back with the *kee-kee run* or a drawn out series of yelps, ascending at the end, the "lost hen" call. Turkeys on a hilltop generally flush downhill and probably will reassemble at a lower elevation, so drop down the hill to the next level and call from there. Young birds should start responding to your call within a few minutes. Older birds take longer, mature gobblers may have more patience than you have and may never come.

But fall or spring, the basics are the same—good concealment, absolute immobility once you're in position . . . and infinite patience.

Most saints would make good turkey hunters.

10

Mourning Doves: Gray Harbingers of Autumn

It wasn't a good year for the pair of doves. The male felt the first stirrings of ardor one warm February morning and flew to a telephone wire. A few patches of dirty snow lay sheltered in the north-facing road ditch, but the air was warm. The male, fresh from a long flight from the frost-rimed bean stubble of Swampeast Missouri, enjoyed the warmth soaking into his gray-brown feathers. He flipped his long tail (his Latin name *Zenaida macroura caroliniensis* means "the long-tailed dove from the Carolinas") to keep his balance.

The male cooed, a soft sound, but one which carried an amazingly long distance. He was a big, healthy male, nearly six ounces in weight, a foot long, head to tail-tip.

Presently, he attracted a female, a third lighter in weight, but almost identical in appearance.

Everything looked promising for the young lovers. No other males intervened, which would have precipitated a feather-filled fight. After a bit of love play, the female submitted. The male's ardent assault lasted but a few seconds, after which he gave a growling cry of triumph.

The pair nested, carrying their motley assortment of twigs into the crotch of a big old sycamore, well off the ground. The female laid two eggs, a day apart, and both birds began to incubate, taking turns while the other fed. But halfway through the two-week nesting period, something happened.

A massive late-season low-pressure system dipped down from Canada, carrying with it a stunning slap from the sometimes heavy hand of Nature. There was no way the doves could know other than, perhaps, their own wild sensitivity to weather change. Bereft of protection from the quick, harsh storm, they abandoned the nest in order to survive themselves. A fierce wind pushed night temperatures well toward zero and the wind chill well below it.

The tiny spark of life in each of the two eggs simply couldn't cope and winked out, an almost microscopic ravel in the vast fabric of life.

Scratch one nest. The pair re-nested, this time in a red cedar tree, about eight feet off the ground. It was a good choice for a nest, sheltered and hidden. But a prowling raccoon heard the male flutter in for his turn at the eggs and, hungry after the lean long winter, investigated, found the second pair of eggs, and gratefully ate them.

The third nest was at the edge of a field, again in a cedar tree. This time the parents brought off two young. The parent doves took turns incubating, then feeding the voracious nestlings who soon turned from ugly, featherless newborns to not-much-prettier nestlings, covered with quill-like juvenile feathers.

It was a big day for the family when the young flew for the first time. Especially for the first youngster who ventured out of the nest tree into the spring sun. Doves probably don't feel any great joy at exercising the talent of self-powered flight, but even had the young dove rejoiced, it was to be a short-lived exultation. A rapier-swift Cooper's hawk swept out of a nearby tree with the grim efficiency of a well-aimed broadhead, and took the youngster in flight. The young dove saw only a flickering shadow that blotted out the warm sun and then felt talons bite deeply into his back. Then he felt nothing.

By autumn, the surviving dove would be full-grown . . . and headed for a rendezvous with me in early September.

Doves are the first of the autumn birds. They're the only game bird to breed in all the states, save Alaska. Considering that a dove is not quite bright, even by bird standards, the species has been revered through history. I can't imagine why. A dove's very behavior is insipid. But doves kept company with the immortals on Mt. Olympus, and it was a dove that came back to Noah with a green twig, indicating the flood was over. Because of the bird's supposed association with peace, some oppose dove hunting. And that includes hunters. There is a group raised to believe that doves are not game birds, who actively hunt all other "approved" birds with no qualms—but will fight you if you propose dove hunting.

At last count (and it varies, depending on how the political gasses are bubbling), fourteen states prohibited dove hunting. Of those, Montana, Iowa, Wisconsin, Michigan, New York, New Hampshire, Vermont, Maine and Connecticut have no active plans to make dove hunting legal. Minnesota, Indiana, Ohio, Massachusetts and New Jersey all have hopes. North Dakota, South Dakota and Nebraska are recent entries to the dove-hunting ranks.

In 1972, South Dakotans voted two to one to ban dove hunting. Perhaps it happened because the state's sportsmen sat on their hands. Certainly, South Dakota is no hotbed of anti-hunting sentiment. The state has a history of fine hunting and it is an important part of the economy. But dove hunting was banned.

It also certainly was not because of a lack of doves. The state produces an estimated 20 million birds a year. But two-thirds of the voters imposed a ban on dove hunting. Six years later, the legislature reinstated hunting. That antagonized one faction of voters who (with understandable irritation) resented the lawmakers ignoring the apparent will of the people. A second faction opposed South Dakota dove hunting because it opposes all hunting. Another faction is composed of landowners who don't give a damn one way or another about doves, but who don't want hunters on their land, citing vandalism and the threat of rangefires (a real one in sere Sep-tember). Save for the anti-legislature group, these factions exist everywhere there is dove hunting.

South Dakota has become a battleground where the dove hunting issue is fought over almost annually. In 1980, South Dakotans voted nearly two to one to legalize dove hunting again.

Between 1968 and 1978, the (at that time) sixteen hunting states of the Eastern Management Unit showed a slight population increase, though it was a statistically static situation. The eleven non-hunting states showed an 18.7 percent decline. No one really knows if that means anything or not, since both the Central and Western units showed increases, both in the hunting and non-hunting states.

You could, I suppose, theorize that hunting actually increases doves, since that's what the figures seem to show, but we have enough people proving things with figures that turn out not to be true, so let's not add to the world's problems. Hunting is part of the annual mortality, not added to it. And hunting accounts for about 10 percent of the total dove death toll each year.

If you're easily impressed by figures, ponder that there are 500 million doves at the start of each September and, at season end some forty-five days later, hunters will have taken fifty million of them. Missouri hunters take about a million a year or roughly their share if the annual kill were split equally among the states. But in fact, Texas dominates the harvest with more than seven million. California, North Carolina, Georgia, Tennessee and Alabama hunters each total more than three million, while hunters in Florida, Illinois, Mississippi, South Carolina and Virginia all claim more than two million. Mexico hunters also kill between two and three million doves a year. Little Rhode Island drags the average down with about 6,000 doves total. Oddly, Maryland, a small state, has a higher bag than big old Idaho. It's a matter of conditioning—westerners generally are more oriented toward big-game hunting than bird shooting.

Dove mothers are stupid, but make up for their lack of intelligence by being prolific. Mother Nature takes care of her retarded children as well as she does her bright ones. Survival of the species is what counts in nature, not the individual, and so doves have evolved a system that allows them to survive their natal numbheadedness.

Quail, grouse, most other game birds raise their annual brood all at once, carefully shepherding the young to adulthood. Most times it works. A few may get picked off by predators or weather, but generally the fall family group is substantially what hatched out in the spring.

Not so with doves. Doves lose their kids to nearly everything. If a snake doesn't get the eggs, a skunk or raccoon probably will. If cold rain doesn't kill the ugly

Breeding areas of the mourning dove (dark gray) and wintering range (light gray).

nestlings, then a cowbird baby, hatched in good faith by the mother dove after the hen cowbird laid an egg in the dove nest, will shove the baby doves out of the nest.

So, momma dove lays two eggs at a session, one day apart. From egg to flying dove is an incredible four weeks and no sooner does the mother dove boot her latest child or two out of the nest than she and her mate are at it again. And they talk about the fecundity of rabbits. A dove may nest as many as seven times in a season, though probably four, perhaps five, is closer to normal.

Still, if every female dove brought off ten young each year, we would be smothered in cast-off dove feathers. It obviously doesn't work that way. Most doves die within a year. The birth rate, heavy as it is, is enough to maintain the population. For some unknown reason, dove populations have declined ever so slightly in recent years. Not to worry—the trend is slow and, wildlife managers feel, relatively insignificant at this time.

I was about nine when I first hunted doves—perched on the front fender of my cousin's rattly pickup, a method which not only is illegal, but was downright dangerous, for he had the eyesight of a mole and, had I been jounced off, undoubtedly he would have run over me before he noticed I was gone. Shooting doves off a highline not only abrades the Creature Constabulary, it also powerfully excites the rural electric co-op.

In those days, the late 1940s, there weren't enough dove hunters in my home, Missouri, to start a good argument. By the time I moved back into dove hunting twenty years later, the sport was growing and it has grown ever since. Yet hunting has not contributed to the decline of dove populations. A few years ago, the U.S. Fish and Wildlife Service jumped the daily bag from twelve to eighteen in the Central Management Unit (management units are roughly analogous to waterfowl flyways). The idea was to test the effect of a very liberal bag limit on dove populations. As far as anyone could tell, it made no difference.

DOVE HABITAT

Doves prefer to feed on nearly bare ground since they have relatively weak feet. Traditionally, the best hunting for the birds is in a silage cut—where green corn, just beginning to go brown, is cut for silage. There's a lot of grain shattered and thanks to the miracle of herbicides, the ground is bare. The other most fruitful hunting area is in a wheat stubble field.

Since hunting season opens a month or two after the wheat harvest, either a planted crop such as clover or lespedeza or a fine crop of weeds has time to grow up and obscure the wheat stubble. But there's grain on the ground and enough bare spots for doves to feed. It's easy to see a silage cut, but the wheat fields aren't as visible—unless you've had the foresight to identify them before harvest.

I recently hunted a field of sunflowers and it was a revelation. In fact, I think sunflowers will be tomorrow's super dove plant. Missouri has patches of the familiar

A mourning dove may produce 10 young, two at a time, during the course of a long nesting season. But mortality of nests and young doves is heavy and the adults don't do much more than replace themselves. The typical dove nest is a sketchy affair of sticks, exceptionally vulnerable to bad weather, especially wind. The two young are altricial, meaning they must be cared for by the parents, but the youngsters grow fast and within two weeks after hatching have flown the nest.

Typical Midwest dove hunting area is a corn silage cut. The cut over area has shattered-out grain that attracts doves, while the standing corn makes a find blind for waiting hunters.

flowers on several of its upland areas and I think the idea is only in its infancy, that in years to come we will see sunflowers on all upland wildlife areas where doves are hunted.

Sunflowers are drought-resistant. They can be planted more cheaply than many other crops, they ripen just when doves are flocking to head south. And, my God, do doves love the seeds. Illinois pioneered sunflowers for doves, planting a small black-seeded oil variety called Peredovick. The flowers are planted in rows on herbicide-treated ground. The rows make it easier for hunters to find downed birds, a real problem where there is a heavy stand of plants.

The area I hunted had 2,500 total acres of which only 60 were in sunflowers which had been planted in strips perhaps 20 yards across and as long as the ridgetop or to the field border. There were brush-hogged lanes through the standing sunflowers which created open areas both for doves and hunters.

It's hard to conceive how good the hunting was. In the 1980 season, Missouri suffered a summer-long drought that wiped out the corn crop. Even though farmers cut corn for silage, the ears largely were undeveloped, so there was little waste grain. And because of the dry conditions, there was no burning on wildlife areas. A short rainy spell in late summer encouraged a flourishing crop of ragweed. It was miserable for dove and hunter alike. So, spots to concentrate doves were at a premium. It was a condition not universal in dove range, but possible anywhere, any season. And the best hunting in Missouri was in the sunflower plots. So I believe in them and think they'll become the best single management tool in the dove manager's kit.

It's not tricky to find a place to hunt doves, but it requires persistence and some knowledge of dove habits. The birds are migratory and begin to concentrate in feeding areas about the time the season opens in September—the equivalent of a duck's staging area. Young-of-the-year are more sensitive to weather change than are older birds and a few nights in the 50s or below, especially accompanied by a cold rain, will drive out almost all young doves. Texas is the beneficiary of most migrating mourning doves (and Texas hunters kill three to four times as many doves as any other state group).

So, doves are beginning to think about a grits-and-gravy atmosphere and they concentrate in ever-larger flocks, getting ready to satisfy their travel itch. They have three major requirements: food, water and a place to sleep. You hunt feeding areas, waterholes and roost sites.

The two best shooting sites are feeding and roosting areas. Either can, with heavy pressure, be "shot out," which generally means that the disturbance is too great and the birds move elsewhere, rather than that they are all killed off.

Doves are seed-eaters. I've talked about sunflowers as the ultimate food, but prepared sunflower fields are uncommon. So, we get back to the corn silage cut or the wheat stubble field. If you think doves year-round, you'll try to locate wheat stubble fields during harvest in late June or July. It's also a good time to make contact with farmers, for they're not being beseiged by a thundering herd of wild-eyed hunters.

Once, three of us asked at a dozen farmhouses if we could shoot at the many doves flickering past almost head-high and got turned down every time. No one was impolite, but the answer was no. "I'd like to," said one farmer, "but I got ten guys a day asking and if I let one in, I feel like I gotta let everybody in . . . it just isn't worth the trouble. Sorry."

No one is asking in July. See Chapter 27, Finding a Place to Hunt, for tips on the care and feeding of landowners. While you're checking in with wheat-cutting farmers, ask about silage-cutting plans as well. If your farmer isn't planning to chop silage, maybe his neighbor is.

But just because you know where stubble fields are, it doesn't mean that you'll find doves there. You need to check them out in late August and there is an infallible indicator, erected solely for your convenience by the local electric and telephone companies. It's called the high line in Missouri—telephone and electric wires. If you see doves on high lines adjacent to silage or stubble fields, you can bet the field is being used by the birds. The more doves on the wire, the more in the field. A half-dozen doves on a wire along a quarter-mile stretch can indicate an eminently shootable population in the field.

One of the less esthetic spots to hunt, though a good one, is in a pig yard. The combination of bare dirt and kernals of grain pulls doves in. You have to race the pigs for the downed doves, though.

Also check dead trees for perching doves. Doves feed early in the morning and again in the evening, so that's when you do your checking. The morning hours are from sunrise to 10 a.m. In the afternoon, look from 4 p.m. to dark.

If you have the time (and the permission) walk into the field. If you flush out a gob of doves, you should check carefully to make sure no one but you has seen them, tiptoe quickly back to the car, go home and begin loading shells and *say nothing* to anyone except those you want to help you kill doves. Good dove fields are like good dogs, good women and rare guns at public sales—everybody wants them and they're hard to find.

There often is good dove shooting around such grain spillage areas as storage bins or feed lots, but I suspect you'd have trouble getting permission to shoot. There are other hazards. I once shot in a pig feedlot during a gentle drizzle. My eyes were on the skies in search of flying doves and I stuck the wet muzzle of my shotgun against an electric fence while holding the receiver. Like to fried my sweetbreads. Another time, I had a good shoot in a hog lot, but had to race the hogs for every downed dove. I won about a third of the time.

Another ready-made dove spot is a milo field where the grain has been cut and baled. The big bales make good hiding spots.

A further technique for locating silage cuts is to use an airplane. One year, a dove-hunting friend flew us over our county in mid-August. We spotted several farmers cutting silage. We flew at about 700 feet, low enough to see the cuts. We then marked the locations on a county road map, landed, drove to the farms and asked permission to hunt. It was a quick, effective way to spot potential dove hunting. Several of the fields were to the back side of the farms, invisible from roads.

As a rule of thumb, it takes seven to ten days after a silage cut before appreciable numbers of doves will be drawn in. Dove feeding locations, unlike woodcock coverts, change from year to year, following changes in crops. So, each year is a new problem of detection.

Roosts are tougher to locate than a feeding area. It's great hunting if you can find the roosts. Since doves establish regular patterns while they're in an area, they'll use the same roost day after day until they migrate.

The hedgerow, of dense Osage orange, was the traditional dove roost. But most Osage orange has been ripped out of the Midwest to make room for one or two more rows of some crop. Osage orange earns its keep only as a windbreak and a wildlife haven—but who cares about erosion or a bunch of birds in this day of agricultural exploitation?

Doves may nest in a grove of trees surrounded by pastures, but often the roost is fairly near the feeding area. I suppose you could ''line'' doves the way bee tree seekers follow bees to their hive (although the famed bee line may be a bit straighter than a dove line). Doves go to roost at last light, so it's tough to follow them. Driving has gotten to be an expensive way of scouting for hunting spots, but several hunters I know use low-cost motorcycles for their backroads prowling.

If you do find a roost, don't shoot within a couple hundred yards of it. Stay well away and ambush birds as they fly to it. Shoot near the roost and you risk driving the birds away.

Doves avoid the heat of the day by perching in trees, often adjacent to the feeding field. You can walk hedgerows and flush birds, but it's hard hunting. If you don't have a shooter on each side of the trees, the birds invariably will flush away from you and you won't get any shots. Remember also that this is when vegetation is at its rankest. Bucking high weeds along a hedgerow when the temperature is in the 90s is not my idea of sport. I prefer to fish or loaf during the gut of the day, hunt the cooler feeding periods.

Regardless of whether it's food, water or sleep a dove wants, he'll come to it by a regular route, often a break in the trees or down a slight valley—a natural funnel. You can study the flight patterns in a hunting area for a few minutes and station yourself to maximize your shooting. Be prepared to make some adjustments in your shooting station. Sometimes moving just a few yards will put you within range of far more birds than if you stay put. Keep watching to see if there are more productive flight lines somewhere else. Be flexible.

I've never done much waterhole shooting, since it always seems to be easier to find a feeding area than a waterhole, but doves do need water and they want bare banks. If the weather has been dry, they'll find exposed shoreline on ponds and lakes, but if not, they may go to a river sandbar.

Sandbars are the only spots where I think decoys would be of much benefit. I've never used decoys, but a bunch set out on an exposed sandbar on a big river might pull in a lot of doves, especially if the birds are using fields adjacent to the river.

The toughest shooting of all is pass shooting in a wind, trying to hit a downwind-bound bird. Most dove hunters thrive on that kind of shooting (though one of my friends recently fired forty-two times to get nine doves in a wind—and he regularly hits 50 percent of his shots).

But for an old woodcock/quail hunter like me, the most fun is jump-shooting doves. If there aren't enough hunters to keep the birds moving in a field, you'll frequently see doves land. It's possible to walk them up. Keep your dog at heel, or at least close by, for two reasons. One is that the birds won't hold for a point, so the ranging dog would flush them out of gun range. The other is that doves often flush low and you would risk shooting your dog.

Only rarely can you walk within easy gun range of a sitting dove. As the season goes on and the birds are shot at more, it becomes impossible. So, you sneak up on them. Don't worry about making noise, but if the birds see you, they're gone. So, use standing corn rows or whatever cover is available to get within range, then stand and be ready for a quick shot. The birds flush quickly and will often twist just after take-off. If you wait an instant, they'll settle into straight-line flight.

Although I wouldn't recommend planting it, there is one other crop into which doves fog with abandon—wild hemp or *Cannabis sativa*, the incautious ingestion of which leads one to fly with the doves. It's also called marijuana. Don't discount the possibilities of hunting the grass, so to speak. I'd be leery of taking home vegetative samples, but it's hell for stout when it comes to doves. Wild hemp is widespread in the Midwest. It originally was planted during World War I to provide hemp for ropes. Now it grows wild in a number of states (and in plenty of cultivated plots as well, though not for dove management).

11

Dove Hunting

The dove that had escaped the Cooper's hawk now was fullgrown and had survived a close call with a great horned owl. He was larger than normal, for he'd fed well all summer on shattered wheat and then clover which had been interplanted with the wheat. He weighed just over five ounces, including strips of yellow fat deposited along the top and bottom of his breast. He, too, went to bed early, fluttering to roost in a thick tree along Whetstone Creek in company with several of his fellows. The birds were beginning to flock, a sure sign of the end of summer, though it still was hot.

Mike McIntosh and I planned to be up at 5 a.m., drive to the dove field in time to catch sunrise. Dove hunting in Missouri often lasts only a few days, until a cold snap drives the young birds south. Those who keep hunting closed in the northern states don't realize, nor care, I suppose, that even if hunting were open, it wouldn't make much difference. It takes only a couple of nights in the 50s, especially with chill rain, to drive the young birds out. Cold weather almost certainly would close the tap on good dove hunting within a few days as effectively as regulation now does in the nonhunting states.

Often the toughest part of dove hunting is hunting for a place to hunt. If it's warm on opening day, birds will be scattered. If it's wet, the corn will be standing, not yet cut for silage. If it's cold, birds will be gone. If the land rippers have been about their growly tasks, last year's hedgerow is today's clean barbed wire fence. Or, if it's wheat stubble, the field you watched with drooly anticipation all summer turns up fall-plowed the afternoon before the opener.

But we were hunting on state-owned ground, part of which is managed for doves. The field had been planted to wheat, then burned over. The September sun hung in the morning sky like a molten glob of metal ore. Summer lets go reluctantly in the nation's gut. Summer is an angry, sullen season in Missouri, implacable and mean. I hate it. The weather goes dry and my pitiful garden, which I hewed out of the dense Cole County clay with the indefatigable persistence of Gutzon Borglum, the Mt. Rushmore sculptor, curls up and dies.

Only doves love summer and perhaps that is why I am not as fond of them as I am of the other game birds. That and their pinheaded intelligence. I love shooting and eating doves—just not their choice of weather.

129

There's water in the ditch, milo to pull birds in. These hunters aren't walking birds up, though that sometimes works. They're going to a hide from which to shoot.

And combine rain forest temperatures with dense fogs of corn, ragweed, horseweed and other pollens, plus the average Missourian's tendency toward chronic sinusitis and you have some idea of what we face each September when dove season comes.

You sweat, you sneeze, you rub itching, streaming eyes, you slug down water that has gone warm and flat. You seek vainly for the vagrant cool breeze. You stink and poach in your own sour juices, crouched in a fencerow along a cut-over cornfield or a wheat stubble field. It's so hot that downed birds begin to decompose in mid-air (assuming you're lucky enough to hit one) and usually fall into the only patch of head-high horseweeds around. The dead bird you and the panting dog search for because you, being a good hunter, don't want to lose downed bird, will be the first of a flush of incoming birds that will shut off the instant you find your dead bird and return to your shooting station. There never are more birds in the air than when you have marked down a dead bird and are afraid to take your eyes off the spot lest you lose it. This is an axiom of hunting, carved into the dark granite of the halls of Hunter's Hell.

Chip, the Brittany, was started on doves. His first point was on a downed dove, first retrieve the same. Work with the gray birds of autumn has made him both a fine dead-bird hunter and a fine retriever. But, because of the heat which everyone always says is unseasonable, except that it settles in every September, dove hunting is hard on a dog. It's hard for other reasons, too. No dog likes to crouch amid the humid horseweeds, but that's what Chip has to do, for he shines like a beacon if I don't shove him down among the forbs. I can dress in camouflage; he can't.

Some hunters go all-out for camouflage, even including headnets. I find it seldom makes much difference. I wear comfortable clothing, including T-shirts early in the season, but everything should be dull-colored, preferably green or brown. Sometimes I wear a camouflage hunting hat. I like a stand under a fairly open tree such as a locust—anything to break up the outline. Standing corn is fine.

The sun rose. There were some birds, a few flying our way. I killed two, Mike three. The limit was ten, but it was fairly clear we'd not get near it, for the birds would be absent during the heat of the day and there was no way I would endure this Godforsaken field waiting for the evening flight. That's dove hunting—early morning, late evening. Even doves flee the midday heat, no mad dogs nor Englishmen they.

I was sweating freely, squinting against the low morning light, the sun crouched balefully on the horizon. Ragweed pollen ate at my skin. My eyes streamed from horseweed dust. Butterflies eddied south on hot snippets of wind and gnats danced maddeningly close to my eyes and ears, occasionally stumbling into mucous membranes already tortured by the pollen.

And then a bird came, distinctive, streamlined for swift flight. He pitched over an Osage orange tree into the field, now pausing, now diving, now dodging with the quicksilver elusiveness of Dr. J puttin' his move on.

It looked to be an easy shot, but the bird fluttered and juked as I stood to shoot and I missed. I sighed, humbled again. Dove flight has a flickering quality, like the flame on a wind-tossed campfire, that has humbled more than just neophyte hunters. Not long ago, I talked to a Michigander who told me with some wonder about a Texas dove hunt where he, awash in empty hulls, did not scratch a single bird. This from an old grouse/woodcock quick gun who owns two bird dogs and takes pride in his wingshooting. He used many short, unflattering words to describe doves.

Old-line dove hunters, those who long since have forsaken 12-bore guns because the shooting is too easy, still will have days when they couldn't kill a dove if it were tied immobile inside an ash bucket. First-timers, no matter how good on the trap range or in the field against more predictable birds, probably will go home with confidence frazzled.

Doves are hysterical birds, given to confused tremolo and undecided panic. The sight of a hunter tumbles a dove in flight like a leaf in a whirlwind. Still, you wonder why they're so tough to hit. There never has been a writer yet on doves who hasn't had great fun talking about the frustrations of dove shooting. And yet, with rare exceptions, most dove shooting is not snap shooting, nor taken in heavy brush, nor even with abrasively tricky angles. If a hunter picks his shots, the majority of them will be simple incoming or outgoing shots.

Further, if you play your cards right and stand to shoot at the proper moment, the bird will flutter to a confused midair halt, breast-on, as if twittering in that inane dove fashion, "Take me, sir, I am yours," all maidenly confusion and fatal indecision. That's the way dove shooting appears in memory, yet it can't be that simple. In company with legions of other dove hunters, I shoot far more poorly on doves than on any other game bird.

The national average is said to be about three birds in five shots. If so, I rank below average and I have a hell of a lot of company. You may have gathered that I don't much like doves, unless they're shoulder to shoulder with several of their mates in a rice casserole. Part of my prejudice is because I can't hit them, a distinction they share with golf balls, curve balls and, on a few memorable occasions, the floor with my hat.

Dove guns? How many shotguns are there? Good shooters might choose a full choke and take only long crossing shots to make things interesting. Someone shooting in a silage cut where doves are flying low and fast might choose a more open choke. I remember one memorable hunt where we crouched behind the big round superbales of milo and popped up to shoot at doves flying no more than twenty feet off the ground. It was snap shooting, calling for open chokes. When in doubt, the classic compromise upland bird gun is a double with improved cylinder and modified chokes.

On doves more than on any other upland bird, you should have a barrel selector or double triggers so you have the option of shooting the tight barrel first on an incoming shot or last on an outgoing one. Choice of gauge again is shooter's preference. It doesn't take a lot of shot to bring down a dove. I shoot No. 8 field loads. Most hunters I know do the same, or shoot an equivalent home load.

Dove shooting mostly is pass shooting, the kind of gentleman's shoot you read about taking place in Merrye Olde England, with the birds sailing past the gentry, who pot at them with expensive doubles. It's one of the few upland exercises where you wouldn't risk ripping $200 scratches in your Purdey. Dove shooting has a certain inherent elegance if you want to practice it. You could wear tweeds, for example (if you don't mind tweeds when it's 97 degrees and humid enough to fell a Bantu). You could brace yourself on a shooting stick with a silver ferruled tip and refer to your companions of the hunt as "old chap" rather than "hey, sucker!"

We crouched in the horseweeds and I began to feel the effects of the horseweed pollen that, unseen, peppered the air with allergic aggravation. My eyes itched, my nose tickled and ran.

Chip crouched at my feet, panting heavily in the rising heat. He has the ideal temperment for a dove dog. He lies quietly until I rise to shoot. Then he's eager business until he finds the bird or I call off the search (I've lost only a handful of birds since I started using the dog and have found countless ones I would have lost without him).

The dog allows the hunter to spend more time gunning rather than tromping heavy, pollen-laden weeds, looking for downed birds. If you're prone to allergy as I am, you want to spend as little time as necessary shattering irritants from ragweed, corn, milo and the like. It is no joke to suffer a hay fever attack. It can turn a fine hunt into real agony.

While doves aren't hard to knock down, they can be hard to kill and cripples

Fencerow pass shooters wait for doves.

will crawl under corn leaves or blend in so well with the ground that you'll never find them without a keen-nosed dog.

The ideal dove dog, no matter the breed, has three attributes:

1. A willingness to hunt dead effectively and enthusiastically.
2. A willingness to retrieve doves, at least part of the way back to you. Many dogs don't like to pick the birds up since the feathers come out in their mouths, a response biologists call "feather shock."
3. A lot of patience. Most of the time, the dog is huddled under a bunch of weeds, uncomfortable and unable to see, a trying situation for an eager hunter. It's hot and miserable for both hunter and dog.

Be sure to bring plenty of water both for you and the dog, for good dove hunting weather will wring moisture out of you and it's no kindness to let your dog suffer from thirst.

A shooting stool can be a comfort—a little camp stool is fine, canvas, leather,

A dog is invaluable to find downed doves, but be sure to take along water, for the best dove hunting is during hot, sultry early autumn weather. Doves make a good training ground for a pup.

whatever. One of my friends went down to Tandy Leather and bought a leather-seat stool, tooled it himself, and now squats in comfort, replete with the thrill of artistic creation.

Some of the best recreational reading I've ever had has come during the draggy hours when the birds aren't flying. Take along a pocket book and improve your mind. Reading time is hard enough to come by and I grab it when I can. It beats staring vacantly into the empty sky, mouth agape, letting flies in.

McIntosh knocked a dove down in some really thick stuff and we unlimbered Chip for the search job. No way we could have found the bird without him. Mike had the bird well-marked, a prerequisite to success, for the best dog can't find downed birds if he's not put in the general area where they fell. A dead bird, dropping into vegetation, doesn't leave much scent. Marking downed birds is a learned trick. Never, never take your eyes from the falling bird.

It's better to pass up a shot at a second bird if the first bird you drop is falling into thick stuff. Mark the last glimpse of him with the closest landmark you can find—a stalk of corn, whatever—*and don't take your eyes off it!* Don't look away for any reason. Walk straight to that spot. Don't detour unless there are snapping alligators in a pit at your feet. Don't blink, don't look at the dog, don't look at anything but your landmark. When you get to it, immediately mark it with your hat or a handkerchief. Not with your gun. I've spent a bit of time more than once trying to locate my gun and that's a case where the dog won't help a bit.

Let the dog do most of the looking. Work him in a pattern—circle, zig-zag or whatever will cover the ground thoroughly. Look for feathers. If you find a few, chances are they were knocked out of the falling bird. Allow for drift in the wind. Crippled doves won't run like a pheasant, but can crawl into cover and be very tough to find.

Once you have the bird in hand, you cook him and eat him. There are countless good recipes, and elsewhere in this book you'll find a bibliography of some good game cookery books. Some pluck the entire bird, some merely breast the bird, others save back and legs, but skin the bird. If you pluck, do it soon after you shoot the bird.

September is a month of contrasts, of change. It is the month each year when I grow actuarily older, for I was born on the 25th. Sometimes, if summer hangs on, baking cornfields dry, turning bean leaves to gold, I get a singular birthday present come the 25th. The season still is open.

But it's the beginning and Chip and I sat just inside the fringe of hulking horseweeds, both panting in the dull sun. Not much more of this could I take. I dropped a couple of No. 8 field loads into the double and they made a musical *poonk!* sound that pleased my ear. The sun hung low in the morning sky, a rare fall gem set in a leaden ring of dark storm clouds that threatened to bring an end to my fun. Winter was coming from the northwest. I raised my arms to let the first cooling breeze of it stroke my wet armpits.

The bird flitted into the field at the far corner and I knew from experience that he would pass within range of me. You can study a dove field for a few minutes and see the flight patterns. The birds enter along certain routes. Find such a crossing and you'll outshoot your less perceptive companions every time. Not outhit, just outshoot.

This bird came in through a swale, a natural funnel. He was a typical dove, indecisive, shifting his weight from wing to wing like a slalom skier trying to make the right and left gates on a tough downhill course. Whether this flip-flop flight is the result of indecisiveness, caution or some genetic protection, built-in to the bird to save him from raptors and No. 8 shot is known only to God. Maybe it's the result of the bird's sheer vacuity of brain. He doesn't know what to do because he *never* knows what to do.

The bird closed in on me, dropping lower, seeming once to settle out of range, only to flutter up at some vague alarm, continue on. I crouched low, keeping my face hid, one hand on the trembling dog, pressing him down in the weeds. I peered at the dove from under the brim of my camouflage hat.

Almost within range. A few more wingbeats . . . now! I came up smoothly, the gun settled to my shoulder, the bird lay on the bead and I lifted the muzzle until he disappeared, then squeezed the trigger.

He fell through his drifting feathers, almost into Chip's mouth. Chip picked him up gingerly, for he dislikes, as do most dogs, the mouthful of feathers that accompany a full-throated retrieve.

I took the dove from the dog, limp and warm in my hand, pink-billed, gray and brown of feather. I laid him with his fallen fellows and signalled to Mike that it was time to go.

The dove born in the third nesting, survivor of a hawk attack and later a near-miss with an owl, only four months old, was dead.

Some years are like that. . . .

12

Woodcock–The Game Bird Leprechaun

The lanky farmer paused for a moment, pulled a red bandana out of his pocket, swabbed his flushed brow, and blew like a winded grampus. It was hot, the kind of springtime temperature that sometimes makes Missouri's April feel like deep July. No matter that the nights turn cool and the grass sparkles with near-frost. Now it was hot and grubbing sprouts is mean work at the best of times.

The farmer spit ritualistically on his hands, gripped his single-bit ax, and cut halfway through a sassafras sprout. He moved around the sapling, took another cut, and watched with satisfaction as the tree toppled over, with a breathy swish. As it slapped the ground, the farmer caught a glimpse of movement a foot from where the treetop lay.

Dang snake! was his first thought, and he crept forward, ax hefted defensively, for it's a rare Missouri farmer who isn't ready to do battle with "one of them dang spreadheads" if he gets a chance.

It took a bunch of looking, but suddenly, out of the mottled browns and yellows and tans of last year's fallen leaves, there popped the eyeball of a bird, then the outline of the bird itself. And such a bird! He'd never seen one like it, least not that he knew. Nose like a tenpenny nail, great big eye set back so far in the head it looked as if the bird had its head stuck on backward. The one eye he could see regarded him unblinkingly. There was palpable tension in the bird, an almost visible aura of anxiety, but the bird made absolutely no motion and her colors blended so perfectly with her surroundings that the farmer never would have known she was there, had not the falling tree startled her into that one slight movement.

Although the farmer had no love for snakes, venomous or not, he felt a gut kinship with free-flying birds (save maybe a damned old chickenhawk), a longing as old as man to be as unfettered as the great, sailing birds, or as swift and sure as the quick-winged ones.

So he backed off from the nest, moved to another part of the pasture, and resumed his sprout grubbing.

The woodcock hen gradually relaxed from her terrible fright. Beneath her, four eggs, buff-colored and impossibly large for the relatively small bird who had laid them, were warm and fertile, only a day from hatching. It had been nineteen days since she laid the first of the four, fifteen since the last. She had moved in that time only to feed at dusk, returning to set the eggs through the long days.

Her earlier courtship had been elaborate; nature's finest; the quick copulation anticlimactic, a brief grappling in the dark of a chilly spring night. But, ah! the promises that had been made by the singing male as he spiralled through the sharp air 300 feet above her, twittering his musical wings in promise of unparalleled passion. At the apogee of his balletic flight, he paused, his wingbeats a frenzied tumble of grace notes, then he swooped to earth with the aerodynamic symmetry of a falling leaf, accompanying this daredevil freefall with a liquid sung melody as lovely as a coluratura's showpiece.

Once on the ground, the third-smaller male sidled up to the hen, hopped her with unseemly haste, was finished in an instant, and was gone again. She sprang into flight and never saw him again.

The four woodcock chicks pipped their way longitudinally out of their shells, only birds to do so—all others crack the shells latitudinally. Had anyone been around to do it, he could have measured the bill of any of the chicks through the first few days, subtracted 14 millimeters, divided that by two, and gotten the age in days of the bird.

But he'd have had to be quick to catch them. The hen brooded her babies for the first few days, though they were active almost from birth. Within two days they were probing for earthworms, always close to their solicitous mother. Once a Cooper's hawk glided through the loamy covert and the five birds froze instantly, vanishing as if by magic into the mottled carpet of the forest floor. Even the fierce red eye of the sleek little hawk wasn't keen enough to pick out the incredibly well-camouflaged little bogsnipes.

It's relatively rare when a woodcock hen doesn't raise her hatched chicks. Most other upland game bird mothers lose a few babies along the way, but, while many woodcock nests are destroyed by predators, once the birds are hatched they're almost home free. And, almost all woodcock eggs are fertile. Invariably, the hen lays four on a first nesting and almost always three on a re-nest.

There was a cold, chilling rain two nights after the last chick hatched and the four babies snuggled under the hen's warm breast, her buffy feathering protecting them from the harsh spring rain. Fortunately, the day dawned warm and by noon the woods had dried off.

The little birds grew rapidly. By their third week they were wandering farther from their mother each day. But at night they bunched up, huddled together, perhaps for companionship, at least for warmth, maybe out of habit. But woodcock are solitary birds who migrate singly and are found together in hunting season only because they are attracted by the essentials of a good resting and feeding covert—not by each other.

At five weeks, one of the little birds buried his bill in the soft loam, felt the wriggle of an earthworm and flexed his prehensile upper mandible until he grasped

Two chicks peep out from under their mother, while a third is visible at the bottom of the photo. These chicks are only a day or two old. Their marvelous camouflage makes it difficult to see them and they seldom fall victim to predators.

the worm. Intent on his miniscule wrestling match, he almost didn't see the horned owl. Certainly he didn't hear it, for the owl's frayed, soft feathering is designed for flight so silent he is Death's Whisper to his prey.

But the woodcock's eyes, set farther back than those of any other bird, even behind his ears, caught a flicker of motion and he flushed instantly, his wings twittering. The quick start and the sound confused the owl and he missed the little bird—barely, but he missed. There are no second chances for owls that miss woodcock, for the fastest owl ever made can't catch the slowest woodcock, if the woodcock is forewarned. Hardy little birds, these woodcock. Hardy and fascinating. For example, I've been watching the woodcock sky dance at the edge of my back yard for a decade. Just down the hill is a "singing ground" where the male sweetflies his love of the evening. I know within a few feet where the male will land at the end of each flight and how he will behave. Is it the same bird, year after year? I doubt it, yet some genetic imprint makes this year's bird act exactly the same as did last year's. Maybe it is the same bird. Birds live longer than we think they do. Bird band returns show hummingbirds have lived at least eight years. Canada geese, a hunted and migratory species, with all the threats to life which that combination suggests, have lived more than twenty years.

So why can't woodcock live a number of years? They're remarkably resilient, a surprise in light of how fragile they appear. They easily shed feathers, as do doves, and their skin is quite thin, easily torn. They are delicately boned, easily downed with one pellet of any size. Yet they apparently either die quickly or get well when they're wounded, unlike many game birds.

William Sheldon, in his *Book of the American Woodcock,* which is, as the name suggests, the standard reference on the bird, gives several examples of woodcock with serious injuries which recovered with no aftereffects and says that shock, a common mortality cause in other birds, does not seem to be a problem with woodcock.

HABITAT AND RANGE

All the studies ever done on woodcock conclude that if there is good habitat, there will be good populations of woodcock. All other factors are controlled, either by nature or regulation. Regulate hunting and let natural mortality occur. Natural mortality is no threat to the species—if predation, weather, etc., were a disastrous factor, there would have been no woodcock here when the Indians ruled.

Woodcock need loamy soil that holds earthworms. Nearly 90 percent of a woodcock's diet is angleworms. The birds will eat other insects or vegetable matter, but it's the earthworm that makes the woodcock. It takes loam and earthworms, but also brushy thickets of certain types. A veteran woodcock hunter learns to know these prime areas at a glance. They may not have birds—but they *should* have. The classic holding covert is an alder swamp. You'll find woodcock in the soft, but not muddy or water-covered parts of the swamp. Snipe may hold in the wetter parts.

Benches along rivers and streams, with a profusion of young birches or aspens, are likely. In my part of the country, the birches and aspens might become sycamore or black locust. Crab apple and hawthorn are two other possibilities. You may find woodcock in old forest, but not often and not in abundance. The little guy likes doghair sprouts, especially with little grass or plant cover to hinder his walking around and probing for worms. An old farmstead, reverting to brush, is ideal, especially if it has a small stream winding through it. Some say the birds migrate south along north-south running rivers, which makes sense since they migrate south in the fall, north in spring. Of course, my favorite covert lies on an east-west river, but someone forgot to tell the birds that.

It has been my experience that where hunters look, in good habitat, in woodcock range, they find the birds. And woodcock range is anywhere east of the western borders of Minnesota, Iowa, Missouri, Arkansas and Louisiana, going from north to south. There may be a few birds slopped over into the thickets of Texas, Oklahoma and Kansas, but the Mississippi River valley and the valleys of the great eastern rivers funnel most of the continental population from summer breeding grounds to the wintering range, especially Louisiana where enough woodcock congregate that, for all practical purposes, it is all woodcock.

The birds generally breed in the Lake States, New England and southern and eastern Canada. They breed all the way to Louisiana, but most woodcock are produced from Missouri north and east.

Breeding areas (light gray) and wintering range (dark gray) of woodcock, a bird of the eastern United States.

Few states have a good handle on the number of birds killed by hunters. Sheldon estimates a half-million, minimum, but even twice that would leave the woodcock, in terms of kill, as a minor league game bird. A million woodcock a year—compare that to the thirty-five million bobwhites taken or the fifty million mourning doves. There are more desert quail killed than there are woodcock, yet the woodcock is a favorite of outdoor writers, probably is known to every gunner, whether he's ever seen one or not. Part of that is because woodcock occur where upland gunner/ writers occur—in the Northeast. And they pop up in close conjunction with ruffed grouse, a bird that has caused more outdoor writers to wet their literary knickers than any other.

Not that woodcock don't deserve their glowing press. I love them, unashamedly and wholly. As a professional wildlifer, I dislike anthropomorphizing animals—giving them human attributes or interpreting them in human terms, making Mickey and Minnie Mice out of them. But it's damned tough to spend ten springs watching a jaunty little cock bird performing aerobatics that outdo the Blue Angels, seeing woodcock behave with cocky perversity, and not read a bit of impish fun into what they do. That's human nature. We tend to worry about things we love, whether the worry is justified or not.

There are few other game birds which occasion such affection in those who study them. And, because the birds are hard to fathom, woodcock men universally are cautious about predicting their future. While virtually all woodcock biologists think the birds are underhunted, they also fret over declining habitat, pesticide residues and other threats. Perhaps this caution is because woodcock came so close to the thin red line once before. Audubon saw the equivalent of great flocks of migrating woodcock in the 1840s, but when the market gunners and the swamp drainers combined their dubious, but ghastly efficient talents, the woodcock population declined so drastically that by 1902, A.K. Fisher, writing for the U.S. Department of Agriculture Yearbook, said the wood duck and the woodcock were vanishing species. Neither has vanished, but it's doubtful woodcock ever again will be as abundant as they were in Audubon's time.

13

Ol' Bugeyes is Back

We'd been working on doves all through September, until an early cold snap sent the young birds south and shut the season down. I went bass fishing one weekend, noticing the first leaves falling, the yellow walnut and locust leaves. Virginia creeper flamed up the side of a big old sycamore along the river. The leaves floated past me like chips of gold in the lethargic current.

There was unrest in me, an unfulfilled craving to go hunting. But the bulk of the fall hunting wasn't for a month or more. I took a hefty, but undersized smallmouth bass next to a rootwad, released him.

It was the morning of my wedding anniversary, September 30. The patient lady who has sent me off into the dusks and dawns, in company with various stub-tailed, bouncing, eager dogs, for nearly half our lives, was at home, feeding kids, doing chores, all the endless drudgery that makes a house our home. And I was bass fishing.

A green sunfish assaulted my spinner and shortly lay quivering in my hand. He joined several of his teammates on my stringer.

I was fishing opposite my favorite woodcock covert and I sloshed out of the stream and pegged my stringer in the shallows, lay the rod on the gravel bar. I clambered up the bank, no easy trick in cumbersome waders, waded through the rank weeds to the edge of the sycamore pole thicket where the massed saplings shut out light and left the thick-mulched ground free of undergrowth. I took one step into the thicket and a woodcock flushed, almost from under my feet. Reflexively, I raised my arms, as if cradling the old Smith, and shouted, "Boom! Boom!" The bird topped out, skittered out of sight over the trees.

"Woodcock are in," I told an imaginary dog. Marty and I dined out that night. I ate too much, had a bit extra of wine, and dreamed of little birds flushing excitedly out of a dream-distorted covert.

All in all, it wasn't a bad way to spend an anniversary . . .

Chip is a phlegmatic dog, much of the time—perhaps resigned is more like it. He has adopted a philosophic outlook on life, believes that if you can't change things, make the best of what you have. McIntosh calls him a stoic. If he can't hunt, he drowses in the dog pen (or, if he gets half a chance, on the downstairs couch). Now and then he'll sigh heavily, a sign, perhaps, that he is reliving past hunts, or pining for those not yet accomplished.

But mostly he waits. Waits for me to come home with that damned, dumb fishing rod, set it aside, and pick up the Smith, my vulgar old shell vest, and the keys to the truck. Then he is what he was born to be, a hunter.

While I enjoy probing a woodcock covert with one other hunter (any more is too many), I also enjoy solitary hunting for the little birds. Just as the birds themselves are solitary, so am I. There is a special magic in smoothing down the shot-ruffled feathers of a bird taken with an impossible shot, while Chip's eager nose dredges the last cooling, heady draught of scent, and a late afternoon sun turns the leaf-littered floor of my covert to copper and gold. Sharing that moment with anyone would spoil it. Only Chip . . . and he understands and sits close for a moment, his deep eyes on mine, before he lets them wander back into the thicket where, perhaps, there is another bird.

I parked the car in the frosty early morning. Chip bolted out, all piss and sniff, and I uncased the Smith, put on the shell vest. We moved into the thicket.

Chip and I always have a discussion the first time out each woodcock season. He wants to run; I want to keep him in sight. My side of the discussion gets noisy and occasionally abusive. It is a frustration that erupts in sound that is not enjoyable to listen to, either for the dog or for fellow hunters. While I realize that at least some dog trainers agree with me that the dog has to know you're unhappy, I also know bellowing at the dog is painful to everyone else.

Ideally, I wanted Chip to quarter in front of me, never ranging more than 20 to 30 feet away, either to the front or the sides. Actively migrating woodcock tend to be skittish and prone to flush wildly, though the woodcock holds better to a pointing dog than almost any other game bird.

While a quartering dog is out of favor for most upland birds (because he spends too much time hunting unproductive territory), he is ideal in a woodcock thicket. So, the dog either has to be smart enough to realize it's softball instead of hardball, or he has to be restrained by the trainer and forced to hunt the way he doesn't want to.

There is a lot to be said for hunting woodcock with retrievers or flushing dogs because both work close to the hunter by instinct, while the pointing dogs, even the slowest of them, tend to work too far out. And in my little covert a dog out of sight is a dog lost. Belled dogs are almost a must in typically thick woodcock cover. Little tinklers just aren't noisy enough, at least for ears too long assaulted by rock music. A calf bell (costs about $2) is about right. The theory, of course, is that when the bell stops, the dog probably is on point (or lost or taking a leak or growling at a skunk).

It's hard for a dog to hear with that bell rattling in his ear, so wait until it quits to give a command. Train yourself to pinpoint the bell at all times so you'll know where to look if it quits.

Only one time have I killed a five-bird limit of woodcock in my little covert. Providentally it was the only time Marty ever has chosen to go with me. She trailed me through the tangle and the birds rose in impressive numbers, by twos and threes. Never have I seen that many woodcock holding there.

Chip seems to enjoy retrieving woodcock, a rarity, for most dogs dislike either the taste or the feathers that come off in their mouth. Sir Ralph Payne-Gallwey (what a fine, great British name!) wrote in 1896 about teaching a dog to retrieve woodcock: "It is sometimes difficult to pursuade young retrievers to pick a dead woodcock or snipe off the ground; and when forced by command to do so they will often grin and lift their lips, and make a face like a child taking a dose of rhubarb.

"Starve such a dog till he will munch the bones of cock or snipe for his dinner, and he will, for the rest of his life, never afterwards refuse to retrieve these birds when you shoot them."

Strong medicine. I can't say if it works or not. Chip was a bit reluctant at first to retrieve both woodcock and doves, but does so now with a great deal of enthusiasm and even pride. Woodcock don't bother him at all, while doves do give him a bit of the rhubarb grin, though he brings them in.

And I have a built-in antipathy to feeding the dog pieces of the bird that he is hunting. There's always the chance that some dogbrain short circuit will occur, convincing the dog that he is supposed to *eat* downed birds, not retrieve them.

Also, I am a wee bit squeamish about feeding dogs things like bird heads, then letting them lick my ear. I try to ignore also the fact that they get in the cat box every chance they get. Dog candy.

My little tangle is Everycovert. It has everything that makes a classic woodcock holding area, especially jumbled growth. Chip, for all his blocky Brittany bulk, flowed through the brush like swampfire. I fought the tangle.

And it is tangle. There was wild grape festooned through the sycamore poles. It could have been worse. It could have been rose and catbriar. Grape merely trips and annoys; it doesn't attack.

I heard a woodcock twitter up, invisible through the still-leafy trees. "Chip!" I bawled. "You get your butt back here!" He reappeared, chastened but vibrant from the adrenal jolt that the sight of a game bird always gives him.

One thing about woodcock, birds flushed are not birds lost. Only rarely will a fresh-flushed woodcock, even one shot at, leave the covert, and the flights are short. Chances are that if you spot the bird down or follow its flight line, you'll reflush it.

I stopped to mop my brow, for despite the early fall crispness of the air, I'd worked up a sweat. Chip checked back, panting heavily. "Sorry you tanked up on food all summer, Fatso?" I asked. If he thought ambling through a woodcock covert made him wheeze, wait a month until the quail opener when I'd slack the reins and let him go full throttle. Lots of lard to come off. Woodcock hunting is good exercise for a kennel-flabby dog because he doesn't burn as much energy as he does later working big areas for other game birds.

Come to think of it, there was some suet settled around my belt as well.

A bird suddenly flushed beside me and angled off to my rear. I twisted awkwardly, off balance, trying to catch a glimpse of the bird and bring the gun up through the brush at the same time. There was a flash of brown and I fired, far too late and too far behind. Sycamore leaves patterned down in the embarrassing silence.

I have yet to see an outdoor painting that captures the flavor of the woodcock shot the way I usually encounter it. You know the classic scene—Brittany braced, head high, watching a flushed bird that is just towering at the edge of a stream while a hunter some thirty yards back is taking the slack out of the trigger on his double.

It's all so *open,* bless my soul! Nowhere do I see a grapevine wrapped around the hunter's thigh. Nowhere is there a blackberry vine gouging furrows of flesh out of his arm. Nowhere do I see a birch whip, disturbed by the rising gun, flicking a searing welt across the hunter's cheek.

Only now is a large lump receding from the side of my head. It has been nearly three weeks since a Minnesota woodcock rose almost at my feet in an alder swamp.

Woodcock hold tighter for a dog than nearly any other game bird, which makes them marvelous birds to work young dogs on (far left). My Brittany, Chip, nearly fell over this bird before freezing on point. At left, Chip points a woodcock whose eye and head are visible at the lower right of the photo, while Joel Vance moves in, gun ready for the flush.

The rise was to one side, forcing me to twist agonizingly, even to get a shot. As I brought the gun up, it snagged on the vegetative snarl and I jerked violently to free it. Free it came . . . the stock rose smartly to the side of my head, laying a clout alongside it that would have given religion to a Missouri mule.

I saw my target rimmed in lovely stars. It was the All-America bird, framed by red, white and blue lightning flashes and at least fifty stars.

We were nearing the end of the covert, close to the spot where I'd flushed the bird while fishing the day before. Chip braced on point ahead of me, the solid, no-nonsense point that means he has Bird isolated and none of this speculative caution which means, "I think there's a bird here, but I'm not sure."

I paused for a moment to study the setup; neither dog nor bird were going anywhere. It's no good to advance on a pointing dog only to have the bird flush behind a big tree or through a dense screen of shrubbery. Give yourself the best chance for an open shot. In this case, I had to make a cautious semicircle and come in to the dog from the side.

Only once in my life have I seen a woodcock on the ground, before it flushed. This was not the time. The bird came up to the left of where I thought it would be, wings trilling, reaching for daylight. I did it all instinctively—there's no time to think gunnery—and fired as the bird topped the treetops. It somersaulted into the thicket, leaving a couple of drifting feathers eddying down as an echo of its passing.

Chip found the dead bird, pointed it briefly until he was sure it was dead, then picked it up and brought it to me.

We ambled out of the covert, paused at the truck to sit a moment. Car tires buzzed faintly on the distant highway. A redbird whickered, a woodpecker dipped and swooped from one tree to another. The October sun was hot through my soft old chamois shirt.

I looked at the bird—perhaps one of the youngsters who'd been raised in the farmer's sprout thicket, who never got to see the Southland.

Chip's ears were soft and hot from the sun. He leaned against me, a comforting, warm bulk, his earlier fire banked now by the exercise.

I put the bird back in the shell vest, cased the gun, and we went home.

14

Woodcock Hunting

Woodcock hunting has come a fair piece from the days when hunters not only could, but did kill 100 birds in a day's shoot.

Five birds a day is the limit now—and not often reached, either. It's a cautious limit, cautiously arrived at. Woodcock biologists tend to be conservative, for they know their favorite animal came so close to the ultimate brink.

It would take a highly dedicated and probably lucky hunter to take 100 birds a season today, much less in a day. It's theoretically possible to kill more than 300 woodcock a season, but practically speaking, a third that would be exceptional. The incentives aren't what they used to be anyway. In the 1600s, a Hamburg, Germany, hunter who tumbled 100 annual woodcock was excused from paying taxes for a year. I don't know why, but don't worry about it—it doesn't work that way anymore.

American woodcock shooting, as a sport, dates to about 1800 and caught hold after the invention of the percussion cap. Some of the early shooters deplored the decline of woodcock by the middle of the 1800s and you wonder at the naiveté of the early writers. Frank Forester, a legendary early outdoor writer, bemoaned the shooting of young birds in the summer. A terrible thing, he said. But he also proudly stacked up 125 birds he and a shooting companion took in one day. John Krider, another well-known early writer, also campaigned against summer woodcock shooting—but he and a friend killed 63 woodcock one morning in the 1850s.

Not to ridicule the early conservation crusaders. It's just that their blind spots are far more obvious today than they were then. As if wholesale shooting year-round weren't enough, woodcock were killed for commercial sale and, at the southern end of their perilous migration, Louisianans firelighted them—shot them at night by a primitive form of spotlighting, using blazing pine knots as torches. Primitive or not, a good shooter would take 100 woodcock a night. Let's hope the swamp mosquitoes made him pay for his fun.

I subscribe to the Ron Schara school of woodcock hunting (a credo, by the way, that applies to every kind of successful hunting and fishing). I once asked Ron, a well-known outdoor writer who lives in Minnesota, his secret for productive bogsniping.

"You walk," he said succinctly, "your ass off."

It should be engraved on my final marker.

Sure, there are shortcuts to woodcock hunting, techniques and tricks that may make your hunts more productive and fatten your game bag. But, as is true with nearly every outdoor pursuit, it all boils down to a pair of resilient legs and the willingness to use them.

FINDING WOODCOCK COVERTS

There are two major considerations in woodcock hunting. One is to find woodcock; the other, dependent totally on the first, is to hunt them effectively and efficiently. It's silly to look for woodcock in a pine grove or on an Ozark ridge. True, you may surprise the aberrant woodcock who, for reasons concealed within his screwy skull, has chosen to squat there. Recently, I killed a woodcock in southwest Iowa. True, he held in a patch of pretty good woodcock cover on the banks of a small stream— but he was far west of where most woodcock migrate and his covert wasn't much bigger than a tablecloth and, as far as I could tell, was the only woodcock habitat in the county. I wouldn't plan on ever finding a woodcock there again.

So, you hunt for woodcock in areas that woodcock prefer. That means along stream benches or in brushy, moist, loamy woodlands. Woodcock don't like ground cover, such as grass, that inhibits their prowling for earthworms. Look for a forest floor of fallen leaves. It's not infallible that woodcock will return to coverts in the fall where they rested on their spring migration, but it's a good bet, so scout out coverts at dusk during March and April when the birds are moving north and males are making their courting flights.

It's worth seeing this courting flight anyway, for it is one of nature's finest dramas. The bird that Arthur Cleveland Bent described as "This mysterious hermit of the alders, this recluse of the boggy thickets, this wood nymph of crepuscular habits" puts on a flying show unrivaled by any other bird. Our Missouri birds begin courting early in March, often when there still are patches of snow. From about fifteen minutes before last light to well into the night, the males will be flying with twittering wings and liquid love songs, or "peenting" on the ground. That rasping, cicada-like call carries a long way on a quiet night. Most ornithologists compare the peent to the call of a nighthawk, but Thomas Imhof, writing in *Alabama Birds,* says it's "a short, explosive, nasal, belching noise."

My experience has been that finding woodcock coverts is not that troublesome. I know that traditional literature claims a hunter's woodcock covert is only slightly more sacrosanct than his wife, and while you may get away with diddling his Mama, leave his mudbat fen alone.

Perhaps I'm spoiled by living in non-traditional woodcock hunting country. I find my coverts by asking. I suppose in hidebound woodcock areas you'll get a stony stare if you ask after local woodcock shooting, but in the Midwest, ask and (if the source ever even has *heard* of a woodcock) you'll be given. Hunting potential is scarcely tapped in much of the country; certainly not through the middle of it. Minnesota, for example, is the largest Midwest state. There are some nine million acres of public hunting land. But only one percent of the state's hunters claim they hunt woodcock. One grouse chaser I hunted with sneered contemptuously, "How do you display a woodcock—bore a hole in the wall and stick his nose in it?"

Bud Tordoff has a reputation as a Minnesota woodcock hunter. Uniquely qualified as both a scientist (he's director of the University of Minnesota's museum of natural history) and a hunter, he's worth listening to. The way to find coverts, he says, "is to ingratiate yourself with the best local hunter. But, in my experience, I rarely find anyone as interested in woodcock as I am, so it's mostly a matter of exploring on my own."

That involves acquiring good maps of unfamiliar territory and finding the small streams, the bog edges and other likely-looking spots, then going there and hunting. Andy Ammann, Michigan's guru of woodcock and grouse biology and hunting, found one of his favorite coverts while he was bowhunting for deer. "It's mostly trial and error," he says. "You look for aspen sproutings on clearcuts, or older aspen groves in open country, semi-open aspen with scattered conifers."

Ammann feels Michigan (which is the most woodcock conscious of the Lake States) has many more woodcock and fewer woodcock hunters than the eastern states. "I grew up in New Jersey," says the now-retired woodcock biologist, "and the hunters were very secretive about their woodcock coverts. In Michigan, we don't need to do this so much—we can always find new ones if necessary. And I find scouting out new areas much fun anyway."

A couple of Missouri hunters I know got interested in woodcock by reading about them. There certainly was no tradition of woodcock hunting in the Ozark hills where they live. They explored a nearby creek bottom which had boggy sprout thickets along its edges . . . and began to jump woodcock. One recently kept a season log and discovered he'd moved more than 200 birds during the two-month-plus season. He felt he had jumped at least twice that many the preceding season.

Woodcock respond to weather change and if the fall is a gradual one, the migration may be gradual as well, a trickle that never puts many birds in a covert at a time. But if there is heavy weather to the north, it can bring in a flight that truly represents the historic collective "a fall of woodcock," for it is as if the birds rained from the sky.

"In woodcocks, especially it is remarkable that upon a change of wind to the east, about Alhallows-tide, they will seem to have come all in a night," wrote Charles Morton of European woodcock, "for though the former day none are to be found, yet the next morning they will be in every bush."

So it pays to find an indicator covert, one you know will have woodcock if woodcock are in the country, and check it frequently—every day during the peak of migration—to see when the birds arrive.

If a man thinks woodcock, he can scout some nice territory during the summer. Canoe floating or wade-fishing takes him past some potential coverts. It requires looking up once in a while from paddle or plug, but if you spot a likely-looking spot, hunt it come fall (after your indicator covert tells you the woodcock are in). Like a winning poker hand, you keep the productive spots, discard the losers.

Every town of any size has a local gunner's hangout, a sporting goods store, hardware store, pool hall or liquor store. You probably get more misinformation than straight skinny in such places, but it doesn't hurt to ask Whiskey Joe, the proprietor, about local woodcock hot spots. It also doesn't hurt to buy something from him. Kind of loosens the tongue. Chances are, he'll look at you as if you asked about church services, but it just may be he has heard of woodcock and knows where some can be found.

Once you locate a covert, mark it down, either mentally or on a map. Until plant succession makes the area unattractive to woodcock, they'll be back every year. You can count on it.

GUNNING

If there is a secret to shooting woodcock, it is to fire regardless of the obstacles involved. If you can see the bird (in the normal woodcock tangle) you can kill it. I once took a friend woodcock hunting for the first time and we jumped two birds. Each time I waited for him to fire and he didn't.

"Why didn't you shoot?" I asked.

"I was waiting for an open shot."

"You might as well leave the gun at home and save the weight," I said. The open woodcock shot makes free beer look common. I literally have killed birds that I couldn't see—birds that flew behind a screen of vegetation as I fired. But some of the shot got through and knocked the bird down. It only takes one shot. I suppose a good enough shooter could wait for his target to fly across the small openings (assuming he's canny enough to predict the bird's flight path and quick enough to fire at just the right instant). But I believe in shooting when I'm ready, no matter how obscured the bird.

The last woodcock I killed before writing this was a classic example. Ginger, the pup, is all legs and puppydumb enthusiasm. She bumped the bird in the densest possible growth of sycamore sprouts, a cathair so damned thick I don't see how the bird could open its wings. I fired when the bird was perhaps fifteen yards away, almost entirely hidden by the thick sprouts.

The bird fluttered down as if landing, didn't seem hit. But you never can assume you didn't hit a woodcock. They rarely fly more than fifty to one hundred yards on a first flush, so try to mark them down or at least watch them long enough to get a line of flight, then hunt that. They won't often sideslip like a quail or grouse, so if you follow the flight line, you should put the bird up, or, if he has fallen dead, find him.

But only if you use a dog. Your chances of finding a dead woodcock, even one lying in plain sight, are almost as good as those of having Raquel Welch call you up tonight to go out for pizza.

Ginger pounced on the bird I thought I had missed. It was stone-dead, with one shot through the back, a second in the breast, a third in the leg. Two of the three would have been fatal; the other probably would have brought the bird down.

I caution against carrying a heavy gun, not only because the heavier the gun the bigger the lump it lays on you when you manage to whack the side of your head with it, but because it isn't needed. Think light and fast. A twenty-six-inch double, bored skeet and skeet or something close is ideal. Most shots will be under twenty yards. Some recommend No. 9 shot; I shoot No. 8. You don't need anything larger, nor any hot loads.

The gunner who is ready will get (and make) more shots. The more tangled the covert, the more ready you'd better be. I carry my gun in my right hand, barrel up (I'm right-handed), using my left hand and forearm to fend off the crap. You might consider wearing a glove on your left hand to forestall abrasions. My finger lays alongside the trigger guard (never, never in it). My thumb is on the safety. If it's a bit more open, I rest the gun butt on my hipbone or carry it at port arms. You can sling one under your arm or shoulder it or carry it barrel down if you want to—but it'll cost you shots. Learn to mount the gun the instant you hear a bird flush, then look for it.

A woodcock gun is one you can hit woodcock with. A good shot will hit three of five woodcock, maybe better. They really aren't as tough as they look. If you adopt as a general rule to shoot at the bird, not figure leads, you'll kill more birds.

Dog on point, bird locked to the ground at his nose-tip . . . you have an opportunity that damned few pheasants will give you. The chance to plan your approach. The woodcock will stay where it is like an agreeable upland game bird, not one of those gaudy demented chickens with the legs of Frank Shorter.

If the point is at the edge of a thicket, the bird almost certainly will flush into the more dense cover.

Work your approach so you don't get caught behind a tree or clambering over a deadfall when the bird flushes. Take it easy—no need to hurry.

It's a flustery flush, wingtwitter and confusion. But you make a good shot and the little bird falls dead. Your good dog picks up the bird and brings it to you. Take a moment to salute the little gentleman of the alder swamp. I don't get mushy over quail, nor doves, feel respect, but not regret for my shot pheasants and grouse, am awed, but not saddened by the death of a wild turkey . . . but I have a pang every time I kill a woodcock, for I have lived through the long evenings of spring with them.

I love them as no other bird, not just as superlative targets, but as fascinating experiments by Nature. They defy bird dictum with a cheeky flip of a saucy tail that, like most everything else, doesn't fit the rest of the bird. They're stuck together all wrong; they should be wading around in lake water with the rest of their kin rather than sharing the uplands with Mr. Ruff. A cripple is hard to look in the eye.

I have yet to meet a Born Again woodcock hunter who does not love the bird—not the sport, though that also consumes him, but the bird.

Too many hunters stuff birds they kill in their game pockets without a second thought for what they've done. No need to feel guilt—you wouldn't be smiling with canine teeth if you weren't a predator. But respect, love, a genuine joy in the marvels of creation that result in goofy little birds who illuminate an October day . . . that, you should feel.

15

Bird=Quail

We watched the weather like wind-bit old dirt farmers, checking the time-honored signals by which Nature announces her intentions. Our crop is dependent on it.

Our crop is quail—birds to anyone who hunts them. ''I'm a bird hunter,'' you say to strangers and if they also are bird hunters, they nod. If not, they ask what kind of birds you hunt and you mark them down as questionable characters—perhaps IRS agents or Congressmen.

While there are other hunted birds, there is only one Bird. My Brittany, Chip, points woodcock. He has locked tight on sharp-tailed grouse in the sere gramma grass of South Dakota and stood firm before the first aspen leaves on a Minnesota hillside. He indicates fallen doves and would point pheasants if only the damn things would stand still. He never fails to let me know where crouches the camouflaged cottontail.

But those are mechanical points, without emotional content. It is only when the hot gush of Bird hits his flubbering red nostrils that Chip is truly transfixed. He was born to Bird. That eight ounces of plump mini-partridge is an avian bennie for my tired dog, an upper that transforms him from a trudging portrait of exhaustion to a pup fresh out of the kennel. Never mind that an instant before he was dragging, worn sloppy by hours of fruitless casting. Never mind that he was reduced to throwing half-hearted points at field mice in a trifling attempt to salvage something from the empty day. Now he has Bird jammed up his nose and, by God, there's no doubt about it. He leans into the quivering wall of scent, every nerve keening. His eyes glaze, his nostrils tremble.

That's what Bird does to a quail dog. It does scarcely less to me, this dapper little bird I've trudged countless miles to tryst with over a quarter-century.

Most of my quail hunting is toward the northern fringe of the bird's range. Quail have ranged as far north as my mother's home country, northwest Wisconsin. But now you'll find few quail north of central Iowa. Perhaps it is coincidental, but where the pheasant dominates, the quail fade. I don't know if there ever have been any studies on pheasant-quail relationships (and don't know what good it would

Most of Bob's range is in the eastern part of the country, especially in the Midwest and South, but where you have row crops and nesting/roosting cover, you well may have the bobwhite quail.

do if there were), but I have a gut feeling that pheasants may inhibit quail populations.

I hunt north Missouri where quail are far more subject to the realities of winter than they are in the southeastern states where the nation's most lush quail hunting is found.

Modern agriculture is light years from the gullied Depression broomsedge 80- and 160-acre home places that Grandpa scratched a meager living from. Not only was there cover galore in those days, but a good chunk of the nation's hunting population was getting ready to go off to war. And no one was plowing crop residue under each fall, nor dousing the growing crops with an ungodly assortment of pesticides and herbicides that I think are taking a toll from our soil which we won't realize for a generation or more. I'm not prepared to *prove* that sluicing this fall's quail crop with agribusiness poisons is harmful to it—or to us—but given the choice, I'd rather shoot and eat unsprayed quail.

It's a tough go for birds on a farm where the shadiest spot in a fencerow is the thin line cast by barbed wire, where the ground is fall plowed, the gullies bulldozed in and leveled off, the small fields made into great big ones, the woodlots cleared or pastured with too many cows, the meadows rank with fescue . . . and cowed to the roots to boot. One of my favorite hunting farms sported river bottom fields, separated by thin, but adequate fencerows. For years, we hunted down these fencerows, running up a covey or two in each one.

Last time I was up that way, the old farmer had sold out to a nephew. The fencerows were gone, bulldozed out to create big fields, the land was plowed—no crop residue to feed birds that also had lost their cover. That unfortunately is the norm, rather than the exception.

Still, today's quail hunter has a far greater chance to shoot a limit than did Joliet and Pere Marquette in 1673 when they traveled down the Wisconsin and Mississippi rivers, past the muddy, raging mouth of the Missouri.

There were few quail then. It took a nation of ax-wielding settlers to chop out holes in the arboreal frontier, to let annual weeds and native grass come in to feed and shelter the little five- to nine-ounce birds, tiny cousins to the mighty turkey, the more impressive grouse.

Aldo Leopold quoted extensively from early writers in his *Game Survey of the North Central States* (1931) to make the point that quail populations flourished with the coming of settlers. Any modern wildlife biologist knows that disturbed ground, with plenty of "edge," is ideal for quail. Leave seeds for the birds to eat, whether grain crops or weed seeds, and there's food enough. Leave crop stalks, plus the tangle of annuals and shrubs that follow clearing of the overstory, and you have good cover. And food and cover are what make little quail, along with a bit of avian lechery between cock and hen.

One quote in Leopold's book is especially telling and sounds as if it were written yesterday: "Kumlien (1903) says that quail of Wisconsin ' . . . gradually decreased in numbers until about 1885, [when] they were entirely absent from many localities where they were once common. The clearing away of underbrush and the introduction of wire fences in place of the old-fashioned rails, with their weed-covered space on each side, probably had as much to do with their disappearance as too close or lawless shooting.' "

The reduction of quail habitat often is so subtle that the average hunter has no idea where all the birds went and usually blames the weather, the conservation department or the Democrats/Republicans. One Illinois study showed thirty-six coveys of quail on a farm in 1966. The farmer converted to grass and began fall plowing his remaining crop land. By 1972, just six years later (and those six years were among the best for quail in modern times), the coveys had dropped to six.

What it's all about. A Brittany and a setter locked on point, with another setter honoring. The hunter moving in and, somewhere a few feet in front of the taut dogs, a restless covey ready to spring into the air.

That's hard evidence, folks—no blaming weather, biologists, foxes or politicians.

In Missouri, for example, cow populations have jumped from 27 per square mile in 1940 to about 65 now. Back then, timothy made up 32 percent of Missouri's pastureland and red clover 26 percent. Fescue accounted for only 17 percent. But by 1978, fescue, a plant that is almost a total loss as far as quail are concerned, comprised 92 percent of Missouri's pastureland and the other two plants, both good for wildlife, had declined to a combined 5 percent. Fescue. Lovely stuff—thick as the air downwind of a sewage lagoon on a hot August day, grows anywhere. Cows don't much like it, but prefer it to rocks.

What hunter among us is astute enough to see this gradual change, this slow decline of quail habitat?

Speaking of subtle changes, try this one on for size: under Missouri law, land that is strip-mined for coal must be reclaimed, restored to arability.

This is seemingly progressive legislation (which probably will be overturned when we really get into the intensive strip mining that will be coming in the next few years). The intent of the law is good. But what if the strip-mined land formerly was "brush" land, not farmed for one reason or another—probably marginal farmland, too expensive to clear? It would have been fine quail, rabbit, deer habitat. However, when it is reclaimed, at least in Missouri, the chances are almost 100 percent it will be restructured as permanent pasture, and remember that 92 percent of Missouri pasture is fescue. So, what was good wildlife habitat has become something else. One biologist told me, "The law acts as an incentive for landowners to sell strip-mining rights because they not only get the revenue from mineral rights, but they also get formerly unproductive land put into production."

And so it goes . . .

Out in Kansas, they used to have some eight to ten thousand miles of hedgerows, superb small game cover. More than half of that has been ripped out since the 1940s. Bill Scott, writing a few years back in *Kansas Fish and Game* magazine, quoted an old farmer as saying he'd ripped out fencerows on his place because poachers slaughtered quail in them, and he thought that if he pulled the hedge, the quail would move farther back from the road.

"This seems," Scott commented, "like dropping a firecracker in your car's gas tank to get rid of a rattle in the trunk."

One final note about quail habitat, because we're about to go hunting. I can see you're getting restless and it does look like a good farm down there in the river bottom. One of the rare ones—maybe it was too wet to get in and plow back in October or maybe the farmer doesn't believe in fall plowing. Sure looks good, all those yellow tumbled-over cornstalks, the grown-up field over here and that old abandoned farmstead will have a covey or I'll buy the beer.

But let me bore you with one further study. I have a built-in antipathy toward sentences that begin "A study shows that . . . " because most studies are like the law of physics that states for every action there is an equal and opposite reaction. Quote a study, and someone will checkmate it with an equally authoritative study that says you're full of hog apples.

However, a 1971 North Dakota study showed that 82 percent of the motorists traveling on that state's highways paid no attention to whether the highway right-of-way was mowed or unmowed. But when they were asked whether they preferred the highway edge to be mowed, most said they did.

The point is that if people don't notice unmowed rights-of-way, don't mow them. The energy saving alone would seem to make that reasonable, plus, from a wildlife enthusiast's standpoint, the benefit to critters is enormous. There are some fifty million acres of rights-of-way along roads, pipelines, railroads and the like and they often are incredibly productive of wildlife if left unmowed. I've shot pheasants along a railroad right-of-way, running the birds out of the tall Indian grass by the droves. Ducks and pheasants are notable nesters along prairie-state highways and I know of a prairie chicken flock that survives nicely among intensely farmed bean fields by roosting and nesting in the thin strip of native grass along an old railbed.

John Madson, in the finest single hunting article I've ever read ("Pheasants Beyond Autumn" *Outdoor Life*), tells of a man who hunts late-season pheasants in the brome grass of Interstate 80 interchanges. "He says he does all right," Madson reports. "As near as we can figure it, the only law he's breaking is the one prohibiting pedestrians on interstate highways."

When we're talking quail, we're talking the bobwhite. He is so preeminent among the six United States-dwelling kinfolk.

You'll find bobwhites a legal game in thirty-seven states and two provinces. Hunters annually kill an estimated 35 million bobwhites, compared to 3.6 million scaled quail and 2.7 ruffed grouse. California quail contribute 2.2 million of themselves to the total quail bag, and Gambel's (desert) quail add 1.3 million. But no other quails, grouses or partridge are even close.

The bobwhite dwarfs them all. Add the kill of every other gallinaceous game bird together and the total still is only one-third of the annual bobwhite harvest.

Bobwhites are the kingbird in the southland—north of Missouri-Illinois, etc. he is an occasional. True, there can be spectacular quail hunting in eastern South Dakota and New Jersey hunters take more than 100,000 bobwhites a year. But Bird's kingdom is in Alabama (2 million plus a year), Florida (2.5 million), Georgia (2.4 million), Tennessee (1.7 million), Mississippi (1.2 million), Illinois (2 million), Missouri (2.8 million), Kansas (2 million plus), Oklahoma (3 million) and Texas (naturally, 8 million).

Over in the Carolinas, they know Bob—more than 2 million each annually. Where they say "y'all" and think Havilah Babcock was one of the Prophets, that's where Bob is king. In fact, I have developed a never-fail technique of finding quail habitat in unfamiliar country. Stop at the nearest small-town restaurant. It will be named the "City Cafe" or the "Nighthawk" or something similar.

Ask for biscuits and gravy. If they don't know what you're talking about, box up your pointers and turn the nose of your quail car south. You're too far north.

16

Of Quail and Hunters

The cock bird I hold in my hand, still warm but limp with the final, awesome relaxation of death, started as one of a clutch of seventeen eggs, laid by an industrious hen beneath a honey locust tree at the edge of the old field down below the fading red barn.

She chose well, by accident. Had she set up housekeeping in a working hayfield the chances are a snickering sickle bar would have scrambled her eggs and probably her with them.

Quail attrition is stunning—70 to 90 percent of this year's birds will not see a second spring. The stubbly hunter with the bony dog, the old double whose cracked stock is secured with friction tape and whose faded eye is as keen as that of a sharp-shinned hawk, is only one of the traps laying in the pitted, short path a quail travels from birth to death.

If a traveling black rat snake doesn't methodically swallow the bird's egg, snuffing out his life almost before it has begun, he faces a terrifying array of tooth, claw and natural disaster before the moment when, God willing, one or two of my No. 8 shot send him tumbling into the cornstubble.

This time, no snake came along and no wandering skunk, so in due time fifteen chicks hatched (two eggs proved infertile). Both the hen and the cock had brooded the eggs. She fed only in the warmth of afternoon, never leaving the clutch of eggs long enough for them to chill. She might grab an unwary, spring-stiff insect that wandered close to the nest, but mostly she drowsed away her parturient confinement, her brain waves probably as close to flat as a live brain ever gets.

There were a couple of nasty late April rains, but the hen, though miserable herself, provided insulation for her eggbound babies, keeping off the cold rain, as well as the hot, direct sun.

The chicks began to pip, to break through the large end of their shells, on the twenty-first day and, by the twenty-third day, they tumbled from their calciferous cages, wet, shaky, but alive. My rooster was among them, weighing but a fraction of an ounce. He nestled with his coveymates against his mother's warm breast and

A classic spot for quail—a field corner with a jumble of stuff that offers cover to a quail covey. There's food in the stubblefield to the rear, cover under the ruins of the old building and in the tall weeds.

gradually dried out. A precocious fellow, he was able to move, see and feed himself almost immediately. No robin he (robins and many other birds are altricial, meaning they must be cared for and fed by their parents in the nest for some time).

That covey was lucky. Others on the same farm fell victim to natural but unhappy disaster. A wandering skunk wiped out one clutch of eggs. A farmer in a neighboring hayfield mowed over another. Yet a third was left motherless when the hen, chasing a bug, was nailed by a sharp-shinned hawk. But the cock, whose primary function had been to fertilize the hen, took over the brooding and brought off the clutch. The other two pairs renested. One brought off a brood; the other suffered a second disaster—a grass fire fried the eggs, a fire started by a carelessly thrown cigarette from a hiked-up hotrod driven by a teenage punk whose only demonstrated talent to date was in the field of littering. The parents, two-time losers, finally brought off five young in August.

Come July, the baby quail grew almost visibly. Fueled on a hot diet of insects, they were large enough in two weeks to be able to fly off the ground for short distances. At three weeks, they were large enough that the two parents, both brooding, couldn't cover them. And now there were only thirteen. One drowned in a thundershower. One was squashed by a car as the hen led them, scurrying, across a blacktop road. The rooster survived.

Seven weeks after they hatched, the young birds were almost half-grown and able to fly a hundred yards, something they did one day when a prowling fox made an incautious stalk and failed, by the space of a tailfeather, to catch any of the exploding birds. Quail flushed from a roost literally go in 360 degrees, for they roost tail to tail in a tight circle. If they're scattered out feeding, they'll take off in fits and starts, disconcerting if you level down on one group of birds only to have another flush almost under your feet. If they're running before the dogs as a covey, they'll generally flush in the same direction. But if they're scattered along a fencerow or ditch, they'll split, some going ahead, some over your head and behind you.

Soon after the fox missed them, the assembly call fluted from a half-dozen locations and the birds began to reassemble.

At two months, the quail were a covey rather than a family group. Cocks and hens were distinctly marked now and the birds occasionally crossed paths with another covey along the Mussel Fork and finally joined forces in September.

A cock and hen who had not mated earlier in the year felt the sweet touch of September Song and had a late hatch of ten birds. This late hatch may be 40 percent of the annual production and is the cream of the production year. For a long time, the late hatch was thought to be a second hatch of a pair who already had raised one batch of chicks, but it's pretty well accepted now that the August hatch is from cocks and hens who, for one reason or another, did not bring off an earlier hatch.

If the early hatch is good and the late hatch is good, the season will be a rouser. If the early hatch only is good, it can be only a fair hunting season.

The early broods not only were full-grown by the start of November, they'd undergone a kind of adolescent unease called the "fall shuffle." Something caused the entire quail population to range far more widely than it had all spring and summer. Cover thins out with the first frosts, food may require more looking-for. Maybe it's like children eager to loose the family ties they've worn so long. Whatever, quail coveys mingled, sometimes birds from one covey joined another, the family groups became coveys, rather than families.

QUAIL DOGS

No one who has gone this far with me will expect me to recommend any dog other than the Brittany for use on quail. However, both pointers and setters are far more prevalent among quail hunters than Brittanies are—though the Brits are coming on strong and, I think, will become as established as the other two.

Other possibilities are German shorthairs, viszlas and the other setters (Lewellin or Gordon). You could use flushing dogs, such as springer spaniels, or retrievers, like the Labrador, but only if that's all you have or if you're willing to forego the pleasure of watching pointing dogs at work.

Most upland dog breeds are specialized; there are few generalists. The Big Three, pointer, setter and Brittany, all are generalists. They all run, they all point, they all retrieve. You have to speak in generalities because dogs, like people, have their individual idiosyncracies. While pointers in general are wide-ranging dogs, long-runners who dislike hunting dead and, often, retrieving, you might find a pointer who works thirty feet out, loves hunting dead and retrieving. And, while Brittanies have a general reputation as close-working dogs, I've known some that would race a pointer to the far horizon.

The legginess of the pointer is legendary. I once hunted quail with a northwest Missourian who had a pointer he'd just gotten back from a trainer. Fine blood, handsome dog—looked, as well as acted, like something out of an advertisement for a pointer kennel. Rex was the dog's name and there shone in his wide-set eyes the fierce desires of the true hunting dog.

At least that's the way he looked in the station wagon on the way to the quail fields.

Rex boiled from the dog crate, a galvanized blur. "Rex! Rex! Whoa, Rex!" bellowed the alarmed owner as Rex headed west at a thundering gallop, scarcely deviating for the larger trees and shrubs, merely knocking over the smaller ones.

"Rex! Goddammit! Rex!" shouted my friend. Rex neither slowed nor veered. He vanished over the horizon and my friend, snarling like one of the dogs, took off his cap, threw it on the ground and stomped on it.

About an hour later, Rex reappeared, running still, but more slowly, from the *east!* We theorized, only half jokingly, that he had circled the world. I've hunted behind good pointers—but it is Rex that sticks in my mind as the quintessential pointer.

Rex would have been fitten company for a southern hunter where the dogs are as lean as tundra wolves and as fleet as greyhounds. I've never experienced southern hunting—it's mobilized warfare and I've always been a foot soldier. Even back in the days of Mr. Nash Buckingham and his brethren, the cornpone bird hunter did most of his cruising seated, either on a sleek horse or on the spring seat of a horse-drawn wagon; later on some vulgar old truck. Now, the four-wheel-drive has taken over as man's trusty steed and Dixie bird men ride to their quail hounds aboard snorting gas hogs that eat up ground, both literally and figuratively.

It's okay, I guess. I use a vehicle to get from one hunting spot to another, but from farm to farm. Once I get where I'm going, my hunting is toughing it out on foot.

They tell me walking is impractical in the vastness of an Alabama plantation or a Texas ranch, that you must have transportation to move you from covey to covey. The closest I ever came to that kind of hunting was for scaled quail in southwest Kansas. We rode a Bronco with a capital "B" from guzzler to guzzler. Guzzlers are man-made catch basins that water wildlife.

Mickey was a hard-muscled pointer, now a memory, who had a lot of faults, but could he find birds! Not only is Mickey gone, but so is the old Model 12 Foster is holding. It burned in a fire. Fortunately, Foster still is tromping the fields of autumn with me.

We hunt 300 acres thoroughly in six hours. The best year I've ever had, we'd get up twelve coveys on 300 acres, or not even two-thirds what southerners consider excellent hunting. I'm not sure what this proves except that I must have missed out somewhere along the line. I've heard of twenty-covey days in other states. Oldtimers tell me about twenty-covey days in Missouri, but I suspect half those coveys originated in the recollection of the teller.

So, I'm content with five to ten coveys in a hard day's hunt. It's a good thing, since I suspect as habitat declines, we'll have to learn to live with reduced numbers, at least on private farmland. Perhaps quail will hold their own on paper company plantations or vast ranches or on public land, but in row-crop land, habitat is vanishing at a stunning rate. Missouri has gone from ten birds to six daily in the last few years. The immediate cause was bad winters, but the real cause was the loss of cover which let January chew up marginal coveys. Quail feathers don't protect a bird from zero temperatures when all he has for shelter is a frozen fall-plowed clod any more than they do from No. 8 shot.

WHERE TO HUNT

There are two general types of hunters these days—those who have a place to hunt and those who don't. Most hunting land is privately-owned and always will be. As a stranger, your chances of getting permission to hunt good quail country are two: slim and none. So, that means you must hunt public land, with the other 80 percent of hunters who live in cities or towns.

I can't speak for someone in New Jersey or Tennessee or South Carolina, but in the Midwest states I hunt, I have found birds enough to satisfy me on public land. There are only two secrets to doing it—persistence and a willingness to move farther from the car than the rest of the hunters.

Public land birds, harassed almost daily, move deeper into available cover. You may find them (as I have) in the middle of a substantial woodlot. They're never easy after opening day.

But, by busting more brush, going deeper into the boondocks, I have found coveys that never had a shot fired at them—and done it near the end of the season. Once the snow flies, and the holiday season sings its Siren song of flickering log fires, hearty meals and eggnog with guts, hunting competition thins out dramatically. Where weather can be severe perhaps 75 percent of the hunters quit by mid-December.

Wives take a toll, coralling ex-hunters first for Thanksgiving, then for Christmas shopping. New Year's Eve (which sometimes starts about Dec. 15) cuts a bloody swath. Hunters who thread their perilous way through the tempting shoals of The Holidays are those who find birds knotted up in hard-core cover. So your snot does freeze on your mittens. Do you want to find and shoot at quail or not?

Easy birds go quickly on public land, but the birds never are shot out, even though you'll find hunters who swear they are. How can they explain that the next season there will be about the same number of birds as there were the preceding year, given constant weather and habitat conditions? No, what really happens is that so many hunting parties move through a public area, nose to tail, like a bunch of circus elephants, that the available birds either are kept scattered or move to the most remote, inaccessible possible spots, including some where you'd never think to look for quail—the middle of a sizeable woodlot, for example.

For the best hunting, an area shouldn't be hunted more than once every five or six days. Give the birds a chance to re-covey, rest and feed. Of course, you only have that option if you control the hunting on the land where you hunt.

A hunter doing my kind of hunting will cover no more than 400 acres in a day's hunt. If he has a weekend to hunt, he should work over 900 acres or more, hunting half one day, half the next. That's what we do. We hunt the 400-acre Mussel Fork farm one day, tackle a nearby farm of about the same size the next.

I'd like to take you over the Mussel Fork. You look about halfway reliable and you gave your dog half your sandwich, so you can't be all bad. The Mussel Fork is such a typical quail area that we can talk about principles and techniques for quail hunting and use it as an example. What say we give it a try?

17

A Quail Hunt

This farm is new to you, isn't it? The old Mussel Fork place. I've been here a thousand times. I know where the birds will be. We may not always find them. Maybe we'll miss them as they feed out in the beanstubble or maybe the dog has the rag on or something. But probably the next time we hunt here, the covey that has been here for the past ten years and longer will pop up just where it's supposed to be. Not the same birds, of course. Quail generally don't live out a year. But the same covey location.

Now, I hunted turkeys over there in the hills and heard quail whistling up girl friends earlier in the year, so I know about where a couple of coveys will be. If we'd gotten here at daybreak, we would have heard birds calling to each other and it wouldn't be quite so much a mystery where they are.

This is a pretty typical farm. The spots where we'll find quail here are where you'll find quail anywhere you find quail—anywhere in the range. It may be live oaks down south instead of white oaks here. It may be a prairie grass peninsula into the bean field out in eastern Kansas, rather than foxtail, the way it is here. But the principles are the same. You can save yourself a lot of looking by learning where quail are likely to be and hunting those spots, rather than trying to cover all the ground on an 800-acre farm.

That's what we have here—800 acres. It's enough to make your forty-year-old legs feel eighty by the time the sun gets low and red over the county line hill. I've walked until I had a crotch cramp so fierce it took me to my knees, howling like a coyote. But I got up and limped on after the other guys because I'm too damn stubborn to quit and too damn addicted to quail hunting to let them run up a covey without me.

See that creek down there, the little one winding through the valley? You can tell there's a creek there by the line of trees. There's also a bridge way off in the distance and they usually don't build bridges without a pretty good reason. That's the Mussel Fork. It's the belt around the fat gut of this rich old farm. Most of the birds we find will be near it.

Let's plan this hunt a bit rather than charging off in fourteen directions at once.

We're at the south end of the place. It runs out to Number 11, the blacktop about a mile away. That's where we left your car, by the old falling-down barn. We'll work to your car and I'll guarantee that by the time we get there, you'll fall to your knees and thank me for making you leave the car there so we don't have to walk all the way back up here. You may fall to your knees anyway, thanks or no thanks.

We'll swing back to the south first and hunt out the old, abandoned farmstead on the hill. There is a covey around it somewhere. The farmhouse sits on a knoll, surrounded by grown-up weeds and grass. There's rusty old farm machinery buried in the vegetation. Below the house, where the garden probably used to be, is a small field with horseweeds over your head. Chances are the birds are in this stuff, for they love to sit in there, safe as if in a bank vault. A little feeder creek borders the horseweeds, intermittent and grown up with young willows. Sometimes the birds are along this creek bed. If they flush there, they'll usually split, half the covey flying up around the abandoned house, the other half flying along the feeder creek toward the Mussel Fork.

And about half the time, you won't get a shot, so it's important to look sharp and mark where the birds go or we won't find the scatters. Run if you have to, get to a vantage point where you can watch them pitch in (knowing that usually where they set their wings to land is not where they really land).

Now, if they're not along the little creek, then we may have a chance. Below the house and barn, beyond the tall grass, is a picked cornfield. This is our covey's restaurant. Chances are, they're out in the cornfield now, picking up a little break-fast. They'll feed in the morning, come back into the grass or down by the creek to loaf away the middle of the day. They probably roost either in the grass fronting the cornfield or the horseweeds. We'll work down through the grass first. Let the dogs do the work and be ready. Chip's pretty careful, but it has been a long time since last season closed and he's gotten fat, lazy and careless.

Goddam! There they go! I told you they were in the grass. Right by the fence. Damn dog! You better hang your head, you worthless tub of guts! You know better than that! Now, you settle down or I'll bust you good.

Did you mark them down? Most of them went into the willows right down in the corner by the creek. But a couple dropped into the corn. I saw right where they went—see that bent willow that hangs out over the field. They're about thirty feet out in the field, off that. You learn to use markers like that. Sometimes the birds will run on you after they land, but these birds haven't been hunted yet, so they'll probably be within a few feet of where they went down.

Easy! Chip! Easy! Damn dog needs to run out some of that piss and vinegar . . . whoa! He's got 'em. See, right where I said. Pretty point. Chip, you just redeemed yourself.

Get ready . . . if they both get up, you take the right bird, I'll take the left. If it's just one, you take the shot. There'll be more. No point in making it a competition.

There they go! Good shot!

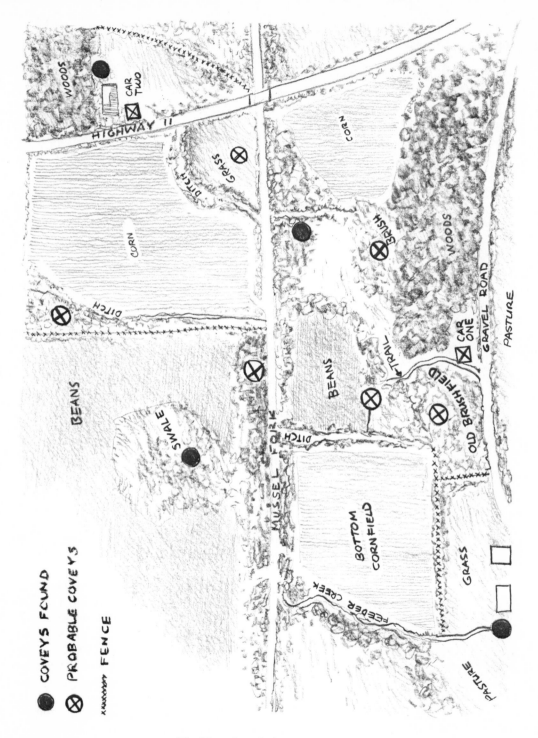

COVEYS FOUND

⊗ PROBABLE COVEYS

xxxxxx FENCE

WOODS

CAR TWO ⊠

HIGHWAY 11

DITCH

GRASS

⊗

CORN

CORN

BRUSH

⊗

WOODS

DITCH ⊗

GRASS

BEANS

⊗

SWALE

MUSSEL FORK

BEANS

⊗

DITCH

TRAIL

⊗

CAR ONE ⊠

GRAVEL ROAD

PASTURE

OLD BRUSHFIELD

⊗

BOTTOM CORNFIELD

GRASS

FEEDER CREEK

PASTURE

The Mussel Fork farm.

It's early enough in the day to have good scent conditions. There's almost always a dew on the ground and until that dries off, the dogs can work better. And if a wind comes up, that'll hinder the dogs even more. But if we get out too early, the birds still will be coveyed in a tight knot . . . maybe 8 to 11 a.m. is best.

This is a pretty easy covey to hunt, one of the easiest on the farm, so we'll go light on them. Hunters can shoot maybe half to 60 percent of the birds in an average covey without creating a problem, but if you leave only three or four birds, there just aren't enough to keep each other warm and you'll likely lose the covey.

But if hunting were to hinder quail, we'd have lost the bird a long time ago, back in the days of no limits or, when limits first were established, bags of two dozen a day.

Not bad—we've been out an hour, jumped a covey, killed four birds, two for you and two for me. A covey an hour is excellent hunting. I should have doubled on that last pair, the ones that got up while you were across the creek. It was that rarity—birds out in the open, going straight away.

Notice I kept the dog on my side. Not so much because he's my dog, but because the wind is blowing this way. Keeps him downwind of the cover. Same in a fencerow—let the breeze blow through it to the dog.

I had trouble with the damn safety. It works hard, which I guess is okay for safety, but bad when you're trying to thumb the sucker off so you can shoot. So I didn't get the first shot off as quickly as I should have and then the second bird jinked into the trees just as I shot.

So you don't believe me. Okay, I won't believe your feeble excuses either . . .

Let's work the creek. Tell you what—I've been here before, so I know how these birds act. You take Chip and see if you can get across the creek and I'll work Ginger on this side. Any bird we flush is going to fly to the other side of the creek and it gets too deep to wade on down a ways. I think it's bred into the bastards. Make Chip hunt in the brush along the creek. If it gets too wide for him to cover while you walk outside, get in there with him.

Sometimes it pays to send a hunter and a dog down the creekbed where it's dry enough to do it—sometimes those coveys hang up under the banks or in the little streamside gullies and you can miss them from up above. But we need another hunter for that, so we'll take our chances. There—you can get across where the stream cuts across that gravel bar. Hope you waterproofed your boots last night.

Can you hear me? Okay, I can see your red cap. Let's move about the same rate, you watch for me, I'll watch for you. Don't shoot at birds headed my way, but give me a holler to let me know. Guess you know that, though. There's a log crossing about a half mile down and you can get back over here then. They've cut the timber up to the bank on your side from there on to the bridge and fall-plowed the field, so you might as well forget that side from there on.

Notice how I'm working the dog. I walk the edge, let the dog work ten to fifteen feet into the fringe. Works most of the time. I might miss a covey that has fed out into the field and if the dog isn't working the edge, he'll miss 'em too—but there'll be more inside the fringe or at it than out in the fields.

If we had a thin snow on, we could see tracks where they eddied out in the field to feed. Last week's wet snow mashed down an awful lot of cover and made our job a whole lot easier. Up to the first big snow or ice storm, there's almost too much cover, too many places for birds to hide.

Now, you see this corner we're coming to? There's everything quail could want here—a patch of open woods for resting cover, along a creek, at the base of a wooded bluff where they can fly to escape. There's a lot of downed trees and grass for cover, and a cornstubble field with a world of shattered-out grain. Just has to have a covey.

Whoops! No sooner said than done. What a pretty point! Look at Ginger honor. She's still trying to sort out what this is all about, but she backs instinctively. It's a good thing. A dog that steals another dog's point and busts birds is not quite as unpopular as the guy who brought him along.

If you were a novice hunter, I'd bet you good money I'd get more shots. I look for avenues of approach to the dogs so when birds flush I can shoot at them. Sometimes a straight line isn't the best approach. Not if it puts a tree between you and the probable covey location. Think open shot. And keep your gun muzzle up, finger off trigger and safety on until you hear the birds go.

Don't look at anything, especially the ground. Even if you see birds on the ground, which you won't, it'll actually cost you time when the birds go.

You can't herd birds, but you can try to keep them close to the edge. If the dog points into the thicket, take turns with your hunting partners going in and fishhooking around behind the probable covey location. You can't push them out into the open, but you may keep them from going far back into the cover.

New hunters freeze when a dog points. I hunt with a nice youngster who is a fine shot, but who doesn't own a dog. When the dogs point, he stops.

There's nothing more fun than a false point. At least Chip keeps you interested when the bird finding is slow. I guess I'd rather have a dog who's too careful than one not careful enough. Let's take a breather here on this log and eat a breakfast bar.

You know, Chip *thought* something was there. He smelled something. No one yet has figured out all the conditions that affect a dog's ability to find birds by scent, since no one yet has gotten inside a dog's nose. My feeling is that hot, dry weather is death for dog work. A windy day scatters scent badly. A crisp morning, with the dew just melting, usually produces the best dog work. It helps if the covey has been working an area to scatter scent, but I suspect a covey still roosted tail-to-tail emits a powerful gust of scent when it shakes itself free of night's grip at first light.

One thing I do know and that's quail always put out some stink. There are basalt beliefs about quail, fallacies so widely held that you couldn't shake them loose with a half-stick of 60 percent dynamite. One is that quail can withhold their scent.

Well, they can't, but an alarmed quail will freeze, its feathers compressed apprehensively. Immobility and the tight sheath of feathers minimizes scent drifting from the bird.

We're shooting pretty good today, doing it right. Most quail shots are going away and a lot of them are nearly straightaway. Brush shooting complicates the easy angles in that the birds dodge obstructions. And if you bump a covey off the roost, they'll come up literally in every direction of the compass since they roost in a circle, tail-to-tail, for warmth and protection.

At one time, before the boss cracked down, another fellow and I shared an office and put up one of those miniature basketball hoops at which you shot foam rubber balls from the sanctity of your desk. It's called "creative relaxation." We had three balls and we separated real quail hunters from those who merely thought they were. We'd take the three balls, crush them together, tell the visiting hunter that a covey rise was coming, then pitch the balls at him. As they expanded, they flew in three directions. The quail hunter instantly would pick one out and catch it. Everyone else tried to catch them all at once and invariably missed every one.

Most good quail hunters shoot with deliberate haste. And the secret, if it is that, to their success is that they get the gun to their shoulder quickly.

There are two ways to shoot quickly. One is to stand there with your jaw dragging the partridge pea when the covey flushes, then snap off a wild shot with the gun halfway to your shoulder. The other is to react at the first stirring in the brush by mounting the gun, then take a bit of time to single out a target and get on it.

Developing that quick reaction is a matter of practice, of years of hunting the little bobs. When you're in good quail cover you always half-expect a flush. When you've scattered a covey and are hunting the singles, you should be ready, not shambling along with your gun tucked under your arm, hands in pockets.

Carrying the gun at port arms is the most efficient when a flush is imminent, but you wouldn't want to do it all day. I often carry the gun at the balance point with one hand, and that's the best argument I know for packing a light gun. Yet I'd rather have a gun with a bit of weight in the front end that gives you the feeling of positive pointing, rather than some 20-gauge feather so ethereal as to threaten to take off and fly with the birds.

The optimum quail gun is a double with twenty-six-inch barrels, bored open—either cylinder and improved or improved and modified. Unless you're a powder tinkerer, No. 8 field loads are perfectly fine—hunters have been shooting them for nearly a century.

We're going to cross the creek here for a reason. You see that two-acre swale way out in the middle of that bean field, over there to the west? See the willow? You oughta try walking this field sometimes when they've had the plow in and then some rain. Any quail you get then, you earn. Dogs like this open stuff. Look at 'em run now. Check how they're trucking about four o'clock.

A single quail comes up as both dog and hunter react. It's hard to see, but the bird is midway between Chip's open mouth (yes, he did try to snap it out of the air), and the muzzle of Foster's gun.

An example of just how quickly quail get somewhere else. The bird already is a considerable distance away as Foster fires and Chip looks on. But he dropped it with a difficult shot into the thick cover.

If we'd hit another covey along the creek, I wouldn't bother with the swale, but it looks as if things might be tough today, so we'd better check out all the possibilities.

This is an almost perfectly circular swale, a wet spot haired-up with willows and collared by foxtail. We'll circle it first with the dogs, then if we don't get the birds up, I'll flip you to see which one of us has to go inside and root 'em out.

This is a covey we'll never shoot out. Most of the time you won't even see them flush—just a muffled roar and a few glimpses of birds scattering through the willows. The singles will come up from under your feet and you'll see some of the wildest shooting since that little misunderstanding at the O.K. Corral.

Nothing on the fringe. Maybe they're out in the field, but I'll flip you to see who takes the dogs in the tangle.

Damn! Never won one yet. Okay, let me go around on the other side and work through. You stay here and maybe I'll run them over you. It's a good theory. Remember the Harvard Law of Animal Behavior: under carefully controlled conditions, organisms do what they damn well please.

Heads up! Here they come! Damn, what a shot! Dead bird, Chip. Look for him. Birrrd! Birrrd! Good dog! Fetch, Chip!

Ah, good dog!

I got one that came up late. Saw the one you got. A super shot. Remember a while ago when we both shot and the bird fell and we both said, "Good shot!" at the same time. I like that about you—hope you do about me. Charley Dickey talks about hunting with "claimers," hunters who are prone to put your birds in their bag. Well, I've always figured that if someone wants meat so badly he'll claim doubtful birds, let him have it. There's no nobility in such an attitude—just that hunting quail is no place for hard feelings or disappointment.

Wish I could hone my saintly qualities enough to keep my mouth shut when someone who's a lousy shot excitedly claims a bird I'm pretty sure I shot. If I hunted with a persistent claimer, I think I'd consider getting a new hunting buddy. So far I've been lucky.

I don't know about you, but I'm so tuned in to quail hunting that I automatically grade farms on their quail potential as I'm driving along. No way to check them out, of course, but I've been at it so long that I'd be willing to put money out to prove I'm right.

You'll find quail on farms with a lot of edge, the meeting place between one type of land use and another—for example, where a cornfield meets a woods or where a grassy plot meets a cornfield or in the fringe around a pond or in a fencerow or in and along brush-choked gullies or along stream banks that face adjoining fields.

Sometimes the birds will be out in the middle of large fields, but conditions that move them there are unpredictable and unless you have field trial dogs, you can burn a lot of hunting time searching for these coveys.

On the obverse side of the coin, farms where the fencerows are clean to bare wire, where the pastures are grazed to the roots, where the cropland is fall plowed, where the fields are big and the woodlot grazed, where there are no brush-choked gullies, where the land is farmed right to the riverbank, will have almost no quail. Fall plowing has become such a serious problem that it's probably the number one environmental threat to quail at the moment. It also is incredibly wasteful of topsoil. The reason for it is to give the farmer a jump on his next year's spring work—if he plows in the fall, he won't have to do it in the spring (and if it's a wet spring and he's late getting in the field, then he will have gained some invaluable time).

But the exposed ground is laid open like a raw wound, vulnerable to the deadly germ of soil erosion. We don't, contrary to gut feeling, have an inexhaustible supply of topsoil and you'll not grow bumper crops of anything on what lies beneath that thin shield of rich earth.

Let's go on back to the creek and work up the next covey. Chip! Ginger! You should have seen Chip work that dead bird. I'll bet he's saved me a hundred birds I'd have lost without him. The damn thing fell in a little tangle of grass and I never would have seen him without the dog.

We're not doing badly at all. You have five birds and I have four. If we can find the covey in the corner down here, you ought to limit out. Six birds is a pretty low limit, but we've had some tough winters. Maybe someday we'll get back up to ten or twelve birds a day. I doubt it though, given the loss of habitat. Maybe eight birds a day.

Did you gut your birds? Good, it's still pretty warm and there's no point in letting the meat stew in its own sour juices. If it were colder, I wouldn't bother to gut quail. Use the ground as a thermometer—if it's frozen, then it's cold enough to eliminate the need for gutting birds.

When we get back to the car, we'll bag the birds in waterproof plastic bags—I always carry a bunch—and put them in the cooler.

By the way, we'll be at the car about noon. We're only making this a half-day hunt. We've ignored some of the good hunting. I don't know about you, but I'm just not in shape. I'm getting tired already.

What we'll do is drive over to New Boston and eat some of the finest greasy hamburgers you ever choked down. Couple of Pepsis, a bag of potato chips and one of those gutbusters and you'll be able to walk till dark.

If we limit out with the barn covey, we can go fishing this afternoon . . . hey, look there! Both dogs locked on. Geez, that's pretty! Almost makes me forget that Chip peed on my guitar case and Ginger ate one of my new shoes.

See where they are? A classic covey location—there's a ditch running perpendicular to the creek and the corner is filled with downed trees and a few little pockets of grass where the birds can rest. Look, there's even a dusting spot here at the edge of the field. See all the tracks and where they've been dusting. That depression is called a dusting cup. I guess they do it to discourage mites or other parasites—don't know if it smothers the little buggers or what, but quail sure do enjoy a dust bath.

Well, I'll be go-to-hell! Nothing there. And here after I bragged those damn dogs up, they false point. Well, there *was* something there. Maybe a fox or something ran them up a few minutes ago. Or maybe it was turkeys. It was a bird point for sure—Chip points all those things he's not supposed to point, but I can tell when he's presenting me with a rabbit and when it's birds.

There are two more covey locations . . . goddamit! A single bird and I missed him. Where do you suppose he came from? How could I miss an easy shot like that?

There's the car. You've got what? Five birds. And I've got four. Well, if I can get a nice double off the barn covey and you can get one, we'll go fishing.

This is a classic-situation covey, too. They've been here since before God. This little field is shaped like an isosceles triangle. There's a thick fencerow down one long leg, full of rose and about five yards thick. Sometimes, the birds will rest in there. The other long leg fronts a jungley woods and that's where you'll most often find them. When they flush, they go right up the hill through the woods and I think into Outer Space for all the luck we have locating the singles.

You see those clouds building up over in the west? I'll bet it's dropped ten degrees since we've been hunting. We've got weather moving in. We almost always have a hell of a snow in the middle of November and this may be it. Those suckers come in quick, too. Get a good big wet snow and it'll knock down a lot of this cover.

When that happens, the quail begin to get squeezed and the hunting gets easier.

It's kind of interesting, but along about the last week of December it'll be colder than a Laplander's linguini and there'll be ice an inch thick everywhere but the deepest cover and that's where the birds will be—and there won't be anybody hunting them. It's the truth. Probably three-fourths of the season's hunting is done during November and maybe a week or so into December.

Most hunters are fair-weather types. Ths quail are out here all the time. But less than 20 percent of the season's bag is shot after Christmas.

See how this fencerow can hold quail? Wild rose thick as dog hair and vines and scrub trees. There's fencewire in there somewhere, but it's not needed. They haven't bred the cow yet that could get through that stuff.

Well, the birds aren't here, so they're along the hill. Ginger! Get in there! Dogs are like people—they don't like to wade around in that crap either, but if they don't they'll miss birds. Only way to train them to hunt cover is to go in with them. Set an example. In fact, we'd better do just that. Don't follow right behind the dog—that halves your chances. If he veers left, you go right. If he goes right, you go left. Spread out and don't forget to kick the brushpiles a little.

If I ever quit talking, we can listen, too. Sometimes you can hear birds chirping in alarm just before they take off. Otherwise you walk into them unexpectedly and when they take off you'll likely salute . . . goddam!

Well, I got one down and missed my double. No excuses this time, other than I'm a poor shot. You got your sixth bird! Super! I'm gonna quit.

Don't know about you, pard, but I'm about to starve. And besides, old friend, I think I just felt a snowflake. . . .

18

The Historic Pheasant

While the American ring-necked pheasant figuratively still has damp feet from wading ashore off the immigrant boat, he's been extant somewhere as long as any game bird, frustrating hunters from the Mongolian steppes to the English moors.

Some writers have traced pheasants back to Jason and the Argonauts. You think you have problems with non-deductible expenses and cabbage worms? Remember, Jason had to dodge the razor-sharp feathers shed by the man-eating birds of Lake Stymphalos on his way to steal golden fleece, shorn from a ghost's ram, and guarded by a sleepless dragon. Worst hunting trip you ever had wasn't that bad.

Somewhere along the way, perhaps between having to yoke King Aeetes' fire-snorting oxen or hanging around the Island of Lemnos (which was inhabited solely by women given to doing God knows what with visiting hunters), Jason picked up some pheasants at the mouth of the River Phasis in Colchis, now the Rion River, and released them when he returned to Greece. So we have the scientific name *Phasianus colchicus* for the English or common pheasant.

Whether the pheasant reaches back through real history into mythology or not, we do know it traces to 250 B.C. when Aristophanes of Byzantium mentions the birds as domestic fowl. Palladius even earlier described how to fatten pheasant for the pot (feed them noodles dipped in oil, which works for people, too, only we call it spaghetti). Ring-necked pheasants apparently made their way from the Orient to southeastern Europe, especially around the Black Sea, before Christ. Pheasants moved north, either as captive or domesticated birds, with the Romans and were in England by 1059. By the 1300s, pheasants were ranging wild in the Rhine Valley; they'd reached Denmark by 1562, just in time to become targets in the fine new sport of wingshooting. For some reason, pheasants held out against introduction to Sweden stubbornly for a long time. They didn't become established in the wild there in appreciable numbers until the 1920s. If nothing else, that long limbo gives hope to wildlifers who long for American pheasants to adapt to new territory.

There are pheasants and there are pheasants, just as there are several species of quail, many of grouse. Most of the birds hunted in North America are ring-necked pheasants, though those of the northeast states often are hybrids, crosses between Chinese ring-necks and either English (Jason's birds) or Mongolian pheasants.

The distinction is one of interest mostly to a biologist, for the birds act the same, no matter the species. Most of the English birds are hybrids themselves. What the English call the "common" pheasant no longer is. It was introduced into Great Britain about the year 1000 A.D., possibly by the Romans, maybe the Saxons. Along came the Chinese ring-neck at the end of the 18th century from southern China. Ring-necks being what they are (nasty, contentious, competitive bastards), they have become the predominant species in Great Britain.

While poachers are catholic in their taste for illegal game, pheasants always have been a favorite target, I suppose because they're big and worth the trouble it takes to get one.

Netting was the first major method used by poachers. Some poachers became adept at calling pheasants during the breeding season, one of those anomalies in hunting ethics which intrigues me. It is perfectly acceptable to call up and kill a gobbling turkey in the spring breeding season, yet it is illegal to do so with a pheasant. Why?

Callers would spread a net between them and the crowing roosters, call the testy cocks toward them, leap up and flush the birds into the net.

Today's wildlife malefactor faces a fine at worst, maybe a few days in jail in some places, though that's not as common as it should be, but the poacher of 1800 had a choice of several penalties (actually, he had no choice, but there were several penalties available). All of them were bad. Many poachers were impressed into the military, the theory being, I suppose, that anyone stealthy enough to fool wild animals might also be good at sneaking around and killing enemies of the Crown. Hard labor or a severe whipping were other possible penalties.

But poaching was about the only way the commoner could hunt, for legal hunters, by definition, were few. The game laws prohibited most Englishmen from sport hunting, including "dissolute persons," a proscription which, if it were enforced in America today, would keep a good many of my friends from going afield.

Still, there were enough sport hunters wandering about the English countryside that they began to get in each other's way, so the shooting butt or battue came into vogue, a stationary hide for the gunner where he would shoot at driven birds. Both partridge and pheasants were the usual targets of the gentleman shooter. Dove hunting is the only American upland bird shooting that in any way resembles shooting from a butt.

So beloved was the pheasant that by the close of the 1800s there were gamekeepers who reportedly shot nightingales so their singing wouldn't keep the pheasants awake. Other keepers wiped out any game that might compete with the exalted pheasant.

If you think your bird dog is superior, consider the qualifications of a good poacher's dog of the early 18th century. The dogs often were a cross between a greyhound and a sheep or cattle dog. They worked at night because that's when Daddy did his dirty work. They had to be superb retrievers, pointers; occasionally they were equipped with a lantern to spotlight roosting pheasants (spotlighting still is a favorite method of game managers for capturing wild birds to use as brood stock in game farms). The poacher's pup must scout not only for game, but for the brush cop as well and must warn its master of the gamekeeper's ambushes. As Charles Trench reported in a fascinating book *The Poacher and the Squire* (Longmans, Green and Co. Ltd., London, 1967) the toughest trick of all for the poacher's dog to learn was that he "must display no sign of recognition if either he or his master were caught and confronted with the other." How you teach a dog to be cool is beyond me—my hounds either are so glad to see me they howl and cry and occasionally pee all over themselves, or they figure I'm going to swat them with a two-by-four and they slink and skulk like city-dump mutts. Either way, no one has any doubt as to who owns the dogs.

Other poaching methods for pheasants included shooting them as they clustered around a bait site, or as they were silhouetted against the night sky on a roost. Poachers spotlighted them on the roost as well, and jerked them to glory with a long pole to which was affixed a noose. Poachers also stupefied pheasants by burning sulphur under the tree. Rat traps baited with peas stuck to the trip pan with pitch also claimed their share of illegal pheasants. One of the weirdest and cruelest methods involved soaking peas to soften them, then drilling a tiny hole through the pea with a needle, threading a horsehair through the hole, then trimming the ends off one-half inch on each side. The poacher scattered the bristled peas, which lodged in the gullets of feeding pheasants and choked or immobilized them.

Another cruel method was to bait a fishhook with a raisin, attach it to a peg driven into the ground. The pheasant swallows the raisin and is hooked like a feathered channel catfish on a limb line. Another anomaly—what makes it all right to take a fish by that method, but terrible if a bird hunter does it? Don't yell at me. I'm just asking.

Most ingenious were two methods which took advantage of the belligerent nature of the rooster pheasant. One involved leaving grain steeped in booze in suitable places. The roosters, acting remarkably like Saturday night cowboys, would get soused, start fighting, and the poacher could walk in and pick up the exhausted, passed-out birds, kind of like the local constabulary mopping up after a roadhouse discussion.

Finally, the poacher might take a snake-mean gamecock to the field. No cock pheasant could resist the challenge of the professional fighter and few survived the encounter.

To cope with this array of dirty tricks, gamekeepers devised their own set of nastiness, the most fearful of which was the mantrap, designed to catch the poacher's leg at the knee.

While we today might sometimes wish for a mantrap to mangle a poacher, the actuality of it is a bit too gruesome for the modern-day ethic, but British gamekeepers still have their little pranks. Most direct is to collar a poacher and beat the living hell out of him. But the poacher also may tumble into a pit while fleeing, or fall over a trip wire (or meet one strung throat-high). Maybe he'll plunge into a stream or a deep ravine when a convenient crossing plank proves to be half-sawed through.

Aside from turkeys, poaching of game birds in this country doesn't appear to be a big problem. Most game bird violations are over-the-limit situations where a legally licensed hunter runs into a honey hole and can't quit shooting. Commercial poachers would much rather concentrate on large animals where one shot means a lot of meat, rather than one or two small birds.

PHEASANTS IN AMERICA

America's introduction to the pheasant was a long one, filled with false starts. Because the bird was so familiar to British colonists, it was natural that they tried to introduce it here. It didn't work. George Washington is alleged to have stocked some. Benjamin Franklin's son-in-law tried them in 1790. But it was ninety-one more years before an American stocking finally paid off.

There always seems to be one atom-cracker, someone who, through luck or inspiration, kicks loose a key log and unjams a problem that has plagued everyone else.

Such a man was Judge Owen Nickerson Denny, U.S. consul to China. You can, depending on whether you just somersaulted a cock pheasant into the foxtail, amid a glittering shower of his own feathers, or missed him cleanly, call Judge Denny a saint or a sinner.

Why Denny's pheasants grew from a spark to a conflagration defies explanation, just as does the question of why pheasants breed like garbage dump flies in some places and don't in others. Aldo Leopold theorized pheasants are successful only to the limits of the glaciers, a matter of calciferous soil. Others blame it on a temperature tolerance barrier.

It was 1881 and Denny was determined to bring the pheasant to America, more specifically his home state of Oregon. There were sixty birds, caged in the hold of the *Otago,* wild-caught and, as it turned out, not packaged for a long sea voyage. They were bedraggled when they deshipped in Oregon. That first try by Judge Denny was as successful as the numerous attempts to stock pheasants had been for the preceding 150 years. It cost the good judge $300 of his own money to feed the Oregon foxes. Most would have given up. Most had. Records of stocking attempts go back to 1730. No one could believe that a bird so widespread in Europe and Asia couldn't thrive in North America. My God, if Charles X (1757–1836) could shoot 8,000 pheasants a year, why in hell couldn't the American gunner shoot even *one!*

Denny shrugged off his $300 fiasco and in 1882 shipped ten cocks and eighteen hens in more spacious cages aboard the bark *Isle of Bute*. The birds were turned

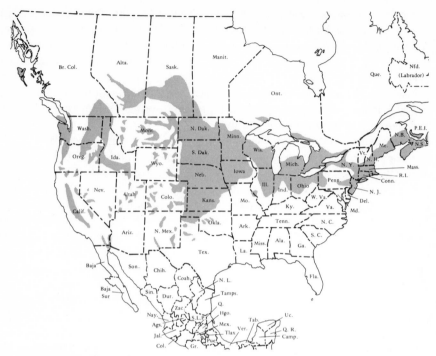

Some set of conditions limits pheasants and theories are almost as prevalent as excuses for missing one of the big, slow-flying birds. Range extension is possible, perhaps even probable—but pheasant biologists have been stung often enough that none will make any rash predictions about what John Ringneck will do.

loose on the Denny home place in the Willamette Valley of Linn County, Oregon. By the time Judge Denny came home in 1884, the birds had spread and were into adjoining counties. And, less than ten years after the successful stocking, there was an open season that accounted for an estimated 50,000 birds. It was the beginning.

Other states began stocking live-trapped Oregon wild pheasants and, after 1911, game farm-raised birds. There was an orgy of stocking, a biological binge that cost a fortune. Pheasants were stocked in every one of the forty-eight states and in every conceivable habitat, from mountaintops to swamps. Remember, in those days no one knew very much about wildlife needs. They were stocking salmon in Missouri's sluggish rivers, too.

A good example of the shotgun approach was that of California. The state raised more than a million birds in the period from 1926–1956 and stocked them statewide, but only in the valleys (especially where there were rice fields) did the birds thrive. Pheasants are a bird of croplands. They will not adapt to deserts, nor forests, nor mountainsides.

It seemed that once the log jam was broken, pheasants caught fire. In 1882, 200 pair of English pheasants were released on Pierre Lorillard's Monmouth County, New Jersey, game preserve and did well.

A year before that, nineteen pheasants were released on Vancouver Island. Some five years later, the island had its first hunt and hunters killed 3,000 birds. Dwight Huntington proved not much of a prophet when he wrote in 1903: "In many of the states, the closed period is now about to expire and the pheasant will be shot with the other game birds, but I doubt much if they will anywhere survive in the Eastern States, save on the preserves. The birds are large and noticeable on account of their bright plumage, and although swift flyers, they are not very difficult marks; and in localities where there are several shooters in each field, the moment the season opens, and often before, with dogs of all sorts, I do not see how the pheasants can possibly escape."

By 1910, George Bird Grinnell said, "The pheasants are not without their opponents. It has been alleged that they destroy or drive off our native game birds, that they injure certain crops and carry disease."

It's hard to believe that pheasants could be considered "pests," but there are farmers to whom any wildlife is a threat, an unwelcome competition, to whom the benefits, whether as a cash crop or for personal enjoyment, are ignored. In 1944, there were so many complaints of pheasant depredation in Iowa that there was a spring season set. The birds were accused of destroying young corn shoots. Perhaps they do, but pheasants and corn coexist amicably all over the country and Iowa now is synonymous with both pheasants and corn.

Do pheasants dominate other wildlife species? John Madson thinks pheasants don't compete with quail, but does report that roosters have driven prairie chickens off booming grounds. The aggressiveness of the pheasant is legendary—after all, they're spiritual and genetic cousins to gamecocks. Ring-neck roosters have chased down and raped domestic hen chickens and turkeys.

Pheasants finally sorted out where they would live and where they wouldn't. Oddly, South Dakota, the state that for many years was the nation's pheasant capital, is the only state never to have had a state game farm to raise and stock the birds.

So, pheasants have become the most prominent of the upland birds, if not the most widely hunted. No one makes long trips, at least in numbers, to hunt quail or grouse, but thousands of hunters annually invade Iowa, the Dakotas, Nebraska to hunt pheasants. Only turkeys command that kind of frantic hoopla and not nearly to the extent the pheasant does.

Pheasants take a bit of hunting, despite what Dwight Huntington thought, so let's take a look at how to go about it.

19

The Hunted Pheasant

There are two pheasant seasons. There is the first hour of the new season and there is the rest of it.

Millions of roosters die in that first hour, blunt-spurred kids hatched out a bare six months before. A pheasant's education comes quickly—either he graduates or he goes home in someone's game pocket. And pheasants who graduate don't just have a B.S. degree (Bachelor of Survival). They earn a doctorate.

Pheasants are agricultural birds, especially fond of row crops. They're never far from grain, whether it's corn, beans or milo. They're legal game in thirty-nine states, epidemic in that flock of states known loosely as The Nation's Breadbasket.

So you want to know where to find pheasants? No problem at all. First, locate a state with pheasants in it, then locate the part of the state that holds birds (for example, in California, you won't find them in the desert or the mountains, but you will in the Sacramento Valley or you won't find them in the Badlands of South Dakota, but you will in the eastern cornfields).

Easy enough—but look at that farm over there. It's a thousand acres of corn and soybeans and fencerows and a few brushy gullies and a creek border that bisects the whole thing, and there are grassed waterways and terraces, and there are two dirt roads with attendant ditches, and there is an old abandoned farmstead with weeds grown up around it, and there is a swale that looks as if it's got water in the middle that is choked with willow sprouts . . . where do you hunt?

You just listed the best places.

There could be pheasants in any of those areas. Early in the season this is especially true. Birds will be spread everywhere on a given farm. Many will be in the cornfields, especially standing corn, which is a horror to hunt (and if you do, don't ever knock down a cornstalk or the farmer will be perfectly justified in knocking you down). Pheasants feed early in the morning and later on in the afternoon, loaf out the midday. If you can find a hilltop come daybreak, you easily can see birds fly into a field—but where a bird lands means nothing, for it may gallop a hundred yards in as many seconds.

So, during the first few hours of morning, hunt in the fields, especially in standing corn. One or two hunters have little chance to run up a rooster in a huge field, but working the edge of smaller ones can be productive. Later in the morning, switch to the holding areas—gullies, fencerows, ditches and grassy swales.

Your success is tied to the kind of crop year it has been. A wet fall delays corn and bean harvest. Don't hunt in beans at all—too easy to knock them off.

Never pass up an abandoned farmstead. Quail and pheasants love the grown-up yards, barn lots and the like—find an old hay rake rusting away by a barn, with foxtail grown up all around it, and if it doesn't have a rooster or a covey of quail huddled near it, there's something wrong.

Pheasants, especially wily oldtimers, often will squat and let you walk right on by them. I think that's why hunters without dogs do more poorly than those with, for the dog isn't fooled just because he can't see a bird. He has his nose. In order to minimize the squatters, you should hunt ditches, waterways and other narrow strips of cover thoroughly. Put a hunter or two on either side of a ditch and a dog in the middle. Don't dilute your chances by following in the pawprints of the dog. If he zigs, you zag. Don't ignore any patch of cover, no matter how small, especially as the season goes on. Kick brushpiles, wade through swatches of foxtail. Cover likely areas thoroughly. If you can train yourself to do it, vary your pace, pause every few yards. The erratic pacing may spook a rooster into the air.

By late season, pheasants will be holding in areas not much bigger than they are. A tuft of grass grown up around a fencepost might well conceal a rooster. Pheasants like peace and quiet and will move into the lea of the wind, so be sure to hunt the quiet side of a hill (especially if it also is the sun side where the birds can bask and listen for danger).

Pheasants will head for heavy cover in bad weather. They dislike wet weather and will be hard to flush. It is then that briar tangles, ditches with overhanging cover, hides under old machinery, even groundhog holes may hold pheasants (and the birds may be almost impossible to boot out). Again, a dog can make the difference.

With the onset of winter, pheasants flock more and do it pretty much by sex. They're harder to find then, but when you do, you may very well find a whole bunch at once. There are some late-season tricks you can use to minimize walking.

First of all, be alert for roost sites, marked by droppings. While the roost may be empty when you're there, chances are the birds will come in to it that night. If you're in an area that permits sunrise hunting, you may score by being there at dawn. Make sure it's light enough to tell a rooster from a hen, though. You might also check the area at sundown, for the birds will be coming in to roost then.

Hunt the densest possible cover and that includes large wooded areas where you'll think you're hunting ruffed grouse. Don't waste much time hunting such areas, though, unless there's some indication they hold pheasants—a sighting of birds flying in or tracks in the snow leading into the woods.

Pheasants are the only game birds hunted with dog where it's feasible to pick roosters from hens. But this hunter is faced with the ultimate challenge as a veritable cloud of pheasants— mostly all hens—explodes in front of him.

Blackberry thickets, willow jungles, frozen cattail marshes all are prime spots. Further, take the advice of an old brook trout fisherman I know who once told me, "I don't wet a line until I get past the cigarette packages, the empty matchbooks, the beer tabs, where the fishermen's path starts to get hard to find." What he meant was that he walked until he'd outlasted the fair-weather fishermen. Do the same for pheasants (or quail or grouse or any game bird). Success goes to him who works hardest. You can figure that the road ditches and the easy spots have been worked over by countless hunters early in the season and what pheasants were there either have been shot or have moved out.

So, head for the distant fencerow, the back side of the farm. If you're on public ground of good size, acquire a map from the operating agency—conservation department, Corps of Engineers, whatever. Failing that, get a county highway map at the courthouse. Once you get to where the "fisherman's trail" thins out, look for your birds in the thick cover. Practice blocking techniques—you and the dog go in one side of a tangle, have your buddy stationed on the other side. A pheasant may make noise flushing, but he can run as silently as blowing smoke—and will run until he sees a damned good reason to fly, like your buddy mounting a shotgun.

PHEASANT HABITS

It might be helpful to review a pheasant's day. For example, if someone were hunting you (let's say with a court summons or a bag of chicken feathers and a bucket of steaming tar), he wouldn't look for you at home in mid-morning. He'd go to your office. Or, at sunrise, he might try to catch you in the open, ambling toward your office.

Pheasants are like that. They have certain fairly predictable habits. They'll roost, for example, in an open field—alfalfa or clover, cornstubble or maybe an open-treed area, like an orchard. Come daylight, the bird will feed, usually moving at the same time toward his resting cover (which will be whatever tangle lies very near the roost).

By 10 a.m. or even before, the bird will be holed up in the jungle and he'll hold there until late afternoon when he sashays out again for another snack, maybe a drink of water, finally back to his roosting area for a good night's sleep.

If you're hunting early in the morning, try to figure out where the pheasant will fly if he's flushed—his escape cover. Then block it off and hunt toward where you suspect the birds will be. Trapped, with you between it and salvation, the cock may sit tight for the dog or may delay flushing until you're well within gun range.

If you're hunting a tongue of cover—a ditch that runs out into a field, for example, go to the wide end and push the birds out to the tip where they'll be forced to fly. Otherwise they'll slip into even stiffer cover, compounding your problem.

DRIVING

The traditional pheasant drive involves enough hunters to start a small-scale Latin American revolution. There are two ways to go about it. One is the simple line of troops advancing on the enemy pheasant until at the end of the field or at some other cessation of natural cover, the herded birds take to the air.

The other is to split the army into two regiments, post one at the end of the cover, and let the first drive the birds toward the blockers.

It goes without saying (though I've already said it once) that no visitor walking standing crops should knock down and trample the farmer's plants any more than you should go into his house and kick over his wife's antique sideboard, filled with Grandma's china. City hunters get blamed for a lot, some deserved, some not, but it only takes one peach-pit-brained hunter lumbering around a farm, tromping crops, leaving gates open, shooting the cows into a Red River stampede to encourage the farmer to post one of those cute, crude signs that says, "Survivors will be prosecuted."

One of the classic pheasant hunting maneuvers is a drive, with a line of hunters moving through a big field toward a second line of blockers— essentially pinching the running pheasants between the two lines until they fly. The hunte at left is likely to be the last one to shoot if he continues to carry his gun back over his shoulder.

Either drive method, in my opinion, lacks appeal. Group hunting is not my kind of hunting. No one knows who shot at or hit what. Birds are hit by four or five different gunners, leaving them looking as if they'd been processed by a corn sheller. There is the considerable danger of shooting someone. Friendships are strained.

I don't think my experiences with large groups are untypical. You can bet that in any crowd of hunters, there will be at least one who shouldn't be there. It may be somebody's kid, out for his first hunting venture and entirely uninstructed, who continually waves his gun muzzle around like a magic wand. It may be some guy who had bourbon for breakfast to top off what he had the night before. It may be a simple bitcher who sours the hunt with his whining. There are all kinds of nasty people afoot these days and it only takes one to curdle a good hunt.

I think you should give your quarry some chance of making a fool out of you. Drives come close to turning it into a sure thing. It all goes back to that indefinable something called *quality*. I don't think it's being snobbish to insist on a sporting chance for the prey—to hunt with a bow or muzzleloader, for example. That adds seasoning to the hunt. The "sure thing" aspect of hunting should be within the hunter, not his equipment.

If the hunter is so skillful as to minimize his chance of failure, then he has mastered his sport. But if the hunter is incapable of trapping a house mouse unless he carries around enough gimcracks to insure success, what has he really accomplished? He hasn't won the game—his equipment has. It's like sticking a straw man atop a fine cow pony. Do you call the straw man a cowboy when the horse does all the work? The real cowboy is the one who can jump on any old nag and herd cows. And the real hunter is the one who hunts successfully regardless of his equipment. He's the one to whom the thrill of the chase is paramount to the exultation at the kill.

That diatribe out of the way, there's no reason you can't drive pheasants. Take a party of four or five hunters and work a pincers movement on a likely spot. Each man knows his job as well as everyone else's. You trust the gun handling of your pards. When the birds get up in a tangled frenzy, you've decided that Charley and Ed will take the right-hand birds, Fred and Al the left-hand ones. Pete can be the official cameraman or can shoot backup, watch for cripples, spot the survivors down or whatever.

One season I hunted opening day in Iowa. We were on a small cornfield that was so jammed with pheasants they were standing on top of each other. There were four of us and Chip, the redoubtable Brittany. We walked the length of the cornfield, occasionally flushing a bird, occasionally getting off a shot. Now, had I used my natal brainpower, a couple of us would have trotted around and blocked the end of that damned field. Because, as we stood perhaps fifty yards from where corn ran into fence, pheasants began to erupt like a swarm of bees. There must have been fifty of them. They came up in a volcanic delirium that seemed to go on forever as we stood there stunned and helpless, just out of gun range. Naturally, every bird flew immediately across the road onto posted ground. Rear-guarding this Chinese fire drill came Chip, puzzled that none of the pretty birdies would squat down for him, the way the little quails do.

GUNS AND GUNNING

Guns? I shoot the same gun at everything, but there's a good case for a long-barreled, full-choke repeater as the quintessential pheasant gun. I suspect a Model 12 Winchester is the end-all in pheasant guns. If you're a good shotgun shot, the tight choke will let you take pheasants a bit out of range for a looser pattern. And the third shot is available for those birds that absolutely refuse to die (which is most every pheasant I've ever seen).

Pitty-pat loads will take all small game birds and grouse, but it takes a high-brass load of No. 6 shot to put a pheasant down. I don't shoot magnum loads in the old Smith because I'm afraid they'll crack the slender stock, but magnums are eminently suitable for pheasants. Generally speaking, a rising bird will die if you aim at the target provided by nature—the ring on his neck. Shoot when the bead crosses it.

That pretty white ring on a rooster's neck makes a perfect aiming point.
Touch off the shot when the bead of the shotgun crosses the ring.

Gervase Markham, the early "shooting flying" writer, advocated camouflage clothing, including a mask, a wreath of oak leaves and garments festooned with branches and leaves.

Nicholas Cox, writing in 1686, talked of wingshooting: "It is now the mode to shoot flying, as being by experience found the best and surest way, for when your game is on the wing it is more exposed to danger; for if but one shot hits any part of its wings so expanded, it will occasion its fall, although not to kill it, so that your spaniel will soon be its victor."

While it's true enough that a pheasant is fairly easily knocked down, killing one often seems as impossible as Shirley Temple body-checking Bobby Hull. I've had birds fold in midair, to all intents deader than a politician's ethical misgivings, only to have them hit the ground running like Frank Shorter. Chasing down a wounded pheasant is an exercise both in physical conditioning and in gun safety, for running with a loaded shotgun is not recommended by any gun safety instructor I ever met.

However, you balance that caution against the probability that your trophy is

As easy a shot as this one looks, the hunter easily could miss it . . . if he doesn't force himself to wait until the bird gets out a little farther. And if he doesn't raise the gun with the pheasant's rise, he might shoot under.

going to run right out of your life, and you make your decision accordingly. Remember, though, it is a moment of frantic activity, and it's easy to get careless and shoot your dog or your hunting buddy or your foot. Never, never run with the safety off or your finger on the trigger. Never! Never! Never!

DOGS

Pheasants are one of the upland birds (along with doves, perhaps snipe) where a flushing dog is every bit as effective and perhaps even more so than a pointing dog. The springer spaniel is the most notable pheasant dog, while retrieving breeds,

Labs, goldens, also are ideal. Since pheasants, especially those who've been shot near, rarely hold well for pointing dogs, the flushing dog serves to panic the bird into the air where the careful pointing dog will go crazy trying to pin down a running bird.

In 1671, Francesco Monari reported that hunters flushed pheasants into trees, using a red dog which resembled a fox enough that the birds panicked, thinking a fox was stalking them. The idea seems to have gone out of favor.

In 1686, a book of advice to sportsmen, encouraged ''a good spaniel that will Range well about and when he hath Pearched the pheasant, to bay soundly, which will cause them to keep the Pearch the better, then whereabouts hearing he is, make up to him as privately as possible, and having espied him (being at a reasonable distance) make your shot; and for your dog's encouragement, let him bring it to you, and make much of him.''

The interesting technique here is a combination of coon hunting and bird hunting—let the dog bay and tree the bird, sneak on it, shoot it (probably with a rifle in those days), then let the dog retrieve it, as in today's upland hunting.

It drives a good pointing dog crazy to get crossways with a bird that won't hold still. In fact, there are many dog owners who will not let their dogs hunt pheasants. In the big field country, where the cornrows stretch endlessly to the horizon, a pointing dog is next to worthless. Pheasants consider the space between cornrows the same way a fleeing mugger considers a dark alley—a good place to duck into and run like hell. In any stretch of ground where pheasants can run ahead of you, they will. Up in northwest Missouri, some hunters walk the grassy railroad rights-of-way. They're loaded with pheasants, nestled in the tall Indian grass. But the damned birds will not flush until they come to a road crossing or other barrier that forces them into the air.

Point to remember: Hunt toward these natural barriers—a lake, a road, a bare field. And hunt right to the very end, for roosters will hug the cover until the last possible instant.

Not that the pointing dog has no place in pheasant work. Far from it. Late in the season, when ice and snow have knocked down much of the natural cover, when the crops are out and the fields bare, then pheasants will group in small patches of cover—a willow-clogged ditch or grass diversion or a tiny woodlot with a tangle of briars. It is in the waning days of the season that you can read the countryside easier than at any other time. It also is a time when you can have it to yourself. The easy birds have gone. The weather often is foul, almost unbearable. I remember once hunting in a fierce north wind so vicious that we literally could not walk into it. We had to back along when we made the turn upwind. But there were pheasants roosted in the tall grass of the fencerow we hunted.

That time of year, most hunters have opted for the fireside. It's holiday time and parties come easier than sleetstorm roosters. Father is expected to put in a little time tree-trimming, playing with the children and the children's mother. Most hunters have left the field. Most cover is gone. Most of the roosters may be gone also—but there are plenty left and they are a challenge to hunt.

The ideal pheasant dog somehow learns a trick that cancels out a pheasant's quicksilver sprint ahead of the gun. The dog, whatever breed, circles in front of the running pheasant, creating a pinch that will force the harassed bird into the air. No one dog species has this bred into it. It's an acquired trick and I don't know how you'd teach it, but I have a feeling that spaniels and perhaps Labs would be the most likely to learn, primarily because I think they're smarter than other bird dogs.

John Madson makes the necessary point that, regardless of dog breed, you're better off with one than without. He quotes statistics that show it takes nearly twice as long for a dogless hunter to kill a cock as it does one with a dog, regardless of breed. That should be incentive enough to hunt with dogs. Madson also talks about the Heinz variety of breeds that have been used for pheasant work, including The Basic Farm Dog, that duke's mixture of collie and shepherd, with maybe some other stuff thrown in for fun. Since farm dogs live around pheasants and generally roam free, they can pick up a lot of hunting knowledge which, if it can be harnessed, can make them as effective as an AKC setter.

Generally, though, retrievers work the big country best. Statistics from Michigan say spaniels find more cripples than any breed, though I have a feeling it's because they seem to be more eager to hunt downed birds than setters and pointers. I suspect the retrievers, especially Labs, will work as effectively as Brittanies or springer spaniels on cripples. I've never yet seen a pointer and seldom ever seen a setter that I considered a good downed-bird dog. So sue me.

Hunting, then, is just that—hunting. Kicking clumps and walking until your legs rebel and muscle knots drive you to your knees, howling like a coyote.

It's probably too simple to mention, but when you're at the farm door, asking (and getting) permission to hunt, ask the farmer if he has any ideas on where the birds might be. Remember—like his dog, he lives there, too.

Take your time. Hunt methodically, hunt thoroughly. Split forces to pinch birds. Hunt to natural barriers. Vary the tempo of your walking. Don't ever assume a downed bird is a dead one.

Somebody—I disremember who—said he prefers to use a game strap to sling roosters over his shoulder, rather than a hunting vest or coat with a game bag in the back. Said the heavy old roosters pulled down on the vest so much, they made his shoulders hurt.

Poor fellow. A game bag so heavy it hurts sure is a hell of a burden to carry.

Someday I may be so lucky . . .

20

The Ultimate Pheasant

The Ultimate Pheasant is no dumb kid whose carefree life ends five minutes after 8 a.m. on a nippy November morning in Adair County, Iowa. He's an old bird whose spurs are black, shiny and as sharp as a buffalo gutter's knife. He weighs about three and a half pounds and is a couple of years old—ancient by wild pheasant standards where the usual lifespan is perhaps a year.

His voice is a bit hoarse and cracked, not from age, but from having honkytonk-bragged his sexual prowess to several generations of disbelieving fellow roosters and an impressive number of pliant hens. Because his corner of Adair County has everything he wants in life—food, good cover and hot hens—he has seen less than a square mile of it, a tangle of brush, cornstubble and foxtail corners. The farmer is considered not quite neat by his well-groomed neighbors.

It seems almost superfluous to describe The Ultimate Pheasant, for surely no upland bird hunter, no matter that he lives outside pheasant range, doesn't know what a cackling, rising ring-necked rooster looks like. Next to waterfowl, pheasants have graced more outdoor paintings, more calendar art, more magazine covers than any other bird.

By nature, The Ultimate Pheasant is a running bird, not a flying one, which may come as a surprise to those who manage to miss him as he leaps into the air, all tail and shrill hysteria. His feet are heavily clawed, his legs exceptionally strong. He won his spurs through genetic achievement, and those sharp weapons can make an unhappy bird dog wish for something relatively easy to retrieve—like a grizzly bear. Even as I write this, the thumb I miss the space bar with is etched with a long, red gash, compliments of an Iowa rooster who objected to being reduced to bag.

Young birds have dull-toned, dull-tipped spurs. Almost invariably, the distance between the front of the leg and spur tip is less than three-quarters of an inch in a young bird, more in an older one (and the older bird's spur is dark, glossy and sharp enough to etch glass).

You may think you're sneaking up on The Ultimate Pheasant, but rest assured he knew you were there long before you suspected his presence. He has exceptional hearing (and "he" includes his drab-colored, short-tailed mate as well). And the yellow eye that peers suspiciously and belligerently out of that distinctive red face patch is keen. Maybe he can't smell you—but with his other superb survival tools, he doesn't need to.

The pheasant is the only upland game bird save the turkey where the sexes are so distinctive that it is possible to shoot only male birds.

Since the birds are polygamous, it takes only a few randy cocks (and that is all ring-neck cocks) to breed the available hen population and insure the coming year's bird crop. Pheasant cocks are mean as hell in general, but during the breeding season they become as pugnacious as Pete Rose stretching a single into a double. In Borneo, natives use "pheasant knives" to kill the local pheasant. They fix a pair of razor-sharp pieces of bamboo in the ground, tied at the apex. The pheasant, resenting any intrusion into his territory, wraps its long neck around one of the upright knives to try to pull it free—and cuts its own throat. Ringnecks are scarcely less contentious.

Chances are, The Ultimate Pheasant was one of about ten eggs, laid anytime from April through July. His daddy was a travelin' man; his mother incubated him for twenty-three days. He was lucky that nothing destroyed his nest, for a third or more of all pheasant nests come to grief. Predators (the skunk being a notable one) feast on the eggs. Or man, especially with a hay mowing machine, takes a heavy toll of birds still in the package. Highway Departments sometimes have mentalities as unyielding as the concrete they pour, and it took years of pleading in some states to get them to delay mowing until after roadside nesting was done. High gasoline prices and limited budgets helped as much as anything in curtailing right-of-way mowing, but in one state I'm familiar with, the Highway Department actually discourages roadside wildlife, considering it a traffic hazard.

It's true that pheasants do get themselves whanged by cars, but they do offer so much pleasure to so many hunters that it seems worth some risk to motorists to continue to encourage pheasant nesting along highways. If we outlawed everything that distracts motorists, we'd better outlaw tight skirts. I know a man who fell in lust at the sight of a comely wench swivel-hipping down the sidewalks and hit a parked lo-boy. Like to killed him.

Mowers not only crunch eggs, but often take the hen as well, for so devoted is she to her maternal chores that she frequently sits tight as the mower passes over her.

It takes the hen about two weeks to lay her clutch, but she doesn't begin incubation until she's finished laying, so all the eggs hatch within twenty-four hours. The little pheasants are precocious—able to run and feed at birth—but need protection from heavy weather for a few days.

The chicks are born downy, looking very much like little domestic chickens, but rapidly grow juvenile feathers which are drab in coloring. The final molt is complete by the time the birds are five months old.

This year's pheasant crop starts to make its way into the world. Somewhere, perhaps, in this clutch of 14 eggs is The Ultimate Pheasant, the rooster who, through guile, trickery, intelligence . . . or just dumb pheasant luck . . . will make the hunter look like the loser in a pie-throwing contest.

Barely out of the egg, pheasant chicks are alert and able to move, hide and feed themselves. Predators and weather are the two big enemies from now until Opening Day.

Pheasant chicks, like all upland bird chicks save the dove, are precocial—they can care for themselves almost from the moment of hatching. Once these little pheasants dry off, they'll be ready to run, hide and grow . . . to baffle the autumn hunter.

Pheasant chicks can fly adequately two weeks after hatching, when they aren't as large as robins. Even though pheasants are runners ("They will betake themselves to their legs and not to their wings, unless forced to it by a close pursuit," sighed George Morgan back in the 1700s), they're no slouch on the wing either. The bird's wings are relatively small with less wing area in proportion to body weight than many other birds. Look at paintings by good artists—you'll think the bird isn't proportioned properly.

But those small wings propel a two-and-a-half-pound cock or a three-pound old battler surprisingly fast. Of course, full-flight speed is almost academic for a hunter whose most common shot is a rising one, before the bird lines out to fly at top speed. Passing or level-flight shots mostly happen when someone else flushes a pheasant past you. In that case, the bird may be hitting close to fifty miles per hour or about the same shot presented by a passing mallard.

The classic pheasant shot (along with the classic woodcock shot) is where the bird tops out on his initial climb and, for an instant, is a hanging target, an art bird magically plucked from an implement company calendar and stuck in the November sky. Quail and grouse almost never give the hunter that fleeting moment of gearshift, but the cock pheasant, ah, yes! He has to pause for a moment to thumb his beak at you and it frequently is his final egotistical error.

But you probably won't get such a sugar shot with The Ultimate Pheasant. If you kill *him,* it's only because of fate's drifting currents. Rarely will it be because you are better at your craft as a hunter than he is at his craft as a survivor. Perhaps someone stops to take a whizz and the pheasant, having let what he thinks are all the hunters go past, rises with a derisive cackle . . . only to confront the lagging hunter who is able to stop drizzling and start shooting.

Maybe it was because you outmuscled him. He has, after all, the brain of a chicken, albeit a cagey one. So, if he feels secure roosted in a tiny swatch of foxtail three-quarters of a mile from the nearest human disturbance, it's only because he's not smart enough to imagine some hunter mule-stubborn enough to trudge there through six inches of snow, over jumbled, greasy clods, in a wind that carries the sting of a swarm of yellowjackets, sustained only by a thin but unflagging optimism.

Opening day in Iowa attracts more than a quarter of a million pheasant hunters. Iowa has less than one percent of its land in huntable public areas, which means that virtually all pheasant hunting occurs on private land. And Iowa has become the nation's leading ring-necked pheasant state. The potential for landowner-hunter friction is obvious.

While the state rightly prides itself on hospitality and while the influx of 50,000 or so nonresident pheasant hunters, in addition to the 200,000 residents, is an economic boon, try telling that to the irate farmer who's down on the creek trying to find out where the half-dozen trespassers got the idea they could hunt on the back side of the "No Trespassing" sign. No doubt there is a lot of acrid grumbling in many rural Iowa homes because of what hunters do. And some of it rubs off on the young bucks of the family. While daddy won't do more than run the trespassers

Here's The Ultimate Pheasant doing what he does best—coming up unexpectedly in an unexpected direction. Judging from the hunter's startled reaction, this Ultimate Pheasant and his girl friend are very likely to make a clean getaway.

out, his ill feelings can get carried to unpleasant extremes by the local boyos. I know—it happened to me on a safari after The Ultimate Pheasant.

We were hassled by a quartet of the local Zit Brigade as we camped at a public lake. ''Go home, out-of-state hunters,'' was the kindest thing they shouted at us as they honked the horn and revved the engine just outside my tent about an hour into what we hoped would be a good night's sleep. After six hours of hard hunting, on public land and on private land where we were invited, after paying $43 for the permit, plus the cost of the trip, I was not inclined to extend the warm hand of friendship to these punks. But, chances are, they were merely translating into action what daddy grumbled ought to be done to out-of-state hunters.

While no responsible hunter should have to put up with trouble from the neighborhood apprentice morons, maybe we should understand what generates it. And if we share communal guilt for such things as pollution and historic mistreatment of Indians, perhaps we also should feel a bit of shame for the actions of our clod-brained brethren.

The antecedents of The Ultimate Pheasant originally were stocked by God or Mother Nature or the Vagaries of Fate—whatever you believe in. In 1900, William Benton of Cedar Falls, up in the north-central part of Iowa, was raising pheasants on a game farm. September is when Midwest weather is unsettled (along with the other eleven months). The dull, smothering heat of August gives way to a few sharp nights, early-turning leaves go yellow and quickly fall.

Sometimes the sky goes black and glassy-green off in the west. Lightning flickers high in towering thunderheads and birds fly low to the ground. There is a sharp, brassy light to the afternoon sky, a hovering tension. You can hear a screen door slam a half-mile away. Sometimes a hook drops out of one of those nasty-looking clouds and a tornado cuts a fearful path through the tan fields. One hit Benton's game farm and suddenly a thousand wild-eyed pheasants found themselves free, if not yet wild. It was the start.

Iowa stocked pheasants until 1934 and opened a season. From these until the 1960s, pheasants were rife in the northern two-thirds of the state, almost unknown in the southern third. Then something happened.

That something was an inspired program of night-lighting wild birds, raising their progeny in a southern Iowa game farm, then stocking the first-generation penned birds in the southern part of the state. The program has been remarkably successful, so much so that what formerly was so-so pheasant hunting now is the best in the state and, arguably, the best in the country.

It was not the first time pheasants proved their fecundity. In ten years, the first successful stocking of twenty-eight ringnecks in Oregon's Willamette Valley pro-created a hunter harvest of 50,000 that still left bountiful seed stock.

So, pheasants can, when they set their contrary reproductive systems to it, breed up a veritable hurricane. There is hope, then, for the eleven states where the pheasant is virtually unknown—Alabama, Arkansas, Florida, Georgia, Louisiana, Mississippi, North Carolina, South Carolina, Tennessee, Virginia and Kentucky.

Missouri has an open season in a few northwest counties, plus St. Charles County, but has an ambitious stocking program in the rest of the northern two tiers of counties, using the same method that Iowa used to populate its southern counties and, in fact, using Iowa birds to do it.

Previous stockings in Missouri of ring-necked, Iranian, Korean, Reeves and hybrids either have failed or barely hang on. The theory now is to use "saturation" stockings, drops of 500 to 1,000 birds in a small area. Perhaps previous stockings were just too small, given a pheasant's short life span anyway. So far, the results are encouraging.

If north Missouri grudgingly gives in to the pheasant (or vice-versa), can central Missouri be far behind? Or the grainfields of Kentucky or any of the other states where The Ultimate Pheasant so far has not turned normally sedate bird hunters into foaming berserkers? The two prevailing theories on this failure to adapt, as previously mentioned, are (1) lack of calcium in the soil; and (2) high ground temperatures.

Neither theory is entirely satisfactory, for there are areas where pheasants thrive that either have little calcium in the soil or else have high temperatures. Most pheasant men toss in a wry little joke to the effect that maybe it's just the pheasant's cussedness that is to blame. Perhaps it's not a joke. One writer theorizes that other upland game birds have had centuries to adapt themselves to the whims of the environment.

The pheasant has been a success in this country for less than a century, an eyeblink in evolution. And planned, intelligent game management is almost as new as yesterday. Only twenty years ago, pheasant biologists were touting the Reeves pheasant, which has turned out to be an utter flop. Live and learn. "Saturation" stockings are only a dozen or so years old. Live and learn.

A viable, if low population of Korean pheasants hangs on in the Missouri Bootheel, a vast, flat, almost coverless land of soybean and cotton fields probably 300 miles from the nearest viable pheasant range. While it's not of huntable size, it hangs on and, who knows, maybe one of these days a Korean rooster and a Korean hen will firkytoodle with just the right genetic dynamite and create another Willamette Valley in Swampeast Missouri.

My Ultimate Pheasant was the third of a nippy early morning in south-central Iowa. The first of the three was far from The Ultimate Pheasant; rather he was an opening day bird, a dummy.

We hadn't gone fifty yards from the car before a young rooster, fated to die before his time, came out of waist-high foxtail, a panicky contrail of Oriental alarums following him. I committed the pardonable sin of being too excited over hunting Iowa's honey hole and I pitched the old 16-bore to my shoulder and scattered feathers and pieces of young bird over half an acre.

This was not the Ultimate, prone to squat as close to the ground as a box turtle or else sprint like a roadrunner. No, this one was young and dumb and the young and dumb die on opening day when the shooting is hot, the heady, cocky feeling of easy victory is overpowering. No one loses on opening day. Come back along about Christmas when the wind is so cold you can't walk directly into it and your fingers go numb inside your gloves and the dog whuffs silver fluff into the bright morning air. That's when you work and when the bird you get, if you're very, very lucky, is The Ultimate Pheasant.

We moved on along the edge of a picked cornfield. Pheasants . . . they are cornshuck creatures, mated to man and his agriculture as surely as a barnyard chicken. Nothing but demented dominckers, psychotic leghorns. My legs still ached from the previous day's hunt, a long one. Six hours through matted orchard grass, sometimes stumbling through the croquet-wicket purple stems of dewberry, cursing with Lincolnésque eloquence the stinging slap of wild plum sprouts. The term "leaden legs" took on new meaning as we stumped down through the tumbled cornstalks. The place was rank with cornstob mantraps, ready to grab tired old feet and twist them in undesired directions.

Chip went spraddle-legged and, once again, this was not The Ultimate Pheasant.

This kind, the kind that lies for the dog like a woodcock, is as rare as fine wine in bottles with twist-off caps. Perhaps it was that the dew still lay on the heavy grass and he didn't want to get his fine, fresh pimp's cloak dampened from a sprint through the coarse vegetation.

Whatever, Chip splayed at the stink of him, forefeet planted, shoulders hunched like a middle linebacker braced to go either way on a shifty running back.

I walked behind Chip, into the field, so that the bird logically would flush over the other hunters. Such foresight sometimes works. The grass convulsed as the pheasant, caught between a rock and a hard place, decided to get airborne. I'm sure somewhere somebody with a talent for arcane statistics has measured the initial thrust of a pheasant flush and compared it to the takeoff speed of other game birds. If the pheasant was found wanting, it was only because whoever measured pheasants in general had not seen this specific one. Even though I was looking down and saw the movement that signalled the bird's first attempt to free itself from the grass, all my brain registered was a confused blur of color, an avian Mt. St. Helens, erupting thunder and fire. I don't care if you've shot 200,000 pheasants, it still takes a while to get all the fused synapses patiently restored to duty after the shock of the flush and begin to think in terms of effective gunnery.

Somehow the gun mounts itself—that's a function of long association with flying birds and flying lead and the often futile attempt to mate the two. The first shot was a panicky salute to my jangled nerves. I forced myself to wait a millisecond, elevated the barrel to compensate for the pheasant's rising trajectory, and touched off the last-chance round.

It wasn't a pretty shot, still low, but a couple of pellets broke a wing and brought the bird down. One of the other hunters ground-swatted the running bird. Don't hesitate—a running cripple is a lost cripple if you don't put aside your natural hesitation to shoot a grounded bird. Just make sure the shot is clear, no dogs or other hunters in the line of fire.

Then we reached The Ultimate Pheasant. Craig Starr, seventeen years old and alive with the keen joy of the hunt, and I ambled down an orchard grass waterway, each of us subconsciously aware of the gratifying weight of pheasant bumping our backs. Chip patrolled ahead with that peculiar drunken sailor gait he's been forced into since some kindly soul, awash with the sweet milk of charity, put a .22 bullet in his back. It cut some muscles, but didn't even dent his spirit.

And then Chip went on point. Save for the grass itself, a thick ankle-deep mat, there was no cover for a half-mile in any direction. Close-picked cornfields lay on either side. No clouds interrupted the pale blue November sky. Assuming the presence of a shootable bird, it was a shooter's dream.

We walked in behind the taut dog. There was a vast heaving beneath the grass and the bird burst into the air, The Ultimate Pheasant, son of a star-crossed union between a junkyard bitch and a pine knot, sporting the gaudy duds of an uptown pimp and the disposition of a drunk logger in a payday shit-kicking contest.

He bore up into the morning, sharply etched on the blue sky. Both guns came up smoothly; we leaned into the shot, mating eyes to gun, seeing every glowing feather on the bird's multi-colored body. It was a straightaway shot, gently rising, easiest shot in the book. No towering pheasant this, no crossing shot on a bird pistoned by the wind. Only an easy, close-in shot on a laboring bird.

We fired four times, emptying the doubles. He spit our high-brass back in our faces, shrieking involved Oriental curses.

He soared on, unweighted by even one pellet, sailed across the half mile of cornfield, landed ever so gracefully at the edge of a tiny patch of foxtail, posed for a moment to let us know he was unruffled by what had happened, a reddish speck in the distance, then ran into the weeds.

We searched the patch, no bigger than a honkytonk dance floor, for fifteen minutes. Fruitlessly.

That was The Ultimate Pheasant . . . .

21

The Lure of Grouse

There scarcely is an upland game bird that hasn't been called "the king of the game birds" or something similarly regal. Pheasant hunters think their quarry goes aloft on angel wings. Charley Waterman calls the quail "the aristocrat of upland game"— not precisely monarchical, but you expect to shoot holes in bobwhite quail that drip blue blood.

But upland bird writers reserve their most flowery encomiums for ruffed grouse. Grouse have been featured in so many bucolic literary coronations that shooting one should qualify as political assassination.

Some of the paeans to the bird are downright embarrassing, but a crusty old pa'tridge hunter still would fight to the last drop of his blood before he'd admit there is another game bird deserving of half as much praise as the grouse. Typical of the lyrical outbursts about grouse is this efflorescence in a 1923 magazine article by Charles Morss: "And in the moulding of him Nature seems to have embodied all of the beauty, all of the charm, all of the inexplicable strangeness and romance of the autumnal woods and produced her feathered masterpiece—the perfect game bird."

One of the most instructive things I've read about grouse in a long time is a letter from a Minnesota grouse hunting friend, Ted Lundrigan. It is an insight into the way grouse hunters think—about the sport, about the country they hunt. Ted was telling about a limit hunt in which the third bird of the day also was his fiftieth of the season:

"It was clear, sunny, with a trace of snow left from Saturday's flurry. I knew the birds would be out. No. 48 was my old nemesis from the deer shack ruins. This bird had tricked me so many times this season. He was a tree rooster, nose diver and smart aleck. Just the Friday before, I took my father-in-law, an old pheasant hunter from southern Minnesota, into the deer shack ruins and No. 48 dove out of a pine just over his head. I threw a futile shot after it. He never took the 20 gauge out of the crook of his arm. He just looked at me, after filling his pipe, and said, 'Wel...l...l...l, I can see these birds are a little fast for me.' This morning, old 48 flushed in front of my Lab. One shot, down and low, and that was it. Too easy. I'll miss him.

"No. 49 was a member of the creek covey. I started this season with 10 birds in that covey. I couldn't find the five remaining birds this morning, but I knew that if they skipped out of their usual haunts, it was likely that they had moved to the Happy Valley cover, an impenetrable tangle of thornapple, trip vines, fallen trees and sharp stumps. No. 49 flushed so close that I had to wait for him to get out and away. He folded and Dixie delivered.

"Dixie was still excited and worked to my left, intent on No. 49. I tried to call her in, but to no avail. In a second, No. 50 came out, low, left to right, and at the extreme end of improved cylinder range. I thought (in the high speed blur of hunter's thinking) *Dixie is marking the bird, try it!* I did. One shot tipped the bird into a broken-wing dive. But I wasn't concerned, nor did I call or whistle. I slid the action open, caught the empty, put it in my pocket. Two heart beats later Dixie trotted out of the brush with No. 50. Too businesslike. I wish I hadn't shot. I wish I had opened the gun and quit . . .''

Doesn't the love of the sport shine through? And doesn't his expertise with grouse? Here is a hunter who knows where his birds will be. And, while those coverts may carry Geological Survey coordinates, this hunter knows them by code names of great meaning to him ("Deer Shack" and "Happy Valley"), but of no value to him who would steal another's covert. And here is a hunter who knows his gun and his dog . . . and most of all, his birds. If they aren't one place, why, they'll be in another. Sure enough, they are.

Mostly, though, it's the love of the sport. Nick Sisley caught it in one sentence of his book *Grouse and Woodcock* (Stackpole, 1980): "No matter who you are or where you hunt, when you pick up a dead grouse and smooth his feathers, wishing you could put him back like a fly-caught trout, it's a moment to remember and treasure, a moment for reflection and thanksgiving."

Until the ring-necked pheasant became established, ruffed grouse often were called "pheasants," especially in southern states. Frank Schley, writing in 1877, talks extensively of "partridges," which now may be synonymous with ruffed grouse but were quail then. His "pheasant" was the ruffed grouse, (or, in some cases, he called them partridges too, which really confused the issue).

It took a hundred years of American wingshooting before common names got commonly accepted. Perhaps the successful introduction of the ring-necked pheasant created such a bastard mess of confusion that by unspoken consent everyone decided to call quail "quail" or just "birds," grouse either "grouse" or "partridge," and pheasants either "pheasants" or "sons of bitches," depending on the shooter's immediate frame of mind.

Grouse of one kind or another inhabit nearly every state. Ruffed grouse are common through the Northeast and the Great Lakes states and south into the eastern mountain states, and are scattered through most of the Midwest. They're in all the Canadian provinces, most of the Rocky Mountain states and far into Alaska.

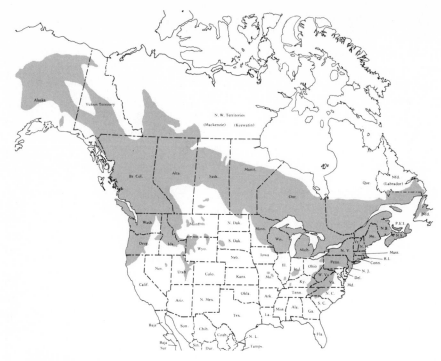

Ruffed grouse inhabit a vast range, excluding only the Southland deltas and the deserts. A woodland bird, the grouse prefers sprouty, cool regions. Missouri is in a restoration project and may extend the grouse's present range some, but that's about as far as hunters can hope for additional opportunity.

Prairie chickens, once so numerous they fled into the skies in vast flocks ahead of creaking "prairie schooners," still are found in a few western states. Other grouse—sage, blue, sharptail and spruce (called "fool hen" by some woods travelers because they can be so unwary you can knock them in the head with a stick) add to the grouse hunter's potential.

It may come as a surprise to those who think grouse surely walk on water to learn that in the late 1800s, some areas of Massachusetts paid bounties of a quarter for every grouse a shooter could ground swat. Grouse ate apple buds (still do, for that matter) and in those days apples were more valuable than grouse. Most grouse in the meat hog days were shot on the ground. The limit was what you could carry home in a tow sack. The average fool hen of 1870 had as much personality as a barnyard chicken.

That largely has changed as the birds have adapted to people trying to kill them.

You may be able to find grouse who perch on low limbs and let you bludgeon them with heavy sticks, but not where I hunt.

The grouse I know have picked up both wariness and personality. Grouse, by their solitary nature, develop independence. No flock bird, they live largely apart from their fellows until it comes time to make more grouse and then it's a hasty courtship, a one-nighter, quickly forgotten. Even though I love quail in the aggregate as no other bird, a single quail has as much personality as a garden slug. But any given grouse, woodcock or pheasant is alternately cocky, jaunty, pugnacious, comic and fun to associate with, like many people I know and like, especially those who frequent roadside inns featuring country music.

I can't say I'm impressed by the relative intelligence of grouse—only by their instinctive wariness and their simple-minded personality. Grouse are creatures of giddy, mindless excitement, motivated more by the aimless gnawings of hunger or other base instinct than by any intellectual purpose.

Actually, all birds fall in that category, for after all, few if any of the world's great philosophers have been birds. Birds simply are not noted for cranial fireworks. But it seems to me that the ruffed grouse and most of the members of the grouse family would, if an examination of general hep-ness were given, tend to lower the grading curve.

A wild turkey will not walk up to a perfectly obvious tent blind and peer inside to see if he knows anyone, but a prairie chicken will. Neither will the turkey stand for having multiple strobe flashes violate the sanctity of his roost or peer at an intrusive camera lens with a foolish grin, but a ruffed grouse will. So, I feel the legendary grouse unpredictability is a sign of an insufficient brain that tends to short circuit at crucial moments.

There isn't even much pattern to a grouse's life. He wanders from bush to bush in search of something to eat. A social creature he is not; it takes excited gonads to get him interested in reproducing his own kind and an aggressive male will mate with any other grouse who submits to him, including another male—certainly not accepted social behavior in the ranks of those who gun for and laud the bird.

My spring grouse woods is eighteen miles away, a forested upland cut by deep gullies. Locals say, "These here hills ain't so high, but them damn hollers sure is deep."

Blue-eyed Mary carpets a creek bottom diffidently pastel, making its visual impact by weight of numbers, not individual glory. A clear-water stream slips languidly over sheets of bedrock. The water occasionally murmurs muted distress at its sudden loss of elevation, but mostly it holds its composure in placid pools.

I spend spring nights in this woods and in the final counting of my days, the discarding of the many misused ones, the careful separation of the eventful ones, those brief intrusions into this fine old forest will revive and live again, tall and proud.

I go there to photograph a cock grouse performing his time-perfected mating ritual atop a mouldering drumming log. It is there, in the small hours when most life is at ebb, that he advertises his dominion and his copulative compulsion. He is a hard bird to fool, for even as he issues a thunderous challenge to rivals and lovers, he senses he also is inviting Great Horned Death to dine on him, so he listens carefully through the momentous mutter of his wings for alien sound. Often he refuses to stand before the unwinking stare of my 200 millimeter eye, the harsh spotlight of my strobe. Even so, those have not been wasted nights, for I absorbed, in a sort of ecological osmosis, a membership in the woods community and a deep peace I cannot find elsewhere.

My old friends of the forest helped me, though not of their own volition. They helped merely by being there. Wildlife isn't philanthropic; neither, however, is it hypocritical. It just is.

Somewhere in the woods is a turkey gobbler, perspicacious, stealthy of footfall, confident in his incredible assortment of keen-edged survival tools. His eyes search the chiaroscuro patterns of the woods with an acuity five times as sharp as mine. His hearing detects the faint scrabble of trundling insects in the leaf mold where my dull ears, seven times less sensitive, would hear nothing but the faint sighing of the wind.

This is the boss gobbler, king of the ridgetop. He sets his great red-toed feet into a high crown limb when the sun flames and fades in the west and tells anyone who cares to listen that he is the most bronzed, the most sleek, the most magnificently fanned turkey gobbler that ever has been fashioned by a beneficent and creative God and a benevolent Nature. He is a strident, bossy bird, with a superfluency of brag, and I sit against a tree in front of my dingy surplus U.S. army pup tent and think, *you big cool dude! You're some kind of bird!*

Not poetic fancy flight, but then this is a stud bird who does not inspire lacey verbiage. He is a four-letter brute. The sun goes down and the boss turkey quiets. I light the tiny candle lantern whose muted flame casts a comforting glow. The very insufficiency of the light strains my eyes and makes them grow heavy and I long for the soft warmth of sleep. If all goes well, my grouse will come to the log which parallels the front of the tent, a dozen feet away. He is the forest's master showman, the Jolson of the Jillikins. What a grand fate for a fine old tree—to topple onto the forest floor, at first unmourned, then to be discovered by a randy cock grouse with ecstacy on his mind, Barnum in his act. Suddenly the crumbling old log becomes a dramatic stage, witness to life ever renewing.

And what a way for a person to awake—to a dawn that spatters the sky with fire, a grouse drumming on his log, a boss turkey gobbling from a dizzyingly high perch, limned by spring's pale green buds, a crow laboring toward the sun, black against gold, a coyote slipping to shelter before daylight dazzles his yellow eyes, a cardinal flicking among the branches like a vagrant ember from a gaudy fire, vibrant and brassy in his enthusiasm.

Frank Schley said back in 1877, "This beating or drumming of the cock pheasant [grouse] is a very singular maneuver and why this bird resorts to this peculiar performance and makes this sound is left only for us to conjecture. Some suppose

A male ruffed grouse in full display (somewhat marred by a missing tailfeather). The bird is fanned and has erected the ruff of feathers around his neck that gives him his name. Object of this gaudy show is a hen.

that the male bird resorts to this means to draw the hen from her hiding place during the period of incubation; others suppose that this sound is produced by the bird when he is in search of worms in a log.''

Early ornithologists, like early scientists of any persuasion, operating on scanty information, often came up with some of the goofiest theories imaginable. It's easy to laugh at someone supposing a grouse thumps on his drumming log to spook up worms, but the bird-watchers of Audubon's day didn't even have Audubon's field notes to draw on. All they knew was that they were watching the strangest bird behavior they could imagine.

The unique drumming of the male grouse is a sound that announces spring as surely as the gobble of the turkey, the strident whicker of redbirds. Even if snow remains cupped in the shaded spots and the first spring beauties and dogtooth violets haven't dared peep out from beneath their old-leaf blankets, the grouse knows that spring is imminent. Grouse drum in every month of the year, but save their serious solos for mating season, spring.

The sound has charmed outdoor enthusiasts since pioneer times. The male grouse chooses a drumming spot—generally a mouldering old log with a downhill opening, like an arena, and escape cover to the rear.

The sound is created by a swooping snap of the wings, forward and upward, beginning slowly and gathering in speed until the sound is a blurred roar. It sounds like a vintage John Deere tractor starting up. The drumroll may last ten seconds and the bird may drum as often as every two minutes at the peak of the breeding season. Young grouse must learn to drum (their early efforts may produce only an embarrassing swishing sound), and as recently as the 1920s, ornithologists still were arguing over how the sound is created.

Some old accounts claim the bird beats his wings on the log which, being usually hollow, boomed like a bass drum. Others claimed the sound was made on the recovery stroke of the wings, still others said the bird flapped his wings against his sides. But essentially, the sound is a sonic boom, much as is the crack of a whip.

Several of the regional names of the ruffed grouse reflect either the drumming sound or the Elizabethan ruff of neck feathers the bird can erect to impress a hen: ruffed heath-cock, shoulder-knot grouse, tippet grouse, drumming grouse, partridge, drumming partridge, birch partridge and, in the South, pheasant, drumming pheasant, mountain pheasant and whiteflesher.

Not only do grouse drum year-round, but at least in the ardent spring, they drum at all hours of the day and night. I once heard a grouse drumming on Wisconsin's Flambeau River just at the peak of the most incredible flaming sunset I've ever seen. The fiery sunset, reflected in the tannin-darkened waters of the river, the quiet solitude of our pine-shrouded campsite and the muffled thumping of the grouse kindled in me a fierce joy that will sustain a spark in my soul the rest of my life.

22

Ruffed Grouse—Naturally

All the posturings, the drumming usually results in a moment of passion for the grouse. A hen comes by, perhaps to see what all the racket is about. She'll have nothing to do with Mr. Macho who struts and postures and otherwise makes himself into the avian equivalent of the fellow who kicked sand in the face of the youthful, puny Charles Atlas.

Faint heart does win fair lady, however, for, when the male quits acting as if he'd just as soon kick his sweetie as kiss her, she submits. The result of the quick copulation is an average of eleven eggs.

The hen will pick a spot next to a stump or tree, probably because of the partial shelter offered. Chances are, the nest will be near a road or a clearing. It's no nest in any constructive sense—the bird squats, laying her eggs one at a time until the clutch is complete, and gradually works a depression into the leaves.

The hen incubates her eggs for twenty-four days. About 40 percent of the nests fall victim to something, but the hen usually will re-nest and, as is usual with a second nesting, there probably will be fewer eggs. As is true with quail, the hen grouse forms a brood patch, a hotspot on her breast, by plucking feathers. Whether the bird covers her buff-colored eggs with leaves when she leaves the nest to feed is one of those unresolved biological questions. Some experts say she does, others say the bird's wings sweep leaves into the nest as she moves off. The hens do throw leaves during their egg-laying and for several days after they start incubation, probably a vestigal nest building attempt, and some leaves settle on their backs, then fall off into the nest when they leave.

Baby grouse are "grouselets," at least to grouse expert Frank Edminster, and that's a charming name. They're charming little creatures, bright-eyed and alert and precocious. They're trying to fly by the time they're a day old and can get into the air and stay there for a while when they're two weeks old. Fueled by high-protein insects, the babies grow rapidly and, in a couple of weeks, begin to eat the fruits, buds and other foods of adult birds. Essentially, grouse are born about June 1 (earlier in the south, later in the north). By mid-September, the young birds are ready for one of nature's goofy phenomenons—one which, if the dice come up craps, results in a dead young grouse.

Grouse, like quail, undergo a "fall shuffle." Apparently the autumnal wanderlust is triggered by weather changes. As is true with quail, the shuffle mostly involves young birds who may move ten miles or more (though three is more nearly normal). The movement is a bit crazed—like that single-minded peripatetic panic which grips lemmings and sometimes squirrels. Grouse in the grip of Shuffleitis sometimes fly into windows or fences.

It certainly isn't that the birds aren't adroit enough flyers to avoid obstacles, as anyone who ever has tried to get a gun barrel on one will testify. It must be some sort of adolescent brain warp.

Grouse, like their small cousins, the quail, explode into flight with a startling roar of wings—a defense mechanism, for the birds also can fly silently when they aren't alarmed. They don't fly fast (probably not more than twenty-five miles an hour in the woods) or far, but in dense brush and amid that thunderous roar, they seem to a hunter to be gallinaceous Quaker Oats, shot from cannons.

Assuming the young bird safely reaches new territory, he settles in not too long before the opening of the hunting season. He may have a few days to explore his new domain and that's what he does.

Although dispersal is Nature's way of breaking up family groups and making grouse the independent, solitary birds they are, they often are found in clots of two to eight birds by hunters. One theory is that the birds are reassembling (though no one knows why). Another is that such coveys are birds not yet dispersed (though that's not a strongly defended theory). Maybe, like grizzled old mountain men, the birds sometimes feel the urge to hold a rendezvous before splitting up again. Whatever, if grouse didn't covey in hunting season, there would be no doubles and a double on grouse is something a hunter will brag about until his friends want to stuff both birds down his throat sideways.

Given the high productivity of grouse, you'd think there could never be a problem with grouse populations, that we should be aswarm with medium-sized brown birds, a scene from a Hitchcock movie. Not so, even in the best of times.

Of the hens in a given area, only 65 percent in an average year will bring off a brood. The rest will lose their nests and not re-nest. Of that 65 percent some will lose some or all of the chicks. Chick mortality is so enormous that perhaps only half the hens which have any kind of brood will succeed in raising one or more chicks.

Given ten hens in a woodlot, averaging ten eggs, you should get one hundred chicks. But let's say that only six of the hens successfully hatch out even one chick. Now we're down to a maximum of sixty new grouse. Except that one female in six won't raise any of her chicks. Scratch one hatching hen and we're down to fifty new grouse.

Grouse researchers estimate that from a quarter to a half of all chicks die within the first month. Whoops! Let's be charitable and estimate that a third of the fifty chicks left will die early. Now we're down to thirty-five young. More of those will die before September, though normally the attrition isn't as dramatic as it is early in life. Say another five gone. That leaves thirty birds (plus the original ten hens) going into autumn.

A few more birds will die before the hunting season opens, victims of fall shuffle craziness or great horned owls or foxes. Disease may lop off one or two. Maybe there will be twenty-five birds (plus perhaps five of the six original hens and the survivors of the original males) crouched in our covert listening to the whuffing of the first chubby, out-of-shape bird dog and the wheezing of the first chubby, out-of-shape bird hunter of the season.

The net profit would appear to be excellent for the year. Hunters will take only a few of those twenty-five new birds. Winter kill will get more. But, by spring, we'll have one of three situations in our woodlot.

Either there will be more breeders than the year before, which will result in an increasing population, or there will be fewer, which will result in a decreasing one . . . or it will be essentially a stable population.

If there are fewer birds, a declining population, it does not mean disaster. Except in the most extreme situations, there is no need to curtail hunting, for hunting is self-limiting. If it is poor, the vast majority of hunters quit, eliminating the hunting pressure on the birds. And if hunting is good, even exerting more pressure than usual, hunters merely skim the cream till they get to the milk—then they quit. Nature tends to keep a stable population, though there are some dramatic swings to either side of that base line. The only thing that really can do in grouse is loss of habitat.

It happens in one of two ways. Either the woods is skinned off entirely, which is what happened in Missouri where the Ozarks were cut to provide ties for the west-reaching railroads, or the woods grows into a mature forest where both food and brushy cover are at a minimum.

Grouse are birds of disturbed forests. Brush, low-growing shrubs, tangles of grape or aspen sprouts or alder or birch—this is the stuff that both concentrates and helps increase the grouse population. Clear it or let it grow beyond a certain age and the grouse decline.

Cecil Heacox in perhaps the most helpful how-to book on grouse hunting I've seen (*The Gallant Grouse*, McKay, 1980) estimates the annual kill of ruffed grouse at six million—an educated guess complicated by the boom/bust phenomenon known as the grouse cycle. For reasons not entirely understood, grouse suffer periodic population flops, then show slow recovery to a peak, then flop again. The cycle operates more dramatically in northern areas and the peaks and valleys come on, roughly, a ten-year schedule. Weather probably is the dominant factor, though not the only one. There's no predicting the bust, but it's wise to check locally before you make a long pilgrimage to some distant hunting hotspot only to find that what was true last year isn't this year.

Only rarely if ever is the bust universal across the entire grouse range. For example, several of us hunted Minnesota successfully in 1980 with the grouse population at or near its peak in that state. At the same time, Michigan hunters were reporting only mediocre success. One theory is that the grouse bust follows a northwest to southeast path (and the recovery as well), but it's only theory, and even if true is about as helpful to know as the fact that a man may have two or three erections a night while he is asleep without knowing it.

Despite the fact that most grouse writing is from and about New England states, three Great Lake states account for more grouse killed than all the New England states combined. Minnesota estimates 630,000 grouse taken, Wisconsin half a million and Michigan a whopping 728,500. Ontario is the only state or province where more than a million birds are taken regularly, every season.

Of the eastern states, Pennsylvania leads with about a quarter of a million birds. New York hunters claim 150,000, and Ohio gunners take about 130,000. Some of the Appalachian states have good seasons, especially West Virginia with 158,000 and Virginia with 112,000. All the wooded Canadian provinces have excellent populations of grouse and, despite high bags, have an underhunted population.

Western states with ruffed grouse generally have relatively little hunting pressure. Washington reports 200,000 birds taken, but Idaho, Utah, Wyoming, Montana— all have quite low kills (and pressure). Even such an unlikely spot as Iowa has good hunting in the rugged northeast river breaks and locals clean up.

An awful lot of ruffed grouse go unhunted in the north country because of the sheer mechanics of hunting them. For example, even as precipitous as West Virginia is, you can conquer it with a good pair of legs and lungs. But the endless bogs and swamps and the sheer trackless areas of much of the muskeg country make it impossible or at least impractical to hunt.

You'd have to have X-ray vision to pick out hens from cocks in the air (or on the ground, for that matter). Grouse sexes simply look very much alike. Whether the bird you just shot is male or female largely is a matter of interest only to another grouse; however, there are hunters who like to know. The traditional test is to check the tail fan. If the middle two feathers interrupt the sharp outline of the band near the feather tips—are hazy in detail, as if they'd been stuck in the fan after being plucked from another bird—chances are the bird is a female.

However, some males also have broken bands. If the middle feathers are 6¼ inches or longer, the bird is a male. If they're shorter than 5¾ inches, it almost certainly is a female. If the feather measurement falls in the gray area between 5¾ inches and 6¼ inches, you can check above the bird's eye. If it has a bright orange ''eyebrow'' over the eye (similar to, but not as prominent as that of a prairie chicken) the bird is a male. If you're still in doubt, perform an autopsy and look at the bird's sex organs—or get back to hunting and quit wasting time.

As far as determining age goes, young of the year (up to nine months) have a sac or pouch near the end of the large intestine called the *bursa Fabricii*. Such information is of use mainly to scientists, either professional or amateur. Perhaps it is interesting to note that you're shooting either old birds or young birds, or females or males—but you can't put them back anyway and the knowledge that the young/old ratio looks either good or bad may make you feel either good or bad. But it still isn't going to change anything. And the young/old ratio tells you what already happened, not what's going to happen next year.

I'd rather spend my time hunting and save my autopsies for that time of fun known as dressing the bird, even though you're undressing him.

23

Hunting Ruffed Grouse

A ruffed grouse will spit in your eye and give you ammonia in a Murine bottle to clean it out.

Witness this scene:

An aging, but still incredibly virile and handsome outdoor writer is catfooting his way through a northern Minnesota aspen stand, his Brittany coursing ceaselessly before him. All is well in the grouse woods, for the hunter is alert, the dog a Mean Machine.

The hunter (who is me, in case the description escaped you) suddenly spies a ruffed grouse perched on a tree limb, some twenty feet up, twenty yards dead ahead—collision of some sort inevitable. The hunter stumbles to a confused halt. His dog prowls on, since the rising scent of the moderately alarmed bird does not sink to ground level.

So this grouse and I regard each other with scarcely concealed suspicion. "Git!" I command, thumb taut on the safety. The bird does not flinch, but begins to stretch its neck skyward until it resembles a rubber bird with its feet glued to the limb, being racked up by a choke chain. "Goddamit! Git!" I shout. I can't figure out what to do. This is the quintessential fool grouse I have read about. Too damn dumb to fly, easy pickings as camp meat. But I'm up here as a sportsman, not a pot shooter. I want to shoot flying. One of my hunting pards refers to perch shots as "taking them in the pre-flight position," but I'm determined to let the bird clear the limb by at least a millimeter before I bust him.

Confounding the situation is the knowledge that whatever I do, it will be wrong. The bird is bound to flush in such a way that either I won't get a shot or it will be a poor one. That's because grouse always do that. Seeing a game bird before the flush always lets a hunter's doubts flourish like okra in Oklahoma and the more time you have to cultivate them, the more they flourish. This bird gave me all the time in the world.

"Throw a stick at him," suggested Mike McIntosh who, by now, could see the bird from his post farther up the hill. I was racked by doubt. Suppose I reached for a stick and the condemned bird decided to fly. Which way would he go? Left? Right? Going away? Incoming? Doubts swarmed me like angry yellowjackets.

I took a tentative step toward the bird. He flushed. Grouse don't sail off a limb. Not under the gun they don't. He catapaulted as if one of the area's native sons, Paul Bunyan, had booted him in the butt. I naturally missed the first shot, sluicing a path several feet behind the bird, tried desperately to get in front of him for the second shot and shot behind him again. Mike fired twice, imitating my futile salute, and finally Spence Turner, the final hunter in the line, downed the bird.

And then I heard a sharp cracking sound above the fervent throb of my profanity and, turning, saw a sizeable tree falling on me. My second shot had bucksawed the tree and now it crashed ponderously and painfully down on my head and shoulders.

You've heard the joke about the fellow to whom terrible things kept happening until he finally looked to the skies and cried, "Why me?" and a thundering, cosmic voice boomed down, "I don't know, Jones. There's just something about you that pisses me off."

Grouse frequently turn the Great White Hunter into the Great American Dope. The only predictable thing about them is that they don't read grouse books, therefore have little knowledge of grouse behavior and habits.

All we can deal with is generalities. Remember: Under carefully controlled conditions, organisms do as they please.

LOCATING GROUSE

So you're going grouse hunting. Be prepared to walk until every muscle below your waist is knotted like a Boy Scout's practice rope, until your silken cheeks have been lashed by sprouts so you look as if you just came in last in a wildcat-wrestling contest.

Most grouse range won't be thick with briars, but there'll be some blackberry and some other thorny stuff. Mostly, it's just thick. Grouse, being bud, fruit and catkin eaters, dine where that food is prevalent and that means thick brush.

Forest clearcuts from five to perhaps twenty years old are ideal. If they're low-lying and moist, they may also hold woodcock. Aspen is the traditional grouse food, but gray dogwood is a favorite. Scientists studying grouse in New York for a ten-year period found that aspen bulked largest in the bird's diet at 12 percent. Cherry was close at 10 percent. Other favored plants included birch, blackberry, hop hornbeam, thornapple, strawberry, apples, beech, sumac, on and on—indicating that grouse eat what there is to eat.

Early in the season, the birds will eat fruits and berries—dogwood, apples, grapes, sumac, pincherries, beechnuts—and catkins of such trees as birch. But those gradually disappear and the grouse are forced to other foods. However, often the new food will be the buds of the fruiting plants—apple or cherry, for example.

It's important to remember that grouse are birds of edge and of disturbed country. A given covert, which started as a clearcut, will grow out of favor. Nothing is forever. So the wise grouse hunter looks for new coverts, especially areas with the same characteristics that made old favorites productive.

You can check what birds are eating by opening the crops of birds you shoot, but that seems to be a chicken-or-the-egg situation. Grouse eat what's where they are. If you kill grouse in a gray dogwood stand, does it mean you'll find grouse in most every gray dogwood stand? You know they're eating gray dogwood, but did the gray dogwood create the grouse honeypot? Or did they eat gray dogwood because that was what was handy when they got hungry?

Learn what attracts grouse as food, but also learn the type of vegetative cover, the size and composition that pulls birds. Adjust for weather. Anyone can identify aspen after leaf-fall, but how about some of the other good grouse plants? It pays to become a bit of a botanist.

Start with these basics anywhere there are grouse. You'll not find many grouse in a mature forest. Big trees are pretty, but not grouse-productive. Look for sapling-sized trees, especially thick stands. Or look for mid-age trees—perhaps fifteen to thirty years old (up to 6 inches in diameter)—with a good screen of whip-sized seedlings in the understory. Grouse are attracted to "edge," as is most wildlife. Edge is where something meets something—perhaps a sprout-clogged valley which ends in a swamp or where a forest meets an old field. Hunt those borders. Hunt along log trails, especially in states where there is clover planted in the trails as grouse food.

Grouse are so adaptable that in good weather you can find them almost anywhere. On one hunting trip we found good numbers of birds around an abandoned farmstead (several in a pine grove, several in an alder swale and even more in the woods bordering the pastures); in a state forest, hunting the sprouty swales among fairly mature trees; in an alder bog; in a birch forest with brushy understory; and in an aspen grove.

Because of local variation, your best bet for a good hunt is a local contact. There is no substitute for experience and on-site information. It may not be as hard as you think. Plead your case to the local conservation department representative. Start well before your trip and find out the person's name and address.

If you come across as a decent, sincere conservation-minded, high-principled hunter, chances are you'll get some useful information, either locations or people to contact. I've never been turned down yet. Quite obviously, a stranger is not going to give you the best hunting spot he knows, but he'll put you in at least good bird country and save you hunting utterly barren spots.

And, assuming you do make a local contact, you should be properly grateful. Whoever helped you, he gave of his most prized possession, his grouse covert. Steal a man's wife, mutilate his cattle, peck knots on his kids' heads, but don't fail to appreciate his covert. That is a mortal sin for which there is no forgiveness.

If grouse are using conifers as roosting cover, the early morning hunter will find them near it. Grouse like to walk around for food and grit and it takes a grouse some time to cover much ground walking, so the general roosting vicinity will be good hunting for the first few hours of the morning.

A thick conifer stand is the worst possible place to hunt grouse. The birds usually flush out the far side of a tree and the best you can hope for is a glimpse. They'll roost in the trees where their scent won't carry to a dog. It's a hunter's nightmare. The best method is a line of hunters moving through the trees, perhaps twenty to thirty yards apart. Someone should get a shot as birds flush.

I'm opposed to large hunting parties, especially on grouse. Three hunters is pushing it and there should be no more than four under any conditions. If the covert is narrow, split up and go in different directions, no more than two together. Don't clump up to the point where several hunters blast away at one poor bird. No one knows who bagged it and there ceases to be much challenge to wingshooting.

In nice weather, you'll find grouse feeding and resting in all the places I've mentioned. But grouse dislike wet weather and when it's raining, they'll head for the thickest conifer stand they can find. The heavier the rain, the more reason for you to stay in the room, play solitaire, watch television and pray for a weather break. However, a light drizzle doesn't slow birds much and they tend to hold much better for a dog. A damp, gray morning, with no wind, probably is the best possible hunting condition. But because light conditions may be poor, a pair of yellow-lens shooting glasses not only will protect your eyes, but will intensify light.

A windy, dry day is the worst for grouse. The birds are spooky, scenting conditions are poor and you'll see a lot of tailfeathers at horrendous distances.

Most hunters quit after deep snow falls for good, though a melting period is a good time to hunt. To my mind, grouse shooting is an October-November sport, which ends as the first deep snow drifts in to the northern states. In the southern portions of grouse range, the season can last much longer. Deer season takes a sizeable chunk out of the November part of grouse season and while I wouldn't quit hunting grouse just because the woods are aswarm with deer hunters, I'd make every effort to look like a thirty-piece orchestra, dressed in blaze orange as I trundled through the woods and I would worry considerably about a brown dog—a shorthair or yellow Lab or vizsla, for example.

Bill Peterson is a moose biologist with the Minnesota Department of Natural Resources (talk about an esoteric profession!) and was our host on one grouse hunt. He largely lives on moose stew and bear chili (or, for variety, bear stew and moose chili). It's a tough world around Grand Marais, on the north shore of Lake Superior, that mean-tempered boss sow of the Great Lakes.

Up in that country, about two good flush-flights from Canada, the grouse wear a slightly frostbitten look and almost all are gray phase birds (all with gray tailfeathers, as opposed to the red phase birds of the southern range or the mixed rufous-gray of even mid-Minnesota birds).

SHOOTING

Peterson believes in hitting what he shoots at and to that end, he packs a double with its barrels cut so short the gun would be equally effective at close-in bird shooting or quelling a riot.

It throws a pattern wide enough to cover a Mack truck at ten yards, but since grouse are not hard to knock down, it's effective. One No. 6 shot will deck a grouse. You can argue that high brass No. 6 is a good grouse load, but probably as many grouse hunters as shoot that will shoot field load No. 8 or No. 7½ shot. Some shoot No. 9 shot because they also run into woodcock; however I use No. 8 shot as a universal load. One possibility, if you shoot like me, is a No. 8 field load in the first, more open barrel, No. 6 duck/pheasant load in the tight barrel. The old saying is that the first shot is to clear away the brush and the second is to kill the bird.

What the first shot actually clears away are the gremlins who jump up and make mischief with your gunnery when a grouse flushes. The second shot is the considered one, gun seated firmly, head down on the stock, eyes on bird, barrel tracking smoothly.

A grouse gun almost necessarily has to be lightweight and fast. The majority of grouse shots will be relatively close and through or into brush. If you're a super shot, you may indeed be able to react and center a grouse with a full-choke gun (and if you're built along the lines of King Kong, you may be able to pack a waterfowl-weight gun all day without pulling your arm down to where the knuckles drag the ground).

In grouse shooting, as in woodcock shooting, you generally can hit any bird you can see. And you must learn to ignore what brush stands between you and the bird. If you feel comfortable with the shot, don't assume you missed—follow the flight line and you may well see your dog fetch a dead grouse. You may be able to hear the bird thump to earth, out of sight, if you don't break out in antique Anglo-Saxon, the way I generally do when I think I've missed.

There are a lot of reasons why anyone shoots poorly on grouse (and anyone who hits one for three shots fired is a pretty good grouse hunter). The bird's explosive flush is unnerving. And it usually happens in thick brush where there may be a moment of confusion before you find your target. Then there are the inevitable obstructions between you and the bird. Grouse fly quickly—not necessarily fast, but quickly. They get airborne and at considerable range damned quickly. They're sprinters. Finally, they may throw in a couple of quick changes in azimuth and elevation to garm up your gunnery.

Any single factor can cause you to miss. All together really work a hardship. And when the rare grouse is pointed, flushes straight-away into a nice, unobstructed opening, the contrast is so vivid you'll probably miss him, too.

All the gunnery tricks I talked about in the chapter on woodcock apply equally to grouse. You must be prepared for a flush at all times. That's virtually impossible in a five-hour hunt, especially as your legs turn to old tapioca, but as sure as you flop your gun backward over your shoulder or cradle it in the crook of your elbow, that's when a grouse will flush.

Port arms is a good, safe, effective position to carry a shotgun. You're instantly ready to mount the gun. You have to learn to start the gun toward your shoulder at the moment you hear a flush, even as you're crouching into shooting position and looking for the bird. Get the gun as close to shooting position as you can as quickly as you can.

If you're smooth with it and your eye comes onto the bird as the gun comes onto your cheek, you should be able to touch off that first round right on the button. But if anything is out of whack—gun not seated right, head up over the barrel, eyes distracted by some obstruction—you'll miss. Still—if you shoot quickly on the first shot, you'll have time for a second shot. And a hasty shot is better than no shot at all; some of the former connect, none of the latter do.

As Dr. Norris said, "He who hesitates has no chance to reconsider."

There is one situation where I recommend caution. Some birds flush out low and there's a real danger of scalping a dog, almost certainly fatally, on such a shot. I'd rather let the bird go than have to give futile apology to my faithful hunting companion.

I told earlier about knocking a tree over on me. Well, not content with one such episode, I did it again the next day. There is a dead bird flying around in Minnesota right now. I did absolutely everything right, yet still didn't kill him. The reason? I shot completely through a three-inch-diameter tree—sawed it off as thoroughly as if I'd done it with a chain saw. The tree couldn't have been more than eight feet in front of me, yet so thoroughly was I concentrating on the flying bird that I never saw it. It's an encouraging mistake, for that's the way good shooting has to be, an intense bond between you and the target.

Skeet shooting helps sharpen your eye, but only if you shoot as if hunting—gun not mounted and not knowing when the target will fly. I suspect clay birds fly faster than grouse, so your best training aid probably is a foot trap operated by a buddy and in a hunting situation (throwing birds into trees or at unexpected angles).

Practice should be with clay birds, not hunting. I never yet knew anyone who could caution himself to do the right thing when a game bird is in the air. You know there always is another clay bird but you may not be as lucky with real birds, so you forget everything you know about shotgun shooting in the heat of the moment.

Most flushed bird shots, grouse included, are almost straightaway and rising. You should lift the gun barrel until it begins to cover the bird, touch off the shot and continue the barrel motion. Same on an incoming bird—start behind and lift until you cover the bird, shoot as you continue the swing. Stopping the barrel travel is one of the commonest causes of misses. But, as I say, you won't remember any of that when the bird is in the air, so the time to drill the proper moves into yourself is in the off-season, using clay targets.

On an incoming bird you run the risk of tearing it up by shooting when it's too close, so consider turning and taking it going away after it passes you. Crossing shots obviously call for some lead, but again, start behind the bird and shoot as the barrel swings through it. Don't worry about the right gap between the bird and the barrel, all that stuff that (I think I may have said this before) you aren't going to remember when the time comes.

A swinging shot to the left for a right-handed shooter is much easier than one to the right where he should shift his feet to get a long smooth swing—either that or contort his body and risk at the least looking like a fool, at the worst a twisted ankle.

GROUSE DOGS

A well-trained setter is the classic grouse dog. There are tales of grouse dogs so sharp they point birds roosted high in trees. Many grouse hunters use only a retriever, kept mostly at heel, whose primary function is to find dead birds. The dog, ranging fifteen to twenty feet out, sometimes does flush a bird, but the bird probably would have been flushed by the hunter anyway.

A good pointing dog can be a revelation, even to an old-line grouse hunter. Ted Lundrigan hunts with a Lab, Dixie, a patient lady with worried eyes. Ted never had seen a pointing dog work grouse until Spence Turner showed up with Samantha. Samantha never had worked grouse, but a game bird is a game bird to a bird dog, whether it weighs eight ounces or twenty.

So, Ted and Spence ambled through the woods, Dixie making matronly casts a few feet in front, Sam flowing along the forest floor like ground fog.

Spence was sidetracked for some reason and Ted and the dogs moved on ahead. When Spence caught up, he found Ted sitting on a log, Dixie at his side . . . and Sam locked on a vibrant point no more than twenty feet away. "She's on point!" Spence sputtered. Ted, reflectively eating a caramel, glanced at the quivering dog.

"Nah . . . she's just resting," he said.

"She's *pointing!*" Spence declared.

With awakened interest, Ted got to his feet, gun cradled under his arm, and the two of them walked to the frozen dog . . . and seven grouse erupted in as riotous a covey flush as you'll ever find in the grouse woods.

While the incident did not destroy Dixie's reputation as an effective grouse dog, it opened Ted's eyes. It's a matter of choice. The grouse dog must work close and have bird savvy. He can't be put off by birds that fairly consistently refuse to hold. He shouldn't chase flying birds or break point to chase a running bird. On the other hand, my Brittany, Chip, assumes any running bird is crippled and vast is his surprise when the bird suddenly takes to wing.

I think a lot of grouse are lost because hunters assume they missed. Cecil Heacox tells about flushing a bird, firing twice at it and then ashamedly explaining why he had missed, only to see their Lab come back with a dead grouse.

It happened to me. Mike McIntosh and I each saluted a grouse and watched as the apparently untouched bird glided into a small pine copse across a pasture. We covered the grove thoroughly but flushed no bird. Then, as we were about to give up, my pup, Ginger, came trotting up with a limp grouse and a worried look, as if asking, "Is this what I'm supposed to do, Boss?"

It pointed out several things—that you can't assume you didn't hit a grouse; that probably a lot of grouse die unclaimed; that a dog makes a hell of a difference in your bag—not so much in the finding of live grouse, but in the finding of dead ones.

Dead grouse—there's a sort of finality about that. No matter that the bird, steaming on a bier of wild rice, will put any barnyard chicken to shame.

No matter that the dog work which pinned him to the ground was flawless, the shot that laid him to his final rest was a marvel of gunnery, taken through a brush screen, at an acute angle, the kind of shot which returns in the last moments before sleep creeps in and brings a wide smile to the face of the weary hunter there in the night.

No matter. Dead grouse. You wish you could retain every instant of the hunt up to the moment where you picked up the limp, warm body of the bird and smoothed its feathers.

But the species goes on. Intellectually I know that. I know it even as I carefully stow the dead bird in my game pouch.

I know it but . . . dead grouse. . . .

24

Hunting the Empty Third

It was a coyote moon out there on the Cimarron, a moon with the pale light of a winter graveyard. I shivered under the cold, prickly stars. A songdog yodeled somewhere out on the prairie and the cold seeped through my coat.

I knew somewhere just beyond the dim crest of the far hill a Kiowa war party surely must be sleeping lightly as its quick ponies shifted uneasily from hoof to hoof, all waiting only for the dawn before moving on.

No matter that we were there to hunt prairie birds; this is a land once bathed in blood. The People they called themselves, the Comanches. Proud and arrogant with the certain knowledge that they were The Chosen, The People. They dominated the plains as no other Indians and the bold sweep of their lightning raids left a trail of Mexican/Texican agony for more than a hundred years.

Young Cynthia Ann Parker was captured by the marauders as a child, a fate considerably better than that of her grandparents. Her grandfather lost his scalp. Her grandmother was merely pinned to the ground by an Indian lance. Young Cynthia Ann grew up to become an Indian wife and mother of Quanah Parker, greatest of all the Comanche chiefs. Every bit as savage as any of his Indian forebears, he killed whites for a quarter of a century . . . before he adopted reservation life, ultimately bought a railroad, fathered twenty-five children, had eight wives, became rich and world-famous and died in bed of pneumonia.

Life on the prairie was seldom easy. It's not easy hunting, either, but the rewards go beyond whopping a few flying birds with No. 8 shot. For most, the prairie horizon is entirely too far away, too unbroken. In a well-known book of early-days reminiscence, Bruce Siberts, who grew up on the Dakota frontier, tells of a friend who finally fled the prairie, grumbling that it was "nothing but prairie and sky, nothing but sky and prairie."

Maybe so—but it also is birds that sail for a mile on the eternal wind. It holds forty-bird quail coveys, no matter that they are funny-colored and topknotted, duded up in a fashion no self-respecting bobwhite ever would be. It is prairie grouse who, almost as much as the buffalo, fueled the taut bellies of restless migrants whose

*Haystacks like this are favored loafing places for prairie grouse. In hot
weather, sharptails will hold well for a bird dog, but the colder the
weather the more likely they are to flush wild.*

lust for Paradise-in-the-West eclipsed their fear of being raped or skinned (or both)
by The People.

There is so much huntable land across the vast belt of prairie, the empty third
of America, that finding a place to hunt is the least of a prairie hunter's worries.
We had 109,000 acres nearly to ourselves—the Cimarron National Grassland in
extreme southwest Kansas, one of nineteen National Grasslands with four million
acres. The Santa Fe Trail ambled through the Cimarron and you still can see the
wagon ruts a century later. The Cimarron was a heartbreaker of a river, for much
of it is dry streambed. William Becknell, first to travel the southern leg of the Santa
Fe Trail in 1821, and his party had to suck the blood from the slashed ears of their
mules to quench their thirst.

Arid or not, the Cimarron is one of the few places in this country where you can,
if things break right, shoot four game bird species in a day—pheasant, lesser prairie
chicken, scaled and bobwhite quail. There's a spring turkey season as well.

Such diversity is common in prairie hunting, whether it's the shortgrass of the
Dakotas or the tallgrass of eastern Kansas. For example, on one South Dakota hunt,

we shot both prairie chickens and sharptailed grouse, saw pheasants, Hungarian partridge, turkeys and mourning doves in a day's hunt.

The nice part of prairie hunting is that it is relatively untapped. Westerners like their meat to fall in big chunks and don't do that much bird hunting. There are a half-dozen grouse species, as many of quail, two partridges, turkeys, doves and a few other birds as well that can be hunted somewhere on what we loosely call "the prairie."

There are many definitions of prairie. You can call the tags of tallgrass in Iowa prairie or you can call the sere shortgrass of the high New Mexico plains prairie or, if an absence of trees is your criterion, you can term the stark aridity of the Sonoran desert as prairie. Each has its wildlife, each its game birds.

There are quail scurrying in the dry, sunbaked arroyos of the desert; there are prairie-plaid-clad grouse clucking fussily in the tallgrass that salutes the endless wind where the west meets the east.

The West can be damned rough on a dog. Hunting often is hot, almost always dry, and a dog can suffer from thirst. In addition, the vegetation frequently is ill-tempered. Cactus can be a real dog crippler, but so are sand burrs and an especially virulent burr called the Texas goathead. As if this were not enough, dogs occasionally are bitten by rattlesnakes. I know two hunters who have had dogs bitten. Both survived, but not without a lot of pain. You can boot a dog against the burrs (though I couldn't keep the boots on the dog), but there's not much you can do about snakes.

However, all the potential pitfalls depend on local conditions. For example, sand burrs were so prevalent in the milo fields near the Cimarron that we couldn't use the dog, but on the prairie itself, we had no problem. My Brittany never ran afoul of the abundant cactus, whether through blind luck or because he'd learned to avoid them.

I can't stress enough the importance of getting local information. That's true anywhere, but especially in the West. Other country may merely inconvenience you if you go unprepared. The West can hurt you or your dog.

If I didn't know anyone at all, I'd start by corresponding with the government representatives concerned with the land I planned to hunt. Ask for marked maps or a local contact. Don't demand—ask, as politely, as humbly as you know how. Stress that you are a sportsman, a concerned hunter, a good guy (and be damned sure you act like one when you get there). Be as specific as possible. Don't ask for "Some good places to hunt." Give some background as to why you are interested in the area such as its history or geology or ecology. You should go on the trip (and let your local contact know) with the attitude that if you kill a bunch of birds, that's fine, but you won't be disappointed if you don't—the chance to see new country is reason enough in itself for the trip.

And don't be upset if your contact is a bit standoffish at first. He doesn't know you from Adam's cat and he wants to make up his own mind before he feeds you into his choice hunting spots.

This is the Cimarron National Grassland of southwest Kansas where we killed four species of game bird in one day—scaled and bobwhite quail, pheasants and prairie chickens. The grassed areas are all right for a dog, but the cultivated areas are infested with vicious burrs.

Lawrence Smith was our contact, wolf-lean, tireless, a rural mail carrier on whom the sun rises across the Cimarron every working morning—and most that aren't. He knows the Grassland by having walked almost every foot of it. A mutual friend set up the hunt and Lawrence said only that he would meet us, talk to us. Had he decided we were not his kind, we would have been sent into the Cimarron on our own, maybe to a fair hunting area, but certainly nothing choice.

But we found shared interests in watching birds that you can't shoot, in conservation, in history and geology. And Lawrence hunted with us, invited us to his home, a home filled with books—not just those which tell you how to shoot things or how someone else shot things, but books about birds, about nature, for Lawrence Smith is what we all should be, a person who cares beyond the strike of the shot string.

I've been fortunate across the years to encounter hunters of high principle and it makes me feel better, makes me forget the road-hunting, pot-shooting slobs who demean the sport.

Nothing I had read would have guided me a fraction as well as Lawrence Smith did around the vastness of the Cimarron. I had maps and articles about the area, but we would have been babes in the wilderness without that kindly man with the prairie wolf legs.

I've hunted two different Grasslands and been through a couple more. Some of them have more water than others, but all were created because they were the sad victims of the 1930s Dust Bowl. Because they are located from Oregon to Kansas, there is considerable variation in topography, geology, in wildlife habitat and species. But all are wide-open areas with very few facilities for recreation-seekers. Some have no camping facilities, but all permit primitive camping. Fire is the deadly enemy of any Grassland, so any camper must be extremely careful with fire.

We pulled into the Cimarron campground after dark, so dawn was our first look at this new land. Great Godalmighty! The world went on forever! Even for an old prairie freak like me, the Cimarron did tend to run on. I could imagine what such a sight would be like to a Georgia quail hunter, fresh off his pine plantation. He'd swear the sour mash finally caught up with him and he'd gone where Congressmen, second-story men and other sinners go when they die.

"Back in the thirties, this was as bare as that road," Lawrence Smith told us, indicating the sandy road down which we walked. "It's taken a long time for this place to come back." Perhaps that's why Grasslands hunting is so ignored—until relatively recently, there was no hunting there. The Cimarron lay in the burned heart of the Dust Bowl and tendrils of its Morton County soil were eddying over Washington, even as lawmakers argued about what to do to reclaim the eroding land. In 1935, the federal government bought the first 53,590 acres of the Cimarron, and in 1938 added another 42,800. Then came the tedious process of reclaiming the soil, re-establishing native grasses on land that never should have been plowed in the first place. Nearly 80 percent of Morton County had been wind-eroded and it was 1940 before the total of wind-scoured acres dropped below 1,000. By 1943, some areas were lush enough to permit limited cattle grazing.

Like most Department of Agriculture areas, wildlife and recreation take a back seat to farm interests, but public sentiment is forcing more wildlife habitat work and the various Grasslands should improve as hunting areas. The Cimarron has one of the nation's largest flocks of lesser prairie chickens and Kansas is one of the few states where prairie chickens are numerous enough to hunt. The birds have made a good comeback in the past few years and flocks of seventy-five to one hundred birds recall pioneer bounty.

The National Grasslands are the most obvious public lands in the West, but are far from the only ones—Bureau of Land Management lands, state lands, Corps of Engineers land all offer a sportsman more hunting territory than he could cover in a lifetime.

We hunted around "guzzlers," watering devices for wildlife that consist of an eighty-gallon tank buried in the ground. A corrugated tin roof funnels the infrequent rain water into the tank. An inch of rain will fill the tank. On the Cimarron, there

Kansas is one of a handful of states that still have prairie chicken hunting. The Cimarron Grassland has lesser prairie chickens and these greater prairie chickens came from the Flint Hills region to the east.

is a four-acre fenced area around each guzzler. "The only problem," Smith says, "is that each guzzler is a sign that says 'hunt here.' They should be in more remote areas."

But in a day of four-wheel drive vehicles, the remote area is almost a thing of the past. Anywhere a wagon could go, so can a four-wheel drive, plus some places the wagon would have come to pieces.

It pays to do some map scouting, using Geological Survey quadrangles and a Grasslands map. The quadrangle will have old farmsteads, perhaps vegetation, rivers, stock ponds and the like marked—all potential concentrating spots for prairie birds—while the Grasslands map will tell you what is public and what is private.

In a nine-hour hunt on the Cimarron, four of us took fifteen quail, two pheasants and a prairie chicken. We flushed at least seventy-five prairie chickens, but the birds tend to flush out of range. Most hunters find a feeding field and wait for the birds to fly in just at dawn. Pass shooting a prairie chicken is a bit like drawing down on one of the Air Force Thunderbirds. Take a variety of guns on a prairie trip. You may be able to use a short-barreled, open-choke brush gun some places, but you almost certainly will be in situations that call for a full-choked gun.

Back in 1970, Paul Johnsgard (*Grouse and Quails of North America,* University of Nebraska Press, 1973) estimated the total grouse and quail kill nationally. All species totalled 47.3 million birds (and another two million in Canada). Of that, 35 million were bobwhite quail. The rest all occur somewhere on the prairie. Ruffed grouse, of course, largely are an eastern and midwestern forest bird, but also frequent the western forests.

Of the many prairie birds, the quails bulk largest in hunter bags. Johnsgard estimated 3.6 million scaled quail, 2.2 million California (valley) quail, 1.3 million Gambel (desert) quail. The two introduced partridges, chukar and gray, total another million birds with bags of 650,000 and 400,000 respectively.

Compared to those totals, the grouses fail to make much of a dent; yet numbers aren't everything—there are as many words extant about King Ruff as about King Bob, yet hunters take only about 2.7 million ruffed grouse to that whopping 35 million bobwhites. Grouse, no matter the species, are harder to take in numbers than are any of the quail. Seldom do you covey-flush grouse, bag limits are smaller, seasons often shorter. Opportunity thus is less.

So numbers shouldn't be the criterion for hunting quality (shouldn't be in any situation, for that matter). My western bird hunting is limited to a few species. Of those few, I'd have to rate the sharptail grouse and prairie chicken as the most sporting. Sharptails, huntable in at least eight states and six Canadian provinces, contribute about a quarter of a million of themselves annually—about the same total as sage and blue grouse, far more than the estimated 85,000 prairie chickens. But there are only six states with prairie chicken hunting.

And, of the six, Kansas is preeminent, with a season both for greater and lesser chickens. It was getting on toward evening as the four of us, now sapless, drained after hiking the long prairie miles, finally got into prairie chickens. We had blue quail, bobwhites and pheasants in the bag, lacked only chickens.

We began to flush the birds off the Cimarron Grassland adjacent to a huge milo

Prairie chickens flush with a roar of wings and glide seemingly forever. Pass shooting is tough, for the birds are fast fliers.

This Cimarron Grassland pheasant came from an old farmstead, a natural concentrating spot for pheasants. Quail were along the river, while scaled quail and pheasants were around the guzzlers and the prairie chickens moved between milo fields and adjacent grassland cover.

field, a few at first, rising with a distinctive cackle like that of a setting hen, then a massive flock. They flew into the milo and Lawrence Smith said he had permission to hunt there, so we decided to follow them, into the lowering sun.

The ground was carpeted with sand burrs, so I volunteered to take the dog back to the car while my two hunting buddies, Foster and Don, followed the birds. The two of them became specks far out in the field, and then I saw the birds rise in the dimming light and heard a shot. Foster had a bird down and still was looking for it when I wearily hiked back to help him look. I finally spotted the bird, dead against a milo stalk.

It was nine hours past our starting point at a guzzler where a covey of blue (scaled) quail scuttled through the wind-ruffled prairie grass. It was six hours past a bobwhite covey bursting out of the Indian grass along the Cimarron River as our noontime chili burbled on a camp stove. It was four hours past a cock pheasant erupting gaudily from a switchgrass hide on an old farmstead.

Aside from our mixed bag of game birds, we had a full stringer of pretty memories to take home. We'd found an untamed land, largely empty of people, with the promise of rich hunting over every rise. We'd explored only a small piece of only one of nineteen National Grasslands with more than four million acres of promise. My Brittany pup made his first wild bird point on a blue quail, a species he'd never see in Missouri.

There were the old farmsteads, rusting slowly in the arid climate, gaunt reminders of the grim Dirty Thirties and the farmers who went bust there and headed for somewhere the wind doesn't blow all the time and it rains more often than the moon is blue.

There was Lawrence Smith, cross between a prairie wolf and a marsh hawk, as adept at sliding through the cactus as the critters he stalked.

There was a prairie sunset that fired the darkening sky with soul-warming glory.

It frosted that night and the song dogs howled into the emptiness.

The National Grasslands

Name	Size (Acres)	Location	Principal Game Species	Where to Write
Little Missouri River	1,033,221 (includes Custer National Forest)	North Dakota	Antelope, whitetail and mule deer, sharptail grouse	District Ranger, Dickinson, ND 58601, Watford City, ND 58854
Buffalo Gap	591,259	South Dakota	Antelope, deer, sharptail grouse, prairie chicken, turkey, rabbit	Wall District Ranger, Wall, SD 57790
Thunder Basin	572,319	Wyoming	Antelope, deer, sage grouse, rabbit, turkey	District Ranger, 118 S. 2nd St., Douglas, WY 82633
Comanche	255,000	Colorado	Upland game, some big game	Comanche Grassland, 910 Hwy. 50 West, Pueblo, CO 81002
Pawnee	193,060	Colorado	Doves early, prairie dogs, deer, waterfowl	District Ranger, 2009 Ninth St., Greeley, CO 80631
Crooked River	170,000	Oregon	Mule deer, rabbit, chukar, Hungarian partridge, pheasant, quail, waterfowl, grouse, antelope	District Ranger, 2321 East 3rd, Prineville, OR 97754
Grand River	155,426	North and South Dakota	Antelope, mule and whitetail deer, sharptail grouse	District Ranger, Box 390, Lemmon, SD 57638

Name	Size (Acres)	Location	Principal Game Species	Where to Write
Kiowa	137,000	New Mexico	Deer, desert sheep, quail, doves	District Ranger, 16 N. 2nd St., Clayton, NM 88415
Fort Pierre	115,998	South Dakota	Antelope, deer, sharptail grouse, prairie chicken, waterfowl, turkey, rabbit	District Ranger, Wall, SD 57790
Cimarron	109,000	Kansas	Quail, prairie chicken, pheasant, turkey	District Ranger, Elkhart, KS 67950
Oglala	94,344	Nebraska	Antelope, deer, sharptail grouse, prairie chicken, turkey, rabbit	District Ranger, 270 Pine Street, Chadron, NB 69337
Rita Blanca	92,000	Texas, Oklahoma	Scaled quail, rabbit, pheasant	District Ranger, Texline, TX 79087
Sheyenne	71,000	North Dakota	Whitetail deer, small game, waterfowl	District Ranger, Lisbon, ND 58054
Curlew	47,599	Idaho	Mule deer, sage grouse, sharptail grouse, dove, pheasant, Hungarian partridge, waterfowl	District Ranger, Malad City, ID 83252
Black Kettle	31,000	Oklahoma	Small game—not promising, scattered land parcels	District Ranger, Cheyenne, OK 73628
Cross Timbers (Now Lyndon B. Johnson)	20,332	Texas	Dove, quail, coyote, deer, squirrel, waterfowl (low populations reported)	District Ranger, Box 507, Decatur, TX 76234

Name	Size (Acres)	Location	Principal Game Species	Where to Write
Caddo	17,729	Texas	Dove, rabbit, waterfowl, some whitetail deer	District Ranger, Box 507, Decatur, TX 76234
Cedar River	6,717 (scattered)	North Dakota	Antelope, mule and whitetail deer, sharptail grouse	District Ranger, Lemmon, SD 57638
McClellan Creek	1,449	Texas	No hunting allowed	Regional Forester, P.O. Box 266, Cheyenne, OK 73628

25

The Prairie Birds

On the face of it, you'd have to say the gray (Hungarian) partridge is the quintessential prairie bird. His hunted range is larger, his bag total more than that of any other prairie bird (leaving out the quails).

But, dammit, he's nothing but a furriner! Comes from one of them danged European countries where everybody's last name winds up with the butt end of the alphabet. So, let's stick with the sharp-tailed grouse as the premier prairie bird, then we'll talk about Huns and some of the other birds.

The difference isn't that much anyway. Gray partridge are hunted in 14 states, 8 provinces, compared to 12 states and 6 provinces for the sharptail. The bag is 650,000 for Huns, 455,000 (split almost equally between states and provinces) for the sharptail.

SHARP-TAILED GROUSE

Seen up close, the sharp-tailed grouse has the slightly frazzled, squinch-eyed, weatherbeaten look of a gimpy old Dakota Territory cowboy—and well he might, for you'll not find him where the warm breezes make winter something that happens only far to the north. No, the sharptail prefers places where the wind cuts the unwary cheek like the bite of a wood rasp.

There are sharptails in almost every northern Great Plains state and Canadian province, through the fabled Yukon, into Alaska—but the Dakotas and the prairie provinces are where a mixture of mid-length grass and drought-tolerant crops give sharptails a place to hide and breed, and a supply of protein-rich grain to carry them through the fierce winters.

Sharptails are there for the hunter willing to walk to a horizon set by the earth's curve and not by a tree or a mountain, the hunter willing to battle extremes of temperature that threaten to lay him low, either with heatstroke or hypothermia. But they're there, those nondescript prairie grouse that flushed in great clouds when

236

the settlers trundled across the bluestem of the eastern Dakotas into the knee-high grama grass, mixing the creaking of poorly greased wagon axles with the repetitive boom of caplock smoothbores. "Some parties brought a load of grouse to town yesterday," reported the *Black Hills Journal* in 1883. "They disposed of them readily and at a good price." In those days, the only limit was the carrying capacity of a horse-drawn wagon. Today, it's three or four birds a day—still a comfortable game bag.

Mother Nature forgot to spill her gaudy palette on the sharptail. You'd think he's a hen pheasant as he rises from the prairie grass, amid dry, scolding clucks as if he disapproves of all hunters. He decorates the hot hills with fuss and wingflap. All sputterwings and the illusion of speed, he's easy to miss. He's as big as a frying chicken and to see those stubby wings blur you'd think he is first cousin to a bottle rocket—but it's all a trick. The best lead is no lead at all.

South Dakota is one of two states (Nebraska is the other) where you can combine hunting for sharptails and prairie chickens, their slightly larger and flashier cousins. Because the ranges of the two birds overlap, the season is loosely called "grouse" and generally runs from September into November, depending on where you hunt. Prairie grouse are prairie grouse and they're not found in conifer forests, or above the tree line. They take grasslands. Grouse populations, like those of any upland bird, are victimized by weather and lack of habitat. When bison and red men roamed the fenceless prairies, the grasses grew tall enough to shroud a grouse, and neither winters nor hunting pressure were severe enough to chew into the vast flock. Now, with the land cowed to a fare-thee-well, it takes good growing seasons to let vegetation get ahead of cow cuspids.

Given a nice wet year and a mild winter, clover and grass will grow tall and tough, and sharptails respond with a dozen chicks per hen, and the grouse population can skyrocket between hunting seasons. It also can plummet when one of those hundred-year winters hits rangeland chewed to the roots.

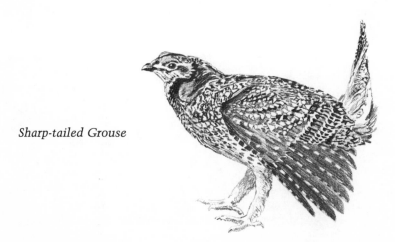

Sharp-tailed Grouse

A mixed bag of prairie chickens and sharp-tailed grouse loafs on top of one of the big haystacks often found in prairie country. The stacks are a good place to hunt for prairie grouse and also provide shade for hunters waiting for the birds to fly in.

This is prairie chicken and sharp-tailed grouse country—the Ft. Pierre National Grassland in South Dakota. What's needed is bird dogs who can pin birds down, for flushed prairie grouse fly a long, long way.

The importance of the sharptail varies from state to state, province to province. Most Yukon Territory sharptails are ground sluiced. Sharptails are so abundant that there is no closed season. In Manitoba, the first hundred miles north from the North Dakota border is excellent. Sharptails make up a third of the Saskatchewan game-bird bag, but they're still underhunted. Alberta also has fine hunting.

An Alaskan upland bird hunter (as rare as a literate politician) has a long (September through April) sharptail season with bags of fifteen daily. But although the Far North is largely unhunted for sharptails, most bird hunters simply can't get there. There's more hunter competition, shorter seasons and lower bag limits farther south, but at least travel is feasible.

The ultimate sharptail weapon is a 12-gauge gun, using No. 6 shot. If it's cold and the birds flush wild, a full choke is best. But if the birds are holding in hot weather, modified or improved cylinder guns are plenty tight.

Sharptails are fairly predictable grouse . . . except when they aren't. They follow general rules . . . except when they don't. Find them in the milo forage cuts early in the morning. But don't expect them to hold for a dog. They'll see you long before you see them and at the ranges they flush, you need artillery spotters to call in fire. Better to arrive at dawn and pass shoot as they sail into the field. On hot days, the birds head for brushy draws, thickets of plum beneath which there is shade. They won't be in heavy ground cover, so look for trees with bare areas beneath them.

HUNGARIAN PARTRIDGE

Now—for the heathen Hun. . . .

Dwight Huntington, were he alive today, would be depressed to learn he'd lost the war. Huntington, writing in 1903, recommended that we drop the terms "quail" and "quail hunting" and call bobwhites and their several kin "partridges." All well and good—except that in Huntington's time, there were no chukar or Hungarian partridges in our uplands and now that there are, it would create a hell of a mess to call a quail a partridge.

Both Hungarian (gray) partridge and chukar partridge are somewhat larger than quail, but smaller than grouse. Gray partridge date back to the 1700s in this country. Richard Bache, a son-in-law of Benjamin Franklin, released gray partridges, probably from England, in New Jersey. The attempt failed, as did subsequent stockings all through the 1800s along the entire Atlantic seaboard. Huns simply aren't adapted to arboreal or small farm conditions.

But when the persistent champions of gray partridge reached the upper Midwest, they struck gold. There were 207 pairs planted near Calgary, Alberta, in 1908–09 and the bird rapidly established itself as a viable game species. Encouraged, other upper Midwest regions planted Huns. Iowa stocked 6,000 in about 1914 and, although most vanished, a huntable population persists in the northwest prairie counties. Minnesota got some of those birds by expansion. Birds pay little attention

Hungarian Partridge

to political subdivisions. Minnesota also paid $6.25 apiece for a thousand Czechoslovakian gray partridge in 1929—and the fact that those birds came from Czechoslovakia proves what a misnomer "Hungarian partridge" is.

The gray partridge, like its gallinaceous cousin the sharptail, is a citizen of big country and one of its defenses is to flush wild and fly far . . . if it doesn't run like a jackrabbit. But gray partridge are unpredictable. They may hold tight for a dog one time, flush in panic the next. As a general rule, the birds feed early and late, like most seed-eating game birds. But, unlike quail, they are not cover-seekers when alarmed; rather they may run to the middle of a bare field, then flush.

In midday, especially if it's warm, they'll covey up in clumps of cover where it's cool. One man hunting such clumps is in for a lot of disappointment, for the birds frequently will run out the opposite side and flush out of sight. So, several hunters should work such brush patches by surrounding them as thoroughly as possible.

Pheasant hunters, used to chasing cock birds down a fencerow to the bitter end, will find the same technique works for gray partridge—walk out a cover strip thoroughly and, for good measure, send the dog out into the field ahead. The ideal cover clump is cool and shady, but not clogged with low vegetation. Gray partridge depend on unobstructed vision. Unlike sharptails, partridge would rather walk to supper and will feed in the grainfield close to their afternoon loafing spot.

If you flush a covey, watch them down. Depending on the amount of cover, you may get a shot at them. If they land in heavy cover, they'll be reluctant to run and may lie to a dog or wait until you're within gun range before they flush.

Partridge shooters used to be two things—quick and deliberate. If that seems a contradiction, so be it. Few if any game birds flush more quickly and, considering that often the bird is well-out when it flushes, it pays to be a quick shooter. On the other hand, because the shots often are at long ranges, many good partridge hunters use full-choked guns and the deliberate shooting techniques of good waterfowlers. Any shot from No. 6 to No. 8 is sufficient to bring down a partridge and many hunters use 7½s.

The ideal partridge dog also is the ideal pheasant dog—one who knows how to handle running birds. If the dog can circle a running covey, chances are the birds, caught between you and the dog, will freeze and let you get close enough for easy shooting.

There is one final method of partridge hunting that almost never is practiced in this country, yet is the standard method of shooting in much of Europe—the driven bird. If you can find someone fool enough to go out and walk miles to flush birds over your gun. Consider having a lot of obedient children.

Gray partridge prefer grainfields, but can be almost anywhere in the West (northern part). They'll flush straight, but probably will bend in an arc before lighting anywhere from a quarter to a mile away. If you flush them repeatedly, more often than not they'll wind up back where you first got them up. Early season coveys are small—a family group—but later on the flocks may be huge.

One thing about it—North American gray partridge never will choose to return to their Middle European roots. Those countries now are all Communist, and the gray partridge is just too damned independent to handle regimentation.

CHUKAR PARTRIDGE

The chukar partridge also is called "chukor," "Indian hill partridge" and "rock partridge." Chukars originally came to North America from India and Turkey. As was true with all the introduced birds, nearly every state and province tried them, and the birds then proceeded to do what they damned well pleased.

Chukars are a favored bird on shooting preserves so you can shoot them in, for example, my home state of Missouri—but not in the wild. Wild populations are limited to the western states, with a few small populations into British Columbia and one small flock extending into the upper part of Baja California.

The desert parts of Nevada, Oregon, Washington, Utah, Idaho and Wyoming have the largest flocks. Western Colorado is fairly well populated. California, Arizona, and New Mexico have small flocks, as does Montana. Essentially, chukar hunting is limited to ten states and British Columbia. Hawaii has a viable population, but on the mainland, Washington, Nevada, Idaho, California, Oregon, Utah, Colorado and Wyoming offer the best and most widespread chukar hunting.

Chukar hunting definitely is hunting where a local contact helps—not as much in finding the birds as in knowing how to approach them.

Charley Waterman, an old hand at hunting the western birds (and, when he is not actively engaged in doing it, one of the very finest at writing about hunting), thinks chukars are among the real track stars of Birddom. But he says you can outguess them, especially by finding a grainfield higher than the eroded canyons in which they roost, pushing them from below with a bird dog at morning or evening.

Chukar Partridge

Chukars tend to stay at the same elevation on a given day, so if you find one bunch, you should find more, which saves some of the legendary up-and-down through horrific near-badlands. Chukars spend a lot of time cackling and, while it may be tough to figure out where the sound is coming from, at least it's a clue.

Just often enough to keep you interested, a chukar flock will hold for a dog. Generally, the birds will be along rimrock, in sparse cover, and hunters work the gullies that serrate the rim. One trick, if you can steel yourself to do it, is not to shoot the first bird up, since it may be an outrider, a distance from the main covey which then will flush out of range.

Most gunners choose at least a modified choke, and 7½ shot is probably the most widely used shot size. The loads should be as hot as you can find them.

Working down on birds forces them to fly, for they generally run uphill, fly downhill. Scatters hold better for a dog than flocks. Most coveys will be fairly close to water, so there should be a creek bottom nearby. Binoculars are a help. A winded hunter, whuffing dejectedly on some rock outcrop amid the sagebrush and cheatgrass, can scour the slopes for moving birds.

South or sunny slopes are good bets on a cold morning, while in hot weather the birds may bunch up in a shaded gully. Check waterholes on a final swing back to the car in late evening; you might catch birds getting a last sip before they go to roost in the rocky draws above.

WESTERN GROUSE

There are a gob of Western grouse, including blue and spruce grouse, both of which are "timber" grouse, not birds of the prairie. Of the two, blue grouse are more widely hunted in the United States, spruce grouse more prevalent in Canada.

Both birds range high in the mountains, feeding heavily on conifers. I recall flushing a spruce grouse in the New Mexico mountains. It took a lot of flushing—both birds are the well-known fool hen—but once in the air, the bird was a good winged target.

Still, both are more often thought of as camp meat rather than as something you'd walk all day just to get a shot at.

Sage grouse have regained an importance they once held as a game bird and definitely qualify as a prairie bird.

Largest of all the grouses, the sage grouse may top eight pounds—more than four times the size of a ruffed grouse. Despite the size and the concomitant meat potential, the sage grouse never has been a favored eating bird. A diet of sage can make older birds bitter-tasting, a problem that can be alleviated by prompt gutting and removal of the crop. H. L. Betten recommends cutting away the neck and backbone of an older bird to eliminate the taint.

In Betten's time, the late thirties, there was only one state with a sage grouse season, Nevada. Today, there are some ten states with seasons and Nevada no longer is the leader. Idaho hunters take more than any group—about 80,000. Oregon, Montana and Wyoming all have bags of about 50,000 while Colorado chips in 12,000 and Nevada 7,000. The two Dakotas barely qualify as sage grouse states.

Because the birds inhabit vast high sagebrush plains, they aren't easy to find. They fly to water at sunrise, so an initial step is to find water holes. You'll see tracks in the mud if the birds have been there. The edges of alfalfa fields are good spots to hunt. You can spot them on sagebrush prairies with a good pair of binoculars. They flush into the wind, like snipe, and you may be able to dash close enough to get a good shot as they try to reach flying speed. Or you can use drivers and blockers on them, like pheasants.

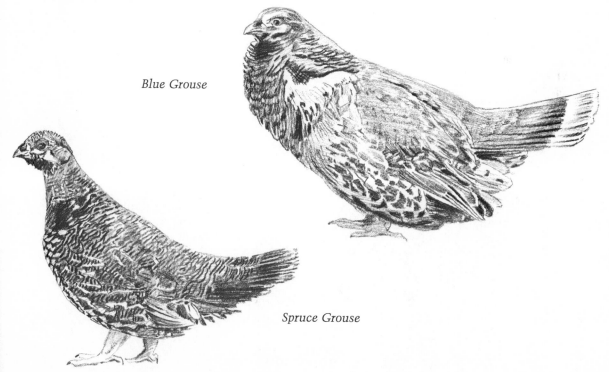

Blue Grouse

Spruce Grouse

Sage Grouse

Like most of the prairie birds, sage grouse are prone to wild flushing, and if you worry about this messing up your cherished bird dog's otherwise well-screwed-on head, leave him at home. If you have one of those rare circling dogs who can pinch birds between you and him, you have not only an animal with several zeroes on his price tag, but a sage grouse dog as well.

A sage grouse "booming" on an arid Wyoming plain. Largest of all the grouses, they can be sporty shooting. That spikey tail is their identifying feature.

WESTERN QUAIL

No question that the bobwhite quail is preeminent. He is far better known than any of his six native kinfolk. Few hunters ever get a shot at any but their territorial quails (which may be as many as three or four in some areas of the West). Almost no hunter, unless he makes a pilgrimage out of it, ever will hunt all seven species.

In addition to the bobwhite, there are valley, desert or Gambel quail, mountain, Massena, scaled or blue, and the masked bobwhite. California has the most with Gambel, valley (the state bird) and mountain. Blue quail share the Mexican border with Massena (also called Mearns), and with masked bobwhites. Farther south, in Mexico, Massena quail are of the Sonoran race rather than the Mearns race—same bird, racial difference of interest only to ornithologists. In fact, for a hunter the only real interest is in differences in hunting techniques. All the quails are seed eaters and they all feed like chickens, scratching and pecking. All quail are flocking birds and all flush with the characteristic roar of wings.

As far as hunting goes, all quail talk to each other and an alert hunter can locate the general vicinity of a covey by listening for the birds to give themselves away.

The valley quail is a far western bird, ranging from northern Mexico northward through the lowlands of California into Oregon and Washington. Anyone accustomed to twenty-bird bobwhite coveys is likely to besmirch his knickers when a hundred-bird covey of valley quail takes to the air. Guzzlers, those man-made waterholes that dot many areas in the arid West, are concentrating spots for the local quail and a knowledgeable hunter will search them out and hunt there.

Most western quail, including the valley, are far more prone to run before flushing than is the bobwhite. If there is an uphill, that's the way the bird will run, so a smart hunter, confronted by sprint-oriented birds, can head them off.

Valley Quail

Dogs find valley quail hunting tough going. It's often in hot, dry desert—toughest possible scenting and hunting conditions for any bird dog. For another, the birds are not as prone to lie to a point as is the bobwhite.

There are two general ways to hunt valley quail—one is gutting it out, busting through every possible sagebrush tangle and eventually stumbling onto the birds. The other is listening for calling birds, hunting the most likely spots, taking it easy. Valley quail don't move much until well after sunrise and will be on the southeast slope in the morning, the southwest slope in the afternoon.

Valley quail enjoy dry conditions and a wet day is a poor hunting day. On a flush, valley quail will fly downhill (unless, of course, they already are in the bottom of a draw). The only exception is if they're close to the top of a hill they may fly over it and down the other side. Like bobwhites they'll head for heavy cover, so a smart hunter will approach a covey location from the uphill side and between the covey and its escape cover, disrupting the bird's normal routine.

If the flushed birds land in thick cover, they'll likely stick to it, but if they land in thin stuff, they'll run immediately uphill. The ideal situation is to come on a covey in a narrow, brushy draw. Work a hunter on each side of the draw and the dogs or another hunter through the middle of the tangle. A bobwhite hunter won't have much trouble spotting potential valley quail cover—it's the western equivalent of what he's used to. Creek edges, brushpiles, old farmsteads, weedy fields and other tangles are ideal for both species, even if they are separated by half a continent.

It's a tossup if mountain, Gambel or valley quail are the most beautiful of the quails. All three are top-knotted, have the jaunty, curling little feather tipping forward from the brow of the male on the valley quail, both sexes on the other two.

All three are lovely birds. California quail have scaled neck-napes and stomachs, gray-blue breasts and the cock has a black-masked face, outlined in white, with a rufous pate. The Gambel cock is similar, but has a yellowish area below the blue breast and a black belly. Mountain quail have blue heads and capes, extending to a brown belly, with scale-marked sides. There is a brown throat patch, from the eyes under the chin, outlined in white and black feathering.

Not many people hunt mountain quail because they're damned hard work. They're found in the mountains of California, Oregon, Washington, Idaho and Nevada. There probably are small populations of the birds in other mountain states as well.

Mountain quail come in small flocks. They run through the dense chaparral and are hard to flush above it, another reason it's almost more trouble to hunt them than they're worth. If you're like me, a resident of the eastern two-thirds of the country, you're not likely to make a trip west just to hunt mountain quail. They'll be a bonus bird, and the best bet for a visiting hunter would be to rustle up a local as a guide.

Chances are you won't be able to use your dog in desert (Gambel) quail country. Deserts and cactus go together like Polish sausage and beer, and cactus country is not good dog country. The desert is harsh, lovely, but unyielding. If something gives, it ain't gonna be the desert.

Mountain Quail

Desert Quail

For desert quail, you need good footgear and good feet and legs to put in them. Desert quail come in sizeable bunches—coveys of fifty are common.

As with the other prairie quails, if you can find alfalfa fields, you should find desert quail. Any legume will attract the fairly small (five or six ounce) birds.

Desert is desert because it's hot and dry, even in hunting season. The middle of the day can be mighty uncomfortable. The birds tend to hold tighter then, if you can bring yourself to stay after them, in shade. They feed early and late and one hunting technique is to find a trail between roost and feeding area and ambush them. As is usual with prairie birds, desert quail are runners.

The Mearns quail is, of all the western quail, most like his eastern cousin, the bobwhite. He's a dog bird. And, since he's in big country, a running dog is ideal— a big ranging pointer, for example. You'll find these quail in grasslands among scrub oak, pinon, and other high plains trees and shrubs.

Their range isn't large in the United States and the birds aren't all that abundant, but of all the western quail, the Mearns (harlequin, Montezuma, Massena, or several other names, take your pick) is least likely to make you win a footrace before you claim him.

Generally, Mearns quail hold in the pine-oak areas of Arizona and New Mexico and on into Mexico, especially where there is wood sorrel and nut grasses and other forbs with bulbs. These succulents provide the quail with water.

Maybe I've seen only the best of it, but on my only blue quail hunt, the birds held as tight as woodcock. In fact, we walked up on them as they roosted in the only tree for miles, like so many Christmas ornaments, and four of us managed to miss eight shots at a range of no more than thirty yards, a trick I've accomplished

Mearns Quail

Scaled Quail

One thing about desert quail shooting (here scaled quail) is that if you can get the birds in the air within gun range, you'll have open shooting.

more than once in a shooting career that would have to improve to be called checkered.

The birds scattered into milo stubble and my pup proceeded to point them one after one, a quail shooter's dream. This came despite the earned reputation of the scaled quail as a distance runner beside whom Frank Shorter would pull up winded and gag up his breakfast.

Scaled quail are slightly larger than bobwhites. The bulk of the range is through west Texas, New Mexico and into Mexico. There are outcrops in Kansas, Oklahoma, Colorado and Arizona. The habitat ranges from grassland, where we found them, to brushy desert. Coveys are large, forty to fifty birds, though family groups are about what they are for bobwhites—a dozen or so.

The birds lack the topknot of most of the western quails. They sport a whitish crest like that of a grouse, which gives them one of their nicknames, "cottontop."

As a general rule, scaled quail are not dog quail—unless you're hunting in the less forbidding part of the bird's range. South and west, into desert, there's a mean array of spikey stuff that will chew up a dog and it's no favor to your bird hound to sic him on quarry that won't hold, in country that doesn't hold scent, in habitat that eats him alive. Another general rule would be to use dogs in ground cover, such as grass, or go without dogs in the desert.

Sharp-eyed hunters cruise in vehicles until they spot a scurrying blue quail covey, then try a quick foot race to the birds to flush them. Or they drive out of sight, sneak back to surprise the birds. Some shoot a running bird, both because it's a sporting target and to goose the rest of the birds into the air.

To a hunter raised on bobwhites, western quail will be a revelation and quite probably a frustration. They live in entirely different country. If you're a stranger, the best approach is to hire a local guide and avoid all the aimless and probably hapless exploring you would do on your own.

26

The Unsung Birds

Old barns . . . they lean tiredly into the centuries, tin roofs creaking with arthritic protest at the pressing weight of their years.

Yet for all their decrepitude, these old citizens of the countryside retain a quiet dignity, and their stolid bulk speaks of a time when there was time, time to do things right.

Sometimes they are forced to give it up—they collapse in a high wind or are consumed by fire. But many still dot the countryside, weathered monuments to the time before "the electric" came snaking over the ridgetops, when A-models clattered along rutted gravel roads that bore state highway markers. You could almost bet an old barn would have a covey of seven or eight quail roosting nearby, probably under a rusty hay rake, itself half hidden by unmowed bunchgrass.

Barns always have attracted wildlife. Some species were unasked-for and unwelcome. No farmer finds love in his heart for the Norway rat, nor the field mouse. But there always are plenty of natural pesticides—ones that fly, stalk or slither. A six-foot black rat snake may give yon dude the screaming whim-whams, but it is one of the most efficient rodent predators that exists.

Up in the loft there was likely to be a barn owl with the face of a boneyard ha'nt, Angel of Death to mice. And, while Br'er Fox may occasionally dine luxuriously on Rhode Island Red, he also snacks extensively on mice.

Rock doves coo softly in the shadowy, cool eaves of the barns. Somehow "rock doves" sounds more elegant than pigeons. Dust motes eddy and whirl in kaleidoscopic frenzy amid the sunshafts that pierce chinks and knotholes in the weathered siding. The barn whispers in a breeze, not secretively, but with a hushed reverence. The voice of an old barn is soothing.

The word "barn" is a combination of two old English words: "bere" meaning barley and "ern" which denoted a place or closet. So barns originally were places that stored grain, not shelters for livestock. That structure was the "byre." The functions gradually merged and most American barns combine grain or other crop storage with livestock shelter.

Though the best of them were built with patient skill, of massive timbers that resist time as stoutly as wood can, yet the grinding of the seasons takes its toll. It costs too much to build old-style barns today, even if the materials were available, and it costs too much to maintain or restore those that still exist.

Technology has bypassed these shambling giants, much as the internal combustion engine leapfrogged the patient plow ox. We don't have time for barns anymore.

And so they lean into the inevitable and finally collapse into the musty pages of history.

PIGEONS AND DOVES

Yet there have been some fine moments around these stolid giants. Pigeon shooting is a matter of circumstance, but given good contacts and a plentiful supply of old barns, you can fill your odd gunning hours with some exceptional pass shooting.

Under no circumstances should anyone shoot pigeons without permission. It may be that the landowner likes pigeons—even those living in a barn that isn't within a mile of a house. You shouldn't be on the land without permission anyway. And it's the epitome of squalid manners to get permission to hunt one species and then shoot everything that moves. Find out specifically what you can hunt (and what you can't). If the pigeons are roosting around an occupied farmstead, it'll be a rare landowner who gives you shooting privileges.

Doves and pigeons are the fastest-flying of all the upland game birds. God only knows what a dove in a tailwind is clocking, but they've been measured at sixty miles per hour in ordinary flight and routinely loaf along at thirty-five to forty-five miles per hour, about what a panicked woodcock or quail is doing at top speed. Turkeys, prairie chickens and crows might hit forty-five miles an hour with the throttle to the firewall. Pigeons have been timed at ninety miles an hour.

What makes doves and pigeons especially difficult is that they most often are shot at when they're at speed, rather than gathering it. The gallinaceous birds take some time to reach maximum velocity after you stick a boot in their butts, but a dove crossing a fencerow is truckin' every time. The only exception is when you rise to shoot at a bird that is fluttering to a landing—and then the bird can turn himself inside out as he puts on an evasive fake.

Pigeon

Rock doves exist wild today on most continents, much as they've always done. The courthouse pigeons are wild ones, despite their city habitat. From rock doves have developed the various domesticated pigeons, the homers, rollers, whatever, that thrill pigeon fanciers worldwide. Byron Dalrymple, in his *Doves and Dove Shooting,* theorizes that because man and pigeons have coexisted and even helped each other for so long, the body of pigeon lovers is fanatically opposed to sport hunting of its favorite bird. It's as if someone proposed a season on wild horses. Think of the outcry from horse lovers. But what's different about a wild horse and an elk? Perhaps that there is no Kentucky Derby with glandularly disturbed gentlemen riding elk . . .

Dalrymple cites many tales of pigeon heroics (pigeons have performed feats that would have shamed Lassie), including carrying wartime messages that saved countless lives. Quite in contrast are tales of horror told by George Laycock in *The Alien Animals.* Though he gives credit to pigeons who serve mankind by flying bull semen into the rugged Formosan hills for the cattlemen there, he also tells of pigeons shitting death in the form of crytococcal meningitis spores, carried in the droppings.

A child of Chicago, I remember the soot-stained, red-eyed pigeons that chortled fatuously everywhere. They were dirty, stupid birds. I sympathize with Robert Benchley who had a running war with pigeons. The famed humorist woke one morning to see " . . . a big bull-pigeon walking about on the window ledge and giving me an occasional leer with its red eyes, all the while rumbling in a deep, bass voice and giving every indication of immediate attack."

I doubt Mr. Benchley would have objected to the promiscuous shooting of pigeons.

Pigeons and doves are no more mystical, religious, intellectual or soulful than any other bird. They are, simply enough, fine sporting targets, and they are good on the table. No game bird offers more and no rational reason exists to prevent them from being shot . . . or, as is all too frequently the case, shot at.

Pigeon shooting usually is a buddy project, at least around barns. One hunter (the one who loses the coin flip) climbs to the barn loft. A good loud noise is enough to send the resident pigeons toward their escape route, usually the loft door. They'll hit that door like a herd of matrons charging into a fire sale. Invariably, the birds will dip sharply several feet just as they clear the loft, as if they'd hit an air pocket. This dip occurs with disheartening regularity just as you shoot . . . and miss.

But barns are only one of several pigeon-producing areas. Bridge pigeons, with almost no natural enemies, can multiply alarmingly. Those soft-voiced coos you hear the birds making are incredibly vulgar suggestions, which usually are accepted. The result is many little pigeons. Pigeons, like doves, lay two eggs at a sitting, and raise several broods per season.

Pigeons have to eat somewhere, usually in a nearby grainfield. if you can find the feeding areas and get permission to shoot, you can have some superb gunsport year-round, since there is no season on pigeons. The same tactics that work on doves will work for pigeons—camouflage, a blind or a good hide and careful studying of the way the birds fly. You can prop up dead birds to serve as decoys. Even if you can't get permission to shoot close to the barn, you may be able to convince the farmer to let your buddy run the birds out of the loft, whereupon they may fly to the field, over your blind.

The pigeon is every bit as difficult to shoot as a pheasant; it's edible; it is, for all practical purposes, if not by regulation, a wild bird.

SANDHILL CRANES

These birds have a wide range over the western two-thirds of the country, all the way from Alaska into Mexico, but they fall into the very marginal upland category—basically, they're shorebirds. Crane hunting is allowed in Alaska, Colorado, Montana, New Mexico, North Dakota, Oklahoma, South Dakota, Texas, Wyoming, Manitoba and Saskatchewan. Another sixteen states and provinces where substantial numbers of sandhill cranes exist do not permit hunting for them.

Sandhill cranes are both wary and shy and have excellent eyesight. Hunters now use decoys and hope to lure them to a blind, à la waterfowl hunting, but in the past the birds were taken by hunters who studied flight paths from resting to feeding fields and took them by pass shooting. The birds fly low early in the season. They aren't hard to hit, but they are hard to kill. Oldtimers used heavy shot and heavy powder charges. A good goose load—No. 4 magnum—is appropriate.

Sandhill hunting is a trophy sport for several reasons: (1) the bird is quite large and impressive; (2) it is difficult to hunt; (3) it is expensive to hunt unless you live in the hunting area; (4) it is uncommon enough to make killing one a chancey thing. The success rate averages about one bird per hunter per season, which is better than that on turkeys, but certainly not startling.

Sandhill Crane

Band-tailed Pigeon

BAND-TAILED PIGEONS

Band-tailed pigeons and white-winged doves are two western species in the same family, but neither is widespread. Where they are, the hunting is superb. They just aren't in that many places.

Band-tailed pigeons are almost exclusively a Pacific Coast game bird, with California hunters accounting for half a million of the estimated 700,000 birds taken annually. Oregon and Washington hunters take virtually all the rest. The total kill of bandtails is less than the kill of mourning doves in Missouri. Still, for hunters with access to shooting them, the shooting can be spectacular.

Bandtails eat a variety of food, but during the hunting season will feed on acorns, pine nuts and waste grain. The birds are erratic in their wanderings and may not reappear in the same place year after year, as doves do. But once settled in, a flock will keep coming back (to a grainfield or oak grove) until it eats all the food. Another peculiarity of the bird is a craving for minerals associated with mineral springs—many hunters shoot over such springs. Hunting in those areas can be rough—the terrain is rugged and the brush thick. It takes a good dog to retrieve cripples. Hunters have reported losing a third of the birds they shoot and that's too many.

The average hunter kills about a daily limit of five in the entire thirty-day season in California. It appears that both hunting pressure and the bird's population have stabilized.

WHITE-WINGED DOVES

Another western bird which, like the bandtail, gets limited hunting pressure, whitewings are taken mostly in the Rio Grande valley, especially in Texas, with an estimated annual harvest of between a quarter and a half million birds. The bulk of the hunting pressure is in the four southern Texas counties of Cameron, Willacy, Hidalgo and Starr.

Biologists studying whitewings find declining habitat a more serious concern than hunting pressure. You can manage hunters far more easily than you can manage habitat, especially if you don't own the habitat. The culprit is that old Western ogre, water. Diversions for irrigation, dams, irrigation wells—all these have drastically lowered the water tables in whitewing country, causing the death of hackberry and mesquite thickets where the birds used to nest.

Some day before too long the West is going to pay a painful price for incontinent mining of water. You can't forever take more than you put in, whether it's money, soil or water. Sooner or later your creditors catch up with you.

The water problem is far too complex and varied to get into in an upland bird book. Whitewing hunting is about as minor a problem as is associated with the declining water resource (unless, of course, you're a freaked-out whitewing hunter). Human suffering is the big problem. If you like real fright, not the kind that Stephen King specializes in, the kind that goes away, read about water problems.

Whitewings are about two ounces larger than mourning doves, on the average. The daily limit is comparable to that for mourning doves (usually ten) and shooting can be every bit as furious as it is for mourning doves in a good field. The season in Texas is short—about five days—and twenty-three days in Arizona.

Whitewings are more flock birds than are mourning doves, and a pair will have two broods a summer, two eggs each—meaning the birds are less prolific than their more widespread cousins.

The whitewing nests in the southernmost areas of the southwest states and migrates to Mexico and Central America. Typical nesting habitat is brushy thickets along the Rio Grande River. Since much of that land has been cleared, the birds have adapted to nesting in the many citrus groves. Hunters over the border in Mexico frequently shoot over sorghum grain fields.

White-winged Dove

Aside from the Rio Grande birds, there is a considerable population of whitewings in Arizona's Sonoran Desert. Because this is a desert bird, waterholes concentrate them and are gunning hotspots. Byron Dalrymple's good chapter on whitewing hunting cautions against waterhole shooting because of the possibility of over-shooting the bird . . . and because anything that has flown twenty miles for a drink should be able to get one.

One technique is to perch on a high point along a flight line and pass-shoot birds going to food, water, or roost.

The vast area north and south of a line from Phoenix to Yuma contains most of the Arizona whitewing hunting—along the Gila River, plus west and south of Tucson.

RAILS

Rails are marginal upland birds. Actually, they're shore or marsh birds and the hunting for them is a bastard enterprise half waterfowl, half upland.

Rails are especially strange to hunt. Despite the most liberal bag of any game bird (usually, if not always, twenty-five), almost no one hunts them. For one thing, they're scrawny little birds and twenty-five makes about one good mess. For another, they're weak flyers who pop up only momentarily as you slog through marsh water, in hot weather, in hip boots, just long enough for a snap shot before they cartwheel back into the tangle.

It's frustrating and exhausting hunting and you'd better be in shape to do it.

A friend of mine sloshed through knee-deep marsh slop all day, finally staggered out on a levee in a wildlife area. Gratefully, he slumped to rest beneath a tree, whuffing and blowing. Canada geese were moving into the area, though the season wasn't open.

Virginia Rail

As a gaggle came especially low over him, he did what every hunter would do. He pointed his gun at the lead goose, and shouted, "Bang! Bang!"

And, from above him, a voice said, "You missed."

There was an amused bowhunter nestled in the tree . . . and that's all I know about rail hunting.

SNIPE

I grew up believing that a snipe hunt involved a bag, a flashlight and a long night swatting mosquitoes while your tormentors laughed themselves sick back in town. That was the folklore practical joke—con some sucker into a "snipe hunt" where he'd hold open a sack to lure snipe, mesmerized by the light, out in the middle of a bug-ridden swamp while the supposed beaters quietly stole back to the nearest beer joint.

Well, snipe hunting may be where woodcock and dove hunting was a few years back—on the brink of better times. Snipe are a traditional game bird, marginally an upland bird since they theoretically are shorebirds. Hunting interest has declined, but there are plenty of snipe around and the bird itself is, though smaller than a woodcock, bigger than a rail, in the same size range as the dove.

Snipe are good eating and tough shooting. The two states with appreciable kills of snipe are Florida and Louisiana. Nowhere else are there enough birds killed to make even a small dent in the population.

Since the birds are wetland-oriented, that's where you'd want to hunt them. Further, since newcomers to snipe hunting probably will have trouble distinguishing the birds from other long-billed shorebirds, the best bet for a beginner would be to visit a public waterfowl shooting area (assuming it has snipe) and talk to the area personnel about what the birds look like and where they are on the area.

Snipe bag limits are more liberal than those for woodcock—eight daily as opposed to five. The good Dr. Lewis, quoted before, wrote that the snipe, in the 1860s, was the most widely distributed game bird in the world. Best snipe shooting in those days was in the spring. For singlyshot birds, a good day's bag was anywhere from fifty to one hundred birds a day.

Hunters used very small shot—No. 10 to No. 12—and a good shooter was one who could hit half the birds he shot at.

Snipe invariably fly into the wind, so hunters then and hunters now hunt with the wind at their backs. Oldtime hunters learned to make the bird's distress call, which would flush them. Another technique is to station one hunter upwind of a snipe hide, then circle another hunter around it to flush the birds toward his buddy.

Incidentally, an aggregation of snipe is a "wisp," a poetic collective noun. Collective names for wildlife often are entertaining, far beyond the commonly used "flock" or "covey."

Common Snipe

You can impress people at slow parties if you know, for example, that a bunch of bitterns is a "siege." We find coveys of quail today, but "bevy" was far more commonly used a half-century ago. Doves can be a "flight," but also a "pitying" or a "true love" or a "dule" which comes from the French word *deuil,* meaning "mourning" or "sorrow." On the other hand, shouting, "Here comes a true love of doves!" at your fellow hunters in a corn-stubble field is likely to get you a bed completely by yourself when it comes time to turn in.

If there is a single prime spot for snipe, it would be a wet pasture, a shortgrass area wet enough to allow probing for worms. Snipe are far more oriented to open country than are their woodcock cousins.

You can find snipe (which usually drop in, as do woodcock, during the night) by listening for their harsh call—but you have to know what you're hearing, of course.

Like woodcock, snipe hens lay four eggs. The Latin name, *Gallinago delicata,* indicates the edible quality of the bird's flesh. Elliott Coues translates it this way: "Latin meaning delicate—not in poor health, but dainty, as the bird is when served on toast." Yes, indeed.

Snipe weigh close to four ounces on the average—about half the weight of a quail, close to the weight of a dove. Their coloration and patterning is similar to that of a woodcock, the game bird they most resemble. The bill, like that of a woodcock, is flesh-colored. The bird is mottled tan, dark brown, off-color white. Snipe fly quickly and erratically, emitting a whistling, high-pitched cry—written as *scaipe!*—when they flush.

Snipe offer the gunner everything he wants in an upland game bird; yet, they're essentially an unhunted bird. Why? Well, the theory is that a thirteen-year closure, from 1941–1953, because of drought and cold weather during breeding that cut into snipe numbers, was long enough to let the snipe hunting tradition fade.

Snipe, like woodcock, are reclusive. Where quail, pheasants, most game birds are common in places frequented by people, snipe aren't. You find them in spots that are tangly, boggy, uninviting. And the peak of their migration occurs before most hunters are geared to the field. The whole month of October drifts by as a prelude to the "traditional" November bird season. There's dove hunting, but generally dove hunters don't frequent snipe areas. Quail, grouse, pheasants—all are November birds and by then the big snipe push is over.

Some of the historic accounts of snipe shooting are stunning—reports of 150 birds a day are common. Shorebird shooting declined because shorebirds declined, victims of intense gunning pressure. Some, such as the plovers, have become rare or endangered where once they came in endless flocks. Snipe suffered, too, but because they're less visible, the flocks never were shot back as extensively as some species.

The range is vast—virtually from the whole of Canada and Alaska for breeding, all the way to South America for wintering. The two ranges, summer and winter, meet in a curving line that runs roughly right through the middle of the United States from east to west. Bisect Missouri (as does the Missouri River) and extend the line to the two oceans and you have pretty well delineated the bird's summer and winter homes.

There's not a whole lot known about snipe, other than broad life history. Since it's not a major game bird anymore, there's not much money available to study its more intimate habits or its habitat and other needs. There's no Snipe Unlimited, nor Snipe Society. On the other hand, there's no immediate threat to the species health either. While snipe, like woodcock, may suffer pesticide damage from ingesting insects and worms that have been sprayed, it doesn't seem to be a looming problem for either species as it has been for some of the raptors.

Habitat loss has been damaging, but not crippling. Obviously, drainage of a marsh will harm marsh birds—but much of the marshlands both birds use are far to the north or are, as yet, unattractive to developers. Snipe are both far more widespread and far less hunted than woodcock, so when wildlife managers begin to worry seriously about the woodcock future, then it is time to think also even farther in the future about snipe.

CROWS

I've always had a great affinity for noisy, scruffy, unconventional types, given over to raucous good fun, the type frowned on by your minister. Thus, there is a lot of resemblance between some of my friends and the average flock of crows.

Crow

Crows, simply enough, are fine birds, given to exuberance and, for birds, capable of superintelligent behavior.

Besides that, you can shoot the tar out of them.

But Heaven forfend that I should consider a crow only as a target. I don't care how often yon crow commits outrage on man's estate, he's still worthy of study and appreciation. So don't badmouth crows. Go yell at a sparrow or a starling. Tell them to go back to England. Cherish the All-American crow.

"No bird has been the subject of more heated controversy than the crow," said Arthur Cleveland Bent, "and none of our birds have been more violently persecuted by man."

The secret of crow hunting lies in making the birds forget their caution. It helps to be a demagogue with a crow call, for the crow who wouldn't dream of racing headlong into a charge of shot under normal conditions will do it when whipped to a frenzy by a skillful caller. People band up into lynch mobs in the name of truth and justice. People and crows have a lot in common. Maybe that's why most people don't like crows.

Crow hysteria perhaps reached a peak in a story told by outdoor writer John Madson in his fine book *Out Home* (Winchester Press, 1979). Madson tells how Bruce Stiles, ultimately director of the Iowa Conservation Department, then a 1930s game warden, was attacked by a horde of crows one day during the waterfowl season. Stiles tried to kill a crippled crow with a stick and the injured bird's distress calls alerted a huge flock of neighborhood crows that then assaulted Stiles, a true-life Hitchcockian nightmare. Stiles fired fourteen shots through his gun at close range, no doubt cutting a wide swath in the enraged mob, but still the birds battered him, until he literally fought his way to shelter in a willow grove.

Crows do not take kindly to insult.

It always has seemed strange to me that a bird which requires so much hunting skill, that takes more know-how from the hunter than quail, pheasants, woodcock or grouse, is rarely mentioned by the upland gunners. What upland birds other than turkeys and waterfowl do you, the hunter, necessarily hunt using skillful calls and decoys? Some do call or decoy doves, but it's not usually necessary. The other upland birds require a rudimentary knowledge of habitat and habits, but ask mostly that the hunter be equipped with a strong back and a weak mind (or a weak mind and a strong dog).

With a crow, you need to know his lifestyle, his whereabouts and his language. You can, if you're good, make and place decoys that will fool him into flying within gun range or you can learn his language and sweet-talk him right into the center of a mist of No. 6 shot.

Or you can, far more easily, catch just a glimpse of a scout crow as he tip-wings away from you, taking with him the silently circling flock you'd hoped to prune.

"If one is biased it is relatively easy to find abundant evidence, either for or against the crow," Bent said. "Only the thoughtless, short-sighted person desires to have the crow completely exterminated, and the overzealous conservationist should submit to a reasonable control of a species when large numbers prove destructive to man's best interests."

That crows can become a pain in the pocketbook is not much in question. Crow has been reviled for a long time. In 1596, Edward Topsell allowed that, "generallie all Crowes are like eunuches bycause they participate not with Ravens or Doves, as eunuches are neither men nor women. These vulgar Crowes lyve not farre from houses, barnes, dunghills, and highwayes, eatinge all things, beinge called Omnivore, devourers of fruit, plants, wormes, garbage, carrion, younge Chickins, and small byrdes, olyves, nutts and other thinges."

Since then ornithologists have learned only how to spell better; they've never summed up Crow more succinctly.

Still, crows are a mixed blessing. One study showed that only 28 percent of the crow's annual diet is animal matter and, of that, two-thirds is insect. So, very, very little would be wild bird nestlings or eggs.

Crow's bad name with the sportsman comes from his supposed widespread habit of eating the eggs and young of other birds, especially waterfowl. Given the choice between a duck and a crow, there's not much doubt which the average hunter would choose.

And where large numbers of crows and nesting ducks coincide, the ducks can suffer.

Scratch a reference book and you'll find a study showing, essentially, that crows eat all the things Topsell said they ate, including lots of "other thinges."

The U.S. Biological Survey found only about one-third of one percent of an adult crow's food and 1.5 percent of the food of nestlings is from wild birds and their eggs. Only about one in twenty-eight crows and one in eleven nestlings had eaten such food. In 1936–37, biologists found no outstanding hazard to waterfowl on North Dakota's Lower Souris Refuge from crows.

Dwight Platt studied crow foods in Kansas for the University of Kansas in the early 1950s. Most of his Arkansas River valley crows ate grains, with wheat the most prevalent, but grain sorghum, sunflower seeds and corn the staples. Crop damages seemed to Platt to be slight. "Crows exert a stabilizing influence on many kinds of prey," Platt concluded. "And on the biotic community as a whole. This study indicates that their effects are especially important in helping to stabilize the populations of grasshoppers and of ground-dwelling beetles, and possibly those of some other insects that have soil-dwelling larvae."

Crows are the most prevalent members of the Family Corvidae, whose largest member is the raven. Where the crow's raucous call is familiar everywhere, the raven, like the loon, is a creature of the cold, inhospitable parts of the country—high desert and the north country. William Hornaday summed up the raven perfectly: "The crow is at all times a cheerful citizen, but the Raven always has a sore throat, and is always going to a funeral." Aside from the crow, the family includes jays, including the familiar blue jay, and magpies.

Crows like to nest in coniferous trees, but they're adaptable to almost anywhere. The female lays four to six eggs, with as few as three, as many as nine. She and her mate both incubate the eggs for eighteen days and share in caring for the young. The young can leave the nest in five weeks.

It's not hard to make a crow decoy. Anyone with a little artistic ability can draw the outline of an acceptable crow, then trace that off on plywood or some similar ¼-inch material. Cut the silhouettes out with a jig, coping or saber saw and paint them flat black.

Bert Popowski is the patron saint of crow shooters and his 1946 book *Crow Shooting* (A.S. Barnes) is the definitive one. In addition to silhouettes or full-bodied decoys of crows themselves, he recommends the well-known owl decoy, plus suspending dead crows to the sides and rear of the blind (the most effective decoy of all). Popowski has such a multiplicity of decoys and setups that it makes a long chapter for him and far too long a chapter here. You can call crows in without decoys, for pass shooting, but a good decoy spread will pull more crows closer than a call alone.

Probably the best combination is several crow decoys with an owl or hawk decoy. Since hawks and owls are protected by federal law, you can't use either a live or stuffed one, except by permit, which you probably can't get anyway. So the most viable alternative is artificial ones. Paper maché owls and crows are cheap, but last about as long as things that are cheap. Still, they're lightweight, compared to wood or more durable decoys. The owl decoy must be visible, which means tying it high in the thin branches of a tree. It should be secure, for crows will hit it if they get a chance and could knock it out of the tree.

Dead crows become good decoys when propped up on the ground, suspended from a tree branch or, one of the most effective lures of all to distant crows, tossed in the air while another hunter calls frantically. It looks like a fight in progress and the distant crows will nearly dislocate their wings getting to it.

Other decoys are possible, but the owl is premier. You can, for example, use a yellow tomcat. It just happens that I have a large yellow tomcat, named Willie Nelson because he is sort of laid back and a very cool cat, but I don't think I would sacrifice his tranquillity to insure a good crow shoot. The idea is you put the cat in a cage—birdcage, for example—and hoist him high in a tree where he is visible to neighborhood crows.

Bert Popowski, talking about this technique, says, "The cage enclosing them should be strong enough to prevent their freeing themselves for sometimes they get quite panicky when a score of crows descend on them, threatening to tear them limb from limb.''

No lie.

You can tie strings to crow decoys that are fastened near the owl decoy and by jerking the string give the crow decoy motion. Tie a couple of dead crows together at the neck, pitch them over a tree limb. Instant decoys. In fact, the more crows you kill, the more decoys you have.

In short, crows are curious birds, attracted by situations which either appeal to their pugnacious side or their instinct for flocking to the site of trouble. They'll come to a call which promises delight, ranging from food to a chunk of love, or they'll rally to a distress call—whether to help out or jeer at the unfortunate is known only to crows.

In Missouri and probably everywhere it is legal to use an electronic caller for crows, a portable record player or tape machine that does all the work for you. You'd spit in the eye of a duck hunter who resorted to such a device, even if it were legal. You'd kick a turkey hunter who took LeRoy Braungardt's superb record to the woods and lured up a twenty-five-pound gobbler.

Why, then, is it acceptable to call up Crow with somebody else's voice?

Do it if you want to, but I'd rather make my own mistakes.

Crow calling is easy in the sense of learning the calls and how to make them, but it's wearing, just as playing a harmonica is. If you're trying to simulate the voices of several crows harassing an owl, you'd run a definite risk of hyperventilating. Nothing worse than calling in a huge flock of crows and passing out as the first one loops into gun range.

The basic crow call is three sharp *caw* calls, loud and demanding, the call of crows looking for company. Slow down the same three notes and drawl them out and you've mastered the feeding call.

The other basic call is the fight call, a growling call that simulates the sound crows make when they're bothering an owl. There are three ways to learn crow calling: (1) listen to crows and see what they're doing while they're talking; (2) listen to a recording; (3) have someone who's good at it teach you (and it helps if you record that so you won't forget).

My crow call has an unfortunate tendency to freeze after I blow it for a while. I don't know why and don't know if they all do this or not. It's an Olt and sounds good except when it quits. It has a slot on the side of the mouthpiece into which you can blow, holding the call sideways, like a flute, to produce a pretty good red-tailed hawk whistle. The hawk whistle, combined with some excited crow cussing, is hard for neighborhood crows to resist.

Obviously, you have to be in crow country to have any luck hunting them. You set up much as for doves—camouflage clothing, a comfortable seat, a rustic blind, either of cut brush or camouflage netting (or within the enfolding arms of a cedar tree).

Most hunters probably don't even know it, but there is a crow season. Some years back, the United States and Mexico signed a treaty giving protection to birds that migrate between the two countries. Crows got included. So, in Missouri, the season is Nov. 1–March 3, which should be enough time for anyone to get crow shooting out of his system.

I certainly wouldn't encourage anyone to shoot crows outside the season under the guise of stopping depredations, though I doubt many raccoon rangers would arrest errant crow shooters. Nonetheless, you owe it to yourself to obey the letter of the law as well as the spirit, and besides Crow needs a little time off for procreation and friendly jawing with owls and hawks without worrying about getting his feathers shot off.

So, Crow is a duck that went wrong somewhere between the blind and the table. He's wily, sporting, demanding. He gives you everything a bull mallard does, except an appetite, so tip your hat to the next crow you see. He's worth it.

27

Finding a Place to Hunt

Once I spoke to a sportsman's club that shall remain nameless because some of its members were large and looked aggressive. I'd been asked to talk about the turkey season and since it promised to be a good one and since these guys allegedly all were sportsmen, how could I go wrong?

It turned out this was a spo'tin' man's meeting, not a sportsman's meeting, and booze flowed like a spring freshet. While I chortled my mellifluous melody of *Meleagris,* there was an incessant counterpoint of the clinking of glasses and a decibel level, bred by raucous conversation, only approached inside a jet engine test tunnel.

The problem was not so much that I got my feathers ruffled, but that the behavior was symptomatic, I'm afraid, of the way these thundermouths acted in the field as well. And I fear that all too many "sportsmen's clubs" are the bucolic equivalent of Ralph Cramden's Royal Order of Raccoons, whose sole purpose is to wear funny hats and have a good time.

It wouldn't matter, except that so much potential group endeavor in a much-needed area goes to waste. Instead of turning some of that primal energy into improving a stream or planting food plots or helping farmers on whom they hunt, these hunters were knocking back booze as if it were going out of style and bitching about rotten landowners and the ignorant conservation department and how they can't find a place to hunt anymore.

There is another way. The Deer Creek Sportsman's Club celebrated its 25th anniversary in 1980. It was organized by nine Air Force personnel stationed at Richards-Gebaur Air Force Base just south of Kansas City. The group leased 3,000 acres in Benton County, a good hunting and fishing area in the northern Ozark hills. Six years after it formed, the group went civilian and now has about eighty members.

It has gone through three ownerships of the club land without losing its lease. The club is family-oriented, and if there is a member you wouldn't be proud to call friend, I haven't met him or her. Considering that Benton County is quite rural and that much of rural Missouri looks on Kansas Citians as creatures not quite as personable as civet cats, the club has had to do a lot of things right to stay in neighborhood good graces that long.

There is an annual picnic, started in 1959, not just for member families, but for area residents. "It gives us a chance to meet and know our neighbors," said Judd Kirkham, Jr., one of the current club members and a second generation one at that—his father also is a long-time member. Some 300 people attend the picnic.

That's the social side of the club activity. A far more critical service is the Deer Creek Volunteer Fire Department, first rural fire department available to the residents of the area, which the sportsmen helped establish and fund.

The club members have planted and maintained food plots since 1959, fenced and carefully sown and cared-for. The members also maintain wood duck nest boxes, and are in the midst of a campaign to save a blue heron rookery. As long ago as 1960, the club used the Air Base to give youngsters gun safety training and now conducts its own NRA safety training program and insists that all youngsters have the course before hunting on the lease.

There are other activities, but that's a good idea of what a sportsman's club can accomplish—not only insuring itself of a place to hunt, but creating good will and acting as a positive force in the community.

If every such club took as active an interest in the production of game, in the sanctity of the natural world, in the careful fostering of good neighbor relations, then we hunters would have far fewer problems today.

Even though there are vast amounts of public land available to hunters and even though no hunter, with a judicious bit of detective work, should have to go hungry for a public place to hunt, the fact is that in almost every state private land predominates. Certainly that is the case in all the eastern, midwestern and southern states. In my home, Missouri, about 95 percent of the land is private.

Even in some of the states where there are extensive government landholdings, private land is far in excess of public—84 percent in Michigan, 92 percent in Virginia, 89 percent in New York, 83 percent in Minnesota. Texas has virtually no public land and private leased hunting is a way of life, with leases going for amounts that you would expect in a state where millionaires are almost a plurality of the population.

The days when finding a place to hunt was as simple as asking at the door are about gone. Farmers face not one or two hunting parties a season, but a procession of red caps. If there is any secret to finding a privately owned place to hunt, it is in being truly humble, grateful and nice. Far too many hunters radiate a subtle aura that lets the farmer know the hunter expects to be granted permission and is going to be cheesed off if he doesn't get it. There are whole books about body language, about reading facial expression and the meaning of voice intonation. You can prejudice your case without saying a word—maybe without realizing you're doing it. And then wonder why the farmer was so grumpy.

The best way to find places to hunt is to start well before the hunting season.

Be nice because you're nice, not because you want something from the landowner. Introduce yourself, say that you admire the fine-looking farm and that you're a bird hunter. "I'd be willing to swap some labor for a chance to hunt here come bird season," you say. "I have a strong back and a weak mind. I'll be glad to buck bales or cut firewood or whatever."

Not many hunters will go to that much trouble, but the exercise would be good for you. One hunter I know used to take his girlfriend along when he was prospecting. They'd go, hand-in-hand, to the farmer's door and she would look as forlorn as possible while they confessed to the landowner that they had no place to hunt. Since she was constructed along the lines of Raquel Welch, no son of the soil under the age of eighty-five had the lack of heart to refuse her.

Far better from a long-range standpoint to establish, then maintain good relations with your farm owners. The rules are many, but most are sheer common sense.

● Always ask permission.

● Follow instructions on where to hunt and be sure to stay well away from livestock and buildings.

● Leave gates the way you found them.

● Cross fences without stretching the wire—crawl under if you have to.

● Don't walk on growing crops or through standing grain (the sole exception being rowed corn and then be damned careful).

● Pick up all litter, including your empty hulls.

● Share your harvest with the landowner and dress the game for him.

● Don't be conspicuous—keep your intrusion to a minimum. Don't block roads.

● Stay in touch in the off season—a Christmas card, a visit when you're in the neighborhood, a phone call.

Thank the landowner with something tangible. I favor books, such as Aldo Leopold's *Sand County Almanac*, because it not only is fine reading, but carries a conservation message. But, if the landowner likes birds, get him a good field guide or a fifty-pound sack of sunflower seeds. Or, if you're workshop handy, make him a string of bluebird nest boxes and put them up for him.

Certain groups of hunters have far less trouble finding hunting territory than others—for example, a doctor or dentist with a rural clientele. It's hard to turn down a hunter who prowls in your vitals. Lawyers likewise frequently know landowners who are obligated to them. Teachers with rural students, agricultural agency representatives, ministers, feed store operators—the list is long and fairly obvious. But the guy with the problem is the one with no handle on the agricultural community and that generally translates to a big city hunter, remote from whatever roots he may once have had.

The bitter truth is that the farmer-sportsman relationship is an enigma wrapped in a conundrum. What the sportsman essentially asks of the farmer is something for nothing. Even though the hunter is the most law abiding, careful soul ever abroad, what can he offer? He is a stranger on the land. What if something happens to him? If he falls down a well or gets an infection from a rusty barbed-wire fence, the landowner may very well be liable. There are places where even if the guy is trespassing, he can sue the landowner if something happens to him. And collect.

And the hunter is there to take something. Something that the landowner fed the rest of the year. Even though you are there with his blessing, there just might be the tiniest spark of resentment.

So anything you can do to even up the sacrifice the landowner makes will help snuff out that budding fire. I know wood carvers who have given landowners (or their wives) tie or lapel pins or other artworks. I've cracked and picked out a pint of walnut meats—a couple of hours of work in front of the television, but a blessing to a farm wife who does a lot of cooking.

While a ''no'' is discouraging, sometimes a ''yes'' can be equally so. There is the story about the quail hunter who stopped at a small farmhouse. He found the farmer calf-deep in a sea of pig effluvia, slopping his sows. The hunter had been troubled by a throbbing cold sore on his lip and constantly chewed and licked at it.

The two exchanged pleasantries for a while, the hunter gnawing his aggrieved lip. ''That's a mean-lookin' lip you got there,'' observed the farmer.

''About to drive me nuts,'' said the hunter.

''Believe I can help you out,'' said the farmer, leaning down to scoop up a fingerload of pig poop.

He rubbed it on the offending lip. The hunter, thinking this a bit of folk medicine, said, ''Will that cure my cold sore?''

''No,'' said the farmer. ''But it'll sure as hell make you stop lickin' your lips.''

Failing a private land contact, the next step is to hunt public land. An invaluable listing of resource addresses is the National Wildlife Federation's *Conservation Directory,* published by the National Wildlife Federation, 1412 Sixteenth Street, N.W., Washington, D.C. 20036, for $4. It lists a huge number of outdoor groups, including all state and federal agencies, plus every esoteric private group you can imagine, from people dedicated to coastal preservation to trappers' groups.

In most cases, the directory is specific enough to list division chiefs within an agency, so you can write or phone a person, rather than a post office box.

Most conservation agencies have some sort of maps of their areas. Despite what you hear, game never is shot out on a public area of any great size, say 2,000 acres or more. Birds may be driven to the area's remotest corners or maybe even off the area itself, but hunting pressure is a self-limiting thing. As the availability of game decreases, so does hunting pressure. Gradually, as the shooters thin out, the game creeps back in. Public land, usually, is managed for game and, given the present rotten trend of land abuse, it often is the only place where a bird can find something to eat and a warm weed to pull over him of a nippy night. Hunger and discomfort works on birds the way it does on people. Birds will risk a shot in the ass just to get a good meal.

Don't overlook small areas (and, if you find a good one, keep your mouth shut about it). The best woodcock covert I know is no more than five acres, a piece of a small river access site heavily used by fishermen, beer drinkers, prophylactic field testers, etc. And by me and one other hunter, who shares with me the determination never to reveal the location.

I once spent an opening day of pheasant season on an Iowa public fishing area of perhaps 300 acres. There probably were two dozen hunters, but I killed a limit in less than half an hour. True, the bulk of the resident pheasant herd headed for private, posted ground shortly after the first shots were fired. But I suspect, later in the season when the privately owned corn had been cut and the ground fall plowed (and the fair-weather hunters were home wrapping Christmas presents), those raunchy old roosters were back on the lake area, crouching grumpily deep in the tangled rose thickets.

You can learn a lot from a bit of judicious map reading. County highway maps contain a wealth of material, especially all the roads in the county, including those rutted trails so beloved by sportsmen. If you're in a quandary as to how to reach some potentially lush area, a county highway map is your best source. It's available from the State Highway Department in the state capital.

Area maps are fine, but a good map of a million-acre national forest would be as big as your living room if it were as detailed as you'd like. Still, they're better than no map at all. But the best maps still are the good old Geological Survey quadrangles. Write the Map Informaiton Office, U.S. Geological Survey, National Center, Reston, VA 22092.

Ask for a free index to the state(s) you're interested in. From that, order the individual quadrangles at $1.25 each. The 7½-minute quads are the most detailed and the best way to go. Ask for green overprinting, which indicates woodland, a bit of information you might not get if you don't specify it.

Take some time to learn basic map reading and it will pay off. Contour lines, for example, give you a pretty good idea of how strenuous your hike will be. And you might save yourself a lot of unproductive walking. For example, if you're looking for stream benches that might hold woodcock, you can find potential areas by locating widely spaced contour lines—or by avoiding areas with steep banks.

You can use maps to find roads or trails (quads often mark trails, including foot trails, that appear on no other maps). Maps help you spot a second car so you'll have a vehicle at the end of a long walk. Maps lay out in easily understood terms the often confusing ridges and gullies that turn yesterday's mountain man into today's lost, whimpering urbanite.

In many eastern, southern and midwestern woods, you can walk your way out of trouble, but in the mountains or in vast sweeps of rolling plains or swamp, you can become seriously lost. Since most hunting seasons are at a time of the year when, in vulnerable country, weather can be unsettled, a simple hunting trip can turn into an ordeal.

Some spooky areas that spring to mind are the vast sandhills region of Nebraska, or some of the wide Dakota prairies, or the dense woodlands of the lake states and Canada, the mountains of the West, or southern swamp country.

But it doesn't even have to be untamed country—John Madson wrote about a prairie blizzard that swept across the upper Midwest on November 11, 1940. The day started warm, quickly turned cold, then became homicidal. Hunters died from exposure all over the Midwest, hunters who had begun the day in shirtsleeves or light hunting jackets and got caught too far from the car by the sudden vicious storm.

I've been marooned twice in such blizzards, neither time, thank God, while I was hunting. The quickness of the weather is that of a big predatory cat and the ferocity is the same—impersonal, implacable and inescapable. While such storms are rare, they do happen. So, if forecasts are dicey, it's wise to carry along foul-weather clothing. Remember, you always can take some off.

It's bad enough to be miles from the car when a storm hits when you know where the car is. Consider being *lost* and miles from the car. It's easy to get caught up in the excitement of the chase and, when the adrenalin drains away, find yourself tired . . . and misplaced. I've done it repeatedly, from the piney woods of Arkansas chasing a will-o'-the-wisp gobbler, to the thick aspens of northern Minnesota, trying to roust grouse. I've always managed to find my way back.

So far.

I'm not a good woodsman, but I'm better than a lot. Those hunters more prone to being lost than I am, then, should make a special effort to have good maps, as well as a compass. Contrary to what I believed as a little kid, a compass does not point to where you want to go. Hunters should know at least that much and preferably a whole lot more about the mechanics of travel by compass.

But in some parts of the country (the iron range country of Minnesota, for example) compasses can be unreliable. So the map can pull you out of a pickle. Iron deposits don't affect maps, but you have to know where you are in order to find out where you want to go. Thanks to Uncle Sam, I have played with quad maps a whole lot more than I ever wanted to, but I still get confused by some aspects of them. Seven of us once hiked several miles up the wrong fork of a stream in Arkansas. The fellow reading the map worked for the U.S. Geological Survey.

Remember that the more detailed the map, the more help it is. A map scale of 1:2,500,000 is an inch to 40 miles—useless. Most highway maps are on a scale of an inch to 19 miles and country highway maps are an inch to 2 miles. But the 7½-minute quad is an inch to 2,000 feet.

In all cases involving state lands, write the state conservation agency (see the list of addresses in this chapter). John Madson tells of a fellow hunting the interchanges along Interstate 80 for pheasants, but such hunting may be illegal some places, dangerous in others and surely frowned on everywhere. Railroad rights-of-way are good for pheasants and quail. Recently I spotted what I'd be willing to bet are excellent woodcock coverts along an Indiana interstate highway right-of-way that was wide enough that it could safely have been hunted.

In the South, paper and timber companies more and more are not only leasing hunting rights, but actually managing their lands for hunting. Respected outdoor writer Wayne Fears manages the wildlife program on Gulf States Paper's 500,000 acres. Clubs pay from $2–$5 an acre annually, which breaks down to a minimum of $80 per hunter. But the management program is superb and the area rich in wildlife. The company pours a million bucks a year into its program, but clears a profit.

A number of states have an extensive system of county forests or other lands. State conservation agencies should have information on the existence and perhaps the location of such lands.

There are several federal agencies with extensive holdings. The U.S. Forest Service controls the four million acres in nineteen National Grasslands, in addition to its 190 million or so acres of National Forest.

The Bureau of Land Management has vast holdings in the West. Generally you can't hunt in National Parks, but there are exceptions (one is the 90,000 acres of the National Scenic Riverway/Current and Jacks Fork rivers in Missouri).

The Corps of Engineers has huge acreages around its many reservoirs, most of which is managed for hunting either by the Corps or by a state agency. River islands may be public property and seldom hunted. Be sure to check ownership first. Don't overlook military posts. Check with the post commandant office to see if there are special hunting seasons. Indian reservations often are open to outside hunting, usually under a fee permit.

So, we have private land and public land. There is one other source of hunting land—your own. A fun farm is an expensive luxury. If you can make the land pay its way and still be good for hunting, wonderful. If you can't, then be prepared to pay a lot for the original purchase ($200 an acre for the scrubbiest stuff available is common), then a lot more for taxes.

Unfortunately, land is taxed the same no matter its use, a stupid system that mitigates against a man dedicating his acres to such nonproductive pursuits as songbirds, nature study and perhaps the occasional game creature.

Landowning then, unless the land is a paying business, is the least likely way to assure upland bird hunting.

Still—anyone with even a bit of ingenuity need never want for a place to hunt.

VANCE'S FAVORITE GOOD GROUPS

DUCKS UNLIMITED: P.O. Box 66300, Chicago, IL 60666.

ENVIRONMENTAL DEFENSE FUND, 475 Park Avenue South, New York, NY 10016 (won't help you find a place to hunt, but has the unofficial motto "sue the bastards" and takes polluters to court).

IZAAK WALTON LEAGUE OF AMERICA: 1800 North Kent St., Suite 806, Arlington, VA 22209.

NATIONAL AUDUBON SOCIETY: 905 Third Avenue, New York, NY 10022.

NATIONAL RIFLE ASSN. OF AMERICA: 1600 Rhode Island Avenue, NW, Washington, DC 20036.

NATIONAL WILDLIFE FEDERATION: 1412 16th St. NW, Washington, DC 20036.

THE NATURE CONSERVANCY: Suite 800, 1800 North Kent St., Arlington, VA 22209.

THE RUFFED GROUSE SOCIETY: 994 Broadhead Rd., Suite 304, Coraopolis, PA 15108.

SAFARI CLUB INTERNATIONAL: 5151 East Broadway, Suite 1680, Tucson, AZ 85711.

THE SIERRA CLUB: 530 Bush St., San Francisco, CA 94108.

WETLANDS FOR WILDLIFE: P.O. Box 147, Mayville, WI 53050.

THE WILDERNESS SOCIETY: 1901 Pennsylvania Ave. NW, Washington, DC 20006.

WILDLIFE MANAGEMENT INSTITUTE: 1000 Vermont Ave., NW, 709 Wire Bldg., Washington, DC 20005.

THE WILDLIFE SOCIETY: Suite 611, 7101 Wisconsin Avenue, NW, Washington, DC 20014 (for professional wildlifers).

NATIONAL WILD TURKEY FEDERATION: Wild Turkey Building, P.O. Box 467, Edgefield, SC 29824.

As a point of interest, Alice Herrington's Friends of Animals claims 120,000 members and Cleveland Amory's Fund for Animals claims 125,000. With the Humane Society of the United States' 115,000, that gives the three major anti-hunting groups a total of 360,000 members—or just slightly more than *one* of the major hunting groups, Ducks Unlimited.

The National Wildlife Federation has more than four million members.

I'd be willing to bet that most people who are anti-hunting belong to one of those three groups, where most hunters (and there are twenty million or so) don't support one of our groups.

Which brings up two equally valid points—there are far more of us than there are of them . . . and more of us should pay for our convictions.

28

About Anti-Hunting

The question of why I hunt is one that occasionally plagues me, though it isn't one of the problems that keeps me awake at night.

There was a time when I didn't hunt and when the idea of killing bothered me. Now I kill, birds and animals, and though I am bothered when I cripple something and don't recover it, the killing does not in any way tempt me to stop hunting. I am more disturbed by hunters who've never questioned their motives or been moved by the fact of death.

I am a predatory animal, possessed of teeth for ripping flesh. I like to eat what I kill and though that is not the major reason I hunt, the food element is important. Man is predatory—but also is the only animal with freedom of choice, who could if he chooses opt for a diet that does not include meat.

Hunters react to the kill differently. Some show no respect for the game. They see only targets and meat. They neither understand nor care that what they kill is a fellow animal, not just an animal. Other hunters are uneasy in the presence of death, especially one they caused. They recognize that not much separates them biologically from the killed animal and feel the shapeless twinges of their own mortality. But of course it isn't bravura to admit to such feelings.

Vance Bourjaily, a fine writer, hunter and philosopher from Iowa, touched on the same theme in talking about the building tension of opening day: "Its discharge has a kind of viciousness as incompatible with the enjoyment of a beloved sport as it is inappropriate to the harmlessness of the birds which are its victims," Bourjaily said. " 'Got the son of a bitch!' we cry ('or missed') as if the bird had done us injury."

At the same time I feel unease at killing something, yet I don't believe in the Hemingway mystique about the bravery of the bull (buck, grouse, whatever). That's a form of anthropomorphism as silly as is the anti-hunter's simpering over the cute human traits of wild things. The bull has no bravery, for bravery must contain fear overcome. The bull isn't afraid. He's not smart enough. He's been bred to unreasoning rage and that's what he shows. It doesn't occur to him that the matador has a sharp sword hidden in that damned red cape and that the sword (if he loses the contest) will turn him into unground hamburger. Now, the matador *is* brave, for he knows quite well that the bull well might slip several inches of sharp horn into his body. So don't admire the bravery of game. Admire its beauty, its elusiveness, its toughness, its trophy qualifications—but not its bravery.

I resent the anti-hunters lumping all us hunters together in a burbling stew. Who is the American hunter? It's a question both simple and complex, one that some of us don't want to examine too closely for fear we'll scrape off some scabs that will expose ugly pus pockets. Visit a public hunting area. See how many of the signs have been shot-speckled or ventilated with slugs. Are the signshooters hunters?

There's nothing I like more than a bit of scotch or a cold beer at the end of a tough hunt. Am I in the same leaky canoe with the hunters who carry a pint in their hip pocket or who suck up a six pack before going out to skillet-shoot a covey of quail or kill doves until the doves quit flying?

People used to shoot buffalo from passenger trains, shoot into passenger pigeon roosts, kill prairie chickens until the birds overflowed horse-drawn wagons. The Marquess of Ripon, an English gentleman gunner, kept a record of his shooting from 1867 on. He dropped 97,503 grouse, 124,193 partridge, 241,234 pheasants, 2,560 woodcock, 2,926 snipe, 3,569 ducks and various other birds and animals for a lifetime total of 556,813.

This awesome record ended on Sept. 22, 1923. Although the Marquess was 72, he hadn't slowed a bit. He was shooting on Dallowgill Moor, near Ripon, and at 3:15 p.m., having shot 165 grouse and one snipe, he dropped dead.

I can't feel too badly about the excess of the Marquess (except some regret that I wasn't a part of it) because he was shooting under controlled conditions and obviously hadn't decimated the available game. Although European nobility had been promoting game management for a long time, the bluebloods acted largely just like Americans when confronted with the teeming wildlife population of this country. They shot it until it was gone.

Even the image of the gentleman hunter has changed. Some of the classic outdoor writers were genteel types who hunted with fine English doubles, wore Harris tweed and had servants to pick up the game and handle the dogs. They were indifferent to the creatures they shot. They equated quality hunting with quantity hunting in monied haunts. Game was never-ending and conservation meant stopping, reluctantly, at twenty-five ducks instead of fifty.

Read the logbooks of an oldtime sportsman's club, whether it was a fishing lodge or a duck club, and you quickly find that success was equated with the size of the bag. Occasionally a writer would wax lyrical about the joys of nature—the beauty of a sunset or the vividness of birds slipping in to the decoys—but mostly that was a sidelight, briefly recalled at the end of a long day of execution.

The idea of the trophy long has been with us, ever since the first scruffy nobleman got the idea of hanging the head of a tough old wild boar on his wall. He probably inherited the thought from some prehistoric savage who sawed off the head of his vanquished enemy to prove his superiority. Who cares? I'm not an anthropologist and really don't have much interest in the origins of trophy heads.

But I do care about the idea of the trophy hunt because it has come to embrace far more than collecting a record book sheep or antelope. Instead of an elk with antlers bigger than your mother-in-law's mouth, a trophy now may be a Giant Canada goose or a wild turkey or one deer a season instead of one a day. And the phrase ''quality experience'' has crept into the hunting lexicon.

I really don't think ''quality experience'' is a euphemism, a conservation department con to make a hunter think he's having a unique experience when all he really is having is an unsuccessful hunt. Pressures on our present resources, both land and wildlife, are so great that there have to be strict limits on game taken. And, in order to make the hunt worthwhile, the hunter must derive satisfaction from other aspects of the experience besides the kill.

Most of today's upland gunners don't know that there were many more species of birds hunted a century ago than there are now. We've subtracted a number of game birds, added but few. The most notable addition, of course, is the pheasant and the most notable subtraction is the passenger pigeon. Everyone has read about poor old Martha, the last surviving passenger pigeon, whose death in the Cincinnati Zoo in 1914 was a media event. She was the final whisper of the thundering roar that was the continental flock of colonial days. The passenger pigeon was the classic example of wildlife exploitation gone mad.

In 1871, just one nesting area in Wisconsin covered 850 square miles and held an estimated 136 million birds. Only 43 years later, the last pigeon, poor old Martha, died in the zoo. That's incredible.

It didn't help Martha that a nation of woodchoppers scythed nesting and roost cover, nor that the beech nut, a diet staple, declined as beech forests were felled. Historians theorized that tornados or other natural phenomena booted the passenger pigeon into eternity, but you can blame it on man. There were floods, tornadoes and forest fires before the shooters, netters, trappers, snarers and woodcutters . . . and there continued to be pigeons.

The historic gunner had plenty of species to choose from if he wiped out one. He always could flush up a robin or visit a nearby cow pasture for a bit of wing-shooting on meadow larks. Both were recognized game species as late as the turn of the century in some southern states. Today's hunter, whether through education or legal proscription, will not endanger any bird through overhunting.

Not to say the danger today isn't man, but it is man armed with a bulldozer, not a 12-bore. I lose my cool at the anti-hunt crew not because they oppose hunting, but because they lay blame in all the wrong places. They're incredibly short-sighted and, even more the pity, don't care to learn. A long time ago, Theodore Roosevelt carried on a feud with a minister named Long, a leading anti-hunting crusader. Rev. Long chastized Roosevelt, the only real conservationist president we've ever had, as ''a man who takes delight in whooping through the woods killing everything in sight.''

TAKING THE BIRDS FROM THE TRAP-NET & CAGING THEM.

Here a gang of passenger pigeon trappers net and crate live passenger pigeons, perhaps for use in pigeon shooting matches. The shame of if was not so much in that it happened, but that it fostered a contemptuous attitude toward game that, to an uncomfortable extent, persists today. Exploitive hunting cannot survive today—and unless we develop an ethical regard for our prey, hunting may be in for serious times.

No doubt Cleveland Amory and the other self-styled wildlife experts of today would applaud Rev. Long as an elder of their tribe. Extravagant fiction is far more entertaining than flameless fact and, after all, Rev. Long wrote stories about wolves leading lost children to safety. Roosevelt summed it up: "The men who misinterpret nature and replace fact with fiction undo the work of those who in the love of nature interpret it aright."

Those who "humanize" nature do it disservice, whether it is someone like Rev. Long and his altruistic wolves, or the Walt Disney studios whose "true life adventures" are highly entertaining, superbly photographed, but which leave many people with the feeling that Charley, the Good-hearted Antelope or whatever is lovable, highly intelligent and . . . well, human. So hunting antelope seems like a crime against person. And the work of the antihunter is that much easier and the lot of the real antelope that much tougher.

How often do Amory and his like attack the developers who are destroying—not harvesting, but destroying—wildlife? Amory subtitled his anti-hunting book *The Incredible War On Wildlife*. Yet no wildlife species is endangered because of sport hunting. Every species on the various rare and endangered lists is there because of other pressures by man—man's intrusions, demands or manipulations, not his hunting.

Let's put the blame where it belongs, hunter and anti-hunter alike. If we lose our wildlife, if we no longer have decent places to go and be alone with the breezes, if hunting declines, it is our own fault. It is the fault of every one of us who opts for personal comfort at the expense of a finite earth.

We can't expect antelope, Disney or otherwise, to play atop the rubble of a strip-mined plains. We can't expect eagles to soar majestically when their brains are seething in pesticide residues. We can't expect endangered Indiana bats to breed in caves covered by many feet of impounded water. We can't expect pheasants to survive bitter winters huddled in the lee of a dirt clod.

I wish all landowners had time to be hunters, for then they might begin to develop a special affinity for the land that does not involve altering it.

Many non-hunting landowners do feel a love for the dirt that crumbles between their fingers, but others own the land, but are not of the land. They don't feel the loss of the quail in the slicked-off fencerow, the absence of the woodcock in the bladed-off sprout patch, the missing pheasant on the fall-plowed cornfield.

Idle land? Oh, hardly. It just doesn't grow corn or cows. But it breeds life at a frantic pace. Idle? Oh, hardly!

The problems wildlife has faced in this country are nothing new. One small town newspaper near my home carried the following time in its "100 Years Ago" column:

"Our genial young friend, Frank _____, only killed 43 wild geese this winter. His excuse for not killing a greater number is that he has been very busy clearing land."

Close to 300 years of wildlife exploitation was summed up in that brief, jocular note. Man's whole attitude toward wildlife is both explicit and implicit. The boss hunter is the one who can kill the most, never mind whether he needs it, never mind whether the resource can stand the pressure. Wildlife is bounty, free for the taking. This piratical approach to wild game is endemic in North America. There is no widespread feeling of stewardship for what is in the forest and the field. If wildlife ever gets on a cash crop basis, as it is in Europe, perhaps we will begin to take as much care of it as we do of the genetic freak that used to be maize.

Landowners will invest in a cash crop. But the second step (and, by far, the biggest one) is to breed an ethical regard for that crop. Somehow, we have to convince landowners that deer jump fences, that raccoons go under them and that even though you pays your money, you don't necessarily get your choices. In other words, even though a landowner builds a brushpile and plants a food plot, he can't expect the quail covey that roosts and feeds there to be his alone. It can and probably will fly across the fence and be decimated by his neighbor's hunters.

No man owns the birds that fly, the beasts that prowl. No more than he owns the air or the water. Yet, just as he logically should have deep concern for the air and water if for no other reason than his own physical well-being, then he also should have deep concern for the wildlife for his mental well-being.

There is a deep-rooted feeling in many Americans that wild things are somehow tainted. Euell Gibbons was considered a genial crazy because he ate wild plants, nevermind that almost everything he enjoyed (not ate, but enjoyed) was richer in taste, vitamins and overall nutrition than almost any plant found sprawling limply in the supermarket bins.

The average cottontail rabbit spends a life of idyllic splendor, nibbling succulents, waxing fat on the finest of foods. He exercises only when forced to by the busy teeth of some predator. His flesh is tender and tasty. His lolloping domestic cousin long has been a favorite on the tables of the world's gourmets. Yet most housewives consider a wild rabbit as dirty and rank.

Let that same housewife sometime go out to a feed lot and watch the hogs rooting in six inches of pig manure, cheek to jowl, tight as ticks on a junkyard dog, and then ask her if she prefers a slice of ham to a wild cottontail. Drag in a woodcock with its dark meat and rich flavor and she'll look at you as if you were asking her to eat a Norway rat. Attitudes . . .

So we need to change our thinking toward both the land itself and the game we pursue.

But food for the body is only an economic justification for keeping wildlife on the land. Food for the soul is what we're really talking about and that's where criticism cuts close to the bone, for no man likes to be told his soul food lacks nourishment.

We are an impatient society and a tree is a very painstaking organism. We dislike waiting fifty years for a tree to reach its glory. Far better that we knock the tree down and plant a cornstalk that leaps to bloom in a season. We don't plant for our children. We plant for our pocketbook. Part of the reason is an economic system that taxes a landowner the same whether he's growing quail or wheat. So, until quail per acre realize income comparable to fifty bushels of wheat an acre, the farmer has a perfect right (in fact, a common sense obligation) to plant wheat or be thought daft. Since quail isn't likely ever to realize the revenue that a farm crop can, the obvious answer is to levy taxes according to the real value of the land, not its potential. If a man chooses to plant trees (or not to knock down the ones already there), he shouldn't have to pay for this aberration with cornfield taxes.

Much of the so-called anti-hunting sentiment is actually anti-hunter. Most of it is earned. Landowners have more patience than I would with hunters who act like the Mongol hordes on someone else's land. We must do everything we can to keep from giving the anti-hunters (or the anti-hunting group) ammunition with which to destroy us. Any upland bird hunter who does not belong to at least one conservation oriented group is leaning on his oar. It doesn't matter whether it's a local sportsman's club or one of the national groups. They all do something to protect and enhance our sport and they all are fueled by member money. Unfortunately, some local sportsmen's clubs become mere social groups, more dedicated to putting booze where their mouth is instead of money.

I got to thinking about some of our ethical problems one day when the birds weren't where they were supposed to be and I spent considerable time sitting on a log. And talking ethics is like wading quickmud for a soapbox revolutionary—ask any minister. But I came up with a personal list of hunter attitudes commonly encountered that need changing if we want to retain hunting. The list probably isn't complete and, like my files, my tax records and my life, is in no discernible order:

1. The feeling that game is "mine." "My bird, my deer, my goose . . ." It's

a common locution, often not intended to mean what it says. Game belongs only to the State in this country and then only for purposes of regulation, not dispensation. Game belongs to itself—not us.

2. The ultimate goal is the limit. Limits are increasingly rare and, in many cases, the limits themselves are attenuated. It's a case of more hunters, fewer acres. Limits are wonderful to reach, but the hunter who is satisfied only when he has killed a limit is a hunter whose outdoor experience is severely constricted. Bad days for him really are bad days, rather than days when the shooting may have been poor, but the company was good.

3. Stocking game creatures solves all problems.

4. Land can be treated casually. Just because a woodlot isn't tidy, a hedgerow isn't trimmed doesn't mean no one cares about it. Just because fence wire is rusty doesn't mean it's abandoned. Just because no one is around doesn't mean a hunter can act brainlessly. A landowner's Back Forty is as important as his living room. You wouldn't trash one; don't trash the other.

5. Easier is better. Too many modern hunters feel it's foolish to walk somewhere when you can rodeo an off-trail vehicle there. You appreciate what you work for and I think the appreciation is directly proportional to how hard you work. Technological advance, which smooths out the knots of a hunt, easily can dilute its keen pleasure.

6. Finally and most important, the feeling that a hunter needs to apologize for being a hunter. Nonsense! Anti-hunting advocates have a perfect right to be anti-hunting, but no right at all to impose their views on anyone else.

A few years ago, sitting by a campfire, my back propped against a tree trunk, listening to a barred owl gurgle and waiting for the moon to rise, I took a pencil stub to a ratty old notebook and came up with some thoughts on why I was there . . .

Smell the respiration of the earth. Can't you smell it! It's composed of starlight and moonglow and things growing.

It's the breath of life out there and you're part of it! Never mind that your old senses have gotten jaded by air conditioning and gas heat and the bland smell of easy living . . . when have you smelled grass growing or crabapples in a spring woods?

You'll never smell it unless you get out there and sniff, fill your nose with the rich stuff of the outdoors, the heady aroma of dead hickory roasting on a cold night's campfire.

Sometime stick your nose right down in a bed of moss under a centenarian oak tree and inhale the black, moist loamy smell of cool spring earth. Beets kind of taste that way, but much food loses that close contact with the earth that grew it, after it's packaged and processed and chemicalled.

Smell the cold coat of a Brittany after an eight-hour hunt through the briar hells and fencerows of December. Smell cows gathered around a hay rick, their breath silver in the gray dawn light.

Hearing? Can you hear the outdoors? Sure you can. Listen to cicadas buzz or barred owls chortle. Listen to the suck and bubble of a river snag caught by the current, playfully ducked time and again through the long hours. Listen to the earth wake in the early morning. Listen to crows rally at gray false dawn. Listen to redbirds taking over the day shift from the nightcallers. Listen to a gobbler's electric challenge. Listen to the steam whistle snort of an alarmed deer, invisible in the last moments of night. Listen to the crunching patter of sleepy squirrels in dry old leaves. Hear the sloshing roll of a big bass as it intercepts a burbling surface lure in the dark of the moon. Hear the thin, icy scream of a red-tailed hawk, exulting in its ability to scribe geometric arcs in a pale blue sky.

Taste? Of course you can taste the outdoors. There's the mellow delicacy of morel mushrooms dipped in eggs and crushed crackers, fried over a spluttering backpack stove. There's the sweet flavor of bluegill filets from fish scarcely out of deep, cold lake water. There's the taste of woodsmoke from a campfire, rich and sharp in the mouth and on the tongue. There's liver from a fresh-killed deer, heaped with onions and fried in old, seasoned ironware. There's the sweet crispness of the ends of timothy, plucked and chewed in a September dove field. There's the tart, hot gush of a sun-warmed tomato.

There's the salty taste of sweat that tumbles down your face on a hot day when the outdoors makes you suffer a bit for its bounty. There's the rush of flavor from a ripe persimmon, soft and silvered with winter's first icy breath.

The taste of the outdoors is in the snap of a crisp apple and its winey juice. It's in the meat of a walnut, mahogany on the outside, white-fleshed, streaked with yellow fat, succulent and rich on the inside. You can taste the outdoors in the wild, smoky flavor of hickory-smoked woodcock, shot amid a tangle of sycamore and grapevines, along a river bench on a cold October day as crisp as clean white wine.

Can you touch the outdoors? I think you can. Feel the rough, wet back of an old oak tree after a summer shower. Feel the first drops of rain as they spatter the river and veil the next bend. Feel the soft, silky ears of your dog as he nestles next to you on the long, dark ride home after a November quail hunt. Feel the warm, sleek feathers of a cock pheasant which rose all fuss and flash from a foxtail patch and fell amid his own shimmering plumage.

Feel clean air going right to the bottom of your lungs as you get your second wind on a long climb up a mountain that puts you with the thin, sharp air and the unseen gods. Feel pleasant fatigue weighing you down as you slouch in front of a campfire, snug in warm clothing, watching sparks eddy and leap. Feel the icy shock of a headlong dive into a spring pool after a hot, tiring hike, the pure, sweet taste of the water rinsing the sweat and dust of the trail from you.

Feel the satin grip of an old fly rod, feel it flex its muscle behind you as it prepares to lay a line on the water with the sinuous grace of a ballet dancer.

Look at the outdoors. You can see it. But only if you lift your eyes to more than the eddying Bivisible, the distant wheeling flock of pintails, the setter flowing over cornshucks in the chill gold light of an autumn afternoon. There's more than those things, though they are part of it. There's a stream buoying that Bivisible, pulsing crystal-cold from beneath fern-shaded mosses. There's a deer, muzzle down in the arrowroot growing in the next eddy. There's a mink, slipping like a brown shadow along the stream edge, eyes glinting with the pale fire of the professional killer. There's cardinal flower, a ruby in a green velvet setting.

There's sunrise and cold mist in the duck marsh. There's a black lab shivering uncontrollably because he, too, sees those distant incoming ducks. There's the familiar stubbly chin of the guy you hunt with, the seamed face, crinkled at the eyes from squinting into a thousand sunrises—a long way, now, from the kid you played basketball with in tiny, hot high school gyms. There's the old Model 12 that belonged to your Dad, and the never-finished pain of knowing that he is not there anymore to share dawns and the sibilant hiss of wings overhead.

There's black earth under the cornstalks, rimed with frost where the sun's gentle touch hasn't yet crept. There's the defiant fire of October trees ending their growing year with a gaudy display before going into the silent sleep of winter. There is the lazy fall of fat snowflakes, the chill shine of stars on a winter night.

There's a dog on point, his every fiber taut. There's a covey flush, frozen for a millisecond against a gray November sky. There's a canoe at the base of a towering cliff whose rocks are streaked with leached minerals into a red-and-black abstract. There's eggs popping in an old black fry pan over an orange bed of coals. There's all this and much more.

These are the moments that shall melt the frost of my years when the future is now. I sometimes wonder what it will be like in those days of infirmity, if any, when I no longer am able to trudge the Green Hills or beat the gumbo at its tenacious worst. Will my bird dog, vibrant with the hot blood and tireless muscles of youth, wonder why I no longer pick up the stained old shell vest and the worn double-barrel? Can I explain to him so he'll understand? Can I explain to myself?

I don't know if it's better not to dwell on what will be, but it certainly is nothing to anticipate. Far better to extract from each sweet moment its full measure of rich joy, to fix in memory the golden colors, the piercing exultation. Far better to have gone than never to have gone at all—for when the burden of years, the chains of infirmity become too heavy, it is too late to retrace the long road to yesterday.

29

Boots, Clothing and Equipment

Footgear can make or break a hunting trip . . . or the hunter's ankle. A simple blister five miles from the car can become a raging wound by day's end that'll take a third of the season to heal. And hot, sweaty feet are miserable, but cold feet are worse.

BOOTS

Good boots, first of all, are going to cost some money. Be prepared for that. And if at all possible, try the boots on. If you do buy by mail, don't hesitate to exchange the boots if they don't fit perfectly. Wear your hunting socks when you make a foot tracing. And break your boots in well before you take them on a hunt. There are those who advocate soaking the boots, then wearing them dry, the theory being they mold to your feet better. I've never done it.

Begin treating your boots immediately. I use Sno-Seal. Take it along on extended hunting trips. Leather benefits from a washing with saddle soap.

I haven't had much luck with the so-called birdshooter boots, the ultra-light boots, often made of kangaroo skin. They're comfortable, but mine have worn out far sooner than I thought they should have. I'd rather clomp around with a bit more weight, but a far tougher boot.

Boots and sometimes gloves are the two items of hunting apparel where the hunter needs to open his mouldy old purse. You can wear an old coat, pants too ratty to use as latrine mops—but footgear and handgear must be high quality.

One of the low points in my life, both literally and figuratively, was when I slipped on snow halfway into a steep-sided gully, fell to the bottom, sprained my ankle and nearly destroyed my fine double on the only protruding rock in loam-rich north Missouri. I fell because I had slick-soled boots.

In my book, lug soles are almost mandatory for most upland hunting conditions. They grip and don't slip in snow, ice or, almost as bad, dry leaves. But you'll say things to them that would make a mule blush when you wear them down a muddy fencerow. Lug soles pick up enough mud to plant a garden that would feed a family of four and, after carrying around a myriagram of malicious mud on each foot for an hour or so, you'll think your legs have petrified.

Seven-inch boots are about right unless you're in snake country. I've hunted snakey areas, but never have come crossways with a venomous reptile. Rattlers are the ones to watch for. Copperheads strike low and almost any footgear will turn their rather short fangs, but a rattler can nail you all the way to the knee.

Snakes are a warm-weather problem, which for the bird hunter translates to very early bird seasons (turkeys or doves), or southern climes. Snakes are denned up for most of the colder seasons, but are busy denning in at least part of those seasons.

I don't want to make a thing of snakes—I've never met anyone who has been bitten by one while bird hunting, but I know two hunters who have had bird dogs bitten, both in western states. Both dogs survived after quite a lot of pain. There's no practical way to keep dogs from being bitten by snakes except to leave them at home when you're hunting snaky areas.

Hunters should follow the usual rules of caution in snake country. Walk noisily and slowly enough that the snake can get out of the way. Don't step over logs or rocks; rather up on them, then look on the other side. In rocky areas, don't stick your hands or feet in places where you can't see, especially on ledges or in crevices.

Your chances of dying from snakebite are far less than from a lightning strike— some 8,000 people are bitten in the United States annually and perhaps a dozen die. But the pain and recuperation certainly will end your hunting season.

CLOTHING

Most bird hunting pain is caused by the multiplicity of thorny plants that inhabits bird country. Common sense dictates you don't traverse a multiflora rose hedge while wearing a goose down jacket, though I know a hunter who once lost his cool when his dog misbehaved and chased the slinking cur down to counsel with him. Only when what he thought was a sudden snow squall turned out to be expensive prime goose fluff did he realize he'd turned his Eddie Bauer parka into high-priced rags.

My personal choice for a garment to carry game and shells is a vest rather than a coat. First of all, most coats are brown, and I came near shooting a friend last season as he stood in chest-high brown grass wearing brown hunting clothing. I swear I never saw him as I leveled down on a low-flying quail. Fortunately, he was safely to one side of the shot, but well within the field of vision. Would I have seen him had he been directly in front of me, beyond the quail? We both hope so.

Smart hunters wear bird pants, the kind with a tough leather or briar-resistant facing. Being a basic dummy and a cheapskate to boot, I usually wear scruffy blue jeans and finish the bird season with legs that look like a road map of one of the smaller eastern states.

Temperature controls what you wear on your upper body. Only rarely is it cold enough to wear down or other really cold weather gear. You send a lot of calories to their doom while battling blowdowns or arguing with briar patches and, no matter the air temperature, you'll stay warm with a wool shirt and a windbreaker. Sometimes a down vest beneath the windbreaker will do when you start out.

A good warm red cap keeps your head warm and when you realize that up to 75 percent of the heat your body loses is through your head and shoulders, you see how important a good cap is. If the weather is merely chilly, I wear only an orange head band to keep my ears warm. If it's really cold, I wear a hunter orange stocking cap, the kind that converts to a face mask in the most bitter of conditions.

Of all the areas where misery strikes, the hands and ears are the most likely. If there is such a thing as a good, cheap shooting glove, I've not found it. Mittens are far warmer than gloves, but are clumsy. Wool mittens can pick up moisture, yet stay warm, but the material gets slick and I've lost some shots because I couldn't get the damn safety slid off.

The best glove I ever used was an old Army combination of a wool glove inside a leather shell. These used to be issued to soldiers and may still be—I look for them in surplus stores, but never find them. The wool liner is easy enough, but the leather shell isn't. Whatever combination you use (and a glove inside a mitten may be the best), make sure it all fits as loosely as possible. Anywhere there is a constriction, it cuts down on the blood flow and you'll get cold.

If you do suffer numbed fingers, pause for a few moments, put your bared right hand under your left armpit and your bared left hand down your britches to clutch your crotch. These are the two warmest spots on your body and you'll quickly thaw your frozen hands. Of course, you have to endure the japes of your hunting partners, but take your choice—cold hands or locker room comedy.

By way of review, let's take the Complete Hunter (You, there! Straighten up!) and work from the head down:

HAT: Anything blaze orange for all upland birds save turkeys and doves. Camouflage or brown for them. Consider a balaclava or face mask for cold weather. Keep your ears warm.

GLASSES: Shooting glasses probably are wise, though I've never used them— but I also have come near poking out an eye a few times.

UPPER BODY: I'm partial to a short-sleeved turtle neck as an undershirt (keeps the neck warm). If you wear a wool outer shirt, the undershirt keeps the wool itch from driving you nuts. I prefer chamois shirts for an outshirt, though wool is warmer. Everything should be hunter orange or at least a bright color.

PANTS: I suppose birdshooter britches are ideal to keep you from the prickly caress of briars, though I've never had the scratch (no pun intended) to afford them—we're talking $30 to $50. I wear blue jeans or occasionally a pair of good ol' bib overalls. Fishnet or other longjohn bottoms are good for turkey hunting where you sit for long periods, but usually too hot for a walking hunt.

BOOTS: Some swear by the rubber bottom/leather upper bird boot, the L.L.

Bean Maine Hunting Shoe being the best-known example. I've always worn full leather.

SOCKS: I like ragg wool. Fortunately, I've never had any foot problems and am not prone to blisters.

ACCESSORIES

Seems like all God's chillun got some kind of weak joint—knee, ankle, whatever. It helps to wrap the offending hinge with elastic bandage or to tape it before the hunt.

Moleskins or Band Aids are good to have on long trips where you may not find a handy store. They should be part of a rudimentary first-aid kit that includes treatment for cuts and scratches, perhaps aid for poison ivy, an elastic bandage for strains or sprains, eye drops and, above all, whatever pain reliever works for you. Other things will occur to you, including any prescription drugs you may need.

It doesn't take long to train a dog to come to a whistle and so save your voice. I use an Acme Thunderer, the best-known and probably the loudest.

There are a jillion compasses, but one of the nicest models slips on shirt or jacket pocket so all you need to do is glance down to see your direction.

Carry a canteen in hot, arid country.

You should have matches and a pocketknife.

In extreme country you probably should have a space blanket in case you get lost.

Take a small cooler, both for food, drink and the like, but also for transporting game home during warm weather. Be sure to carry plenty of watertight, capacious plastic bags so game isn't water damaged by melting ice.

Fruit juices are marvelous during a lunch break or when you're thirsty. Something slightly tart such as cranberry/apple is better to me than a sweet juice. I won't tell you what to eat, but peanut butter and honey is high energy food. Caramels offer instant energy both to dog and man. Lemon drops are good for people.

I carry high-quality dog food packages for a midday snack and a plentiful supply of dry dog food for day's end. You should have a leash for those rare occasions when you're where you don't want your dog suddenly to bolt across four lanes of rush-hour traffic after a rabbit. Be sure to take a bowl for dog water in hot weather.

Dove hunting calls for a small seat, a fold-up camp stool, for example. For turkey hunting, sew a pad to the bottom of your hunting coat so it can hinge down to sit on or up against your back for walking.

Other items that should be with you include a flashlight and spare batteries and bulb and a wind-up alarm clock. I wouldn't be without a book to read.

You should have a pocket notebook and pencils (pens run dry). You also should have a camera. More about each of these items in a moment.

You should have a minimum of one complete set of dry clothing, plus rain gear. Rain chaps are cheap insurance against dew-soaked pants.

Carry boot dressing and gun cleaning equipment. A can of WD-40 or its equivalent is vital. If it's safe to do so, consider leaving your guns locked in your car during very cold weather. This minimizes condensation on the cold metal in the warmth of your room. At least don't leave guns in a case—get them out and wipe them down with oil.

Now, on the notebook—every shooter should keep a notebook or diary of his hunting for a variety of reasons, the most compelling of which is nostalgia. But in addition you can, with a bit of ingenuity, cram those pages with practical information. Small sketch maps pinpoint the location of coveys or other game hotspots that memory, being human, may misplace. I long ago learned that I could think of a twenty-five word or less solution for every one of man's problems, from international strife to overactive bladder—but if I don't write it down instantly, I'll forget it within an hour.

You can list information on shot and powder loads, hunting theories, dog training tips, weather and biological information. Spare pages are for writing down directions to unfamiliar hunting areas and for exchanging names and addresses with the fine folk you meet along the way.

Not the least of the uses of a conscientious diary is to settle arguments and, especially, those disputes with money riding on the outcome. You can't settle the eternal question of who is the better shot by a diary but you damn sure can prove who shot what and with what success on a given hunt.

PHOTOGRAPHY

The late Don Wooldridge, longtime photographer for the Missouri Conservation Department, and a dear and sadly missed friend, told me he considered it impossible to hunt and photograph simultaneously, so he quit hunting. I've tried both for years, but while I don't consider it impossible, it is so nearly that as to be utterly impracticable. You must hunt with patient friends, for the moment when the dog is on point and the hunters eager to move in is the moment when you must say, "Wait till I get focussed!" If the birds flush unsaluted, you're likely to wear your focus ring for a necklace.

There are two elements to good photography. First is a good single-lens 35mm reflex camera and second is knowing how to use it. Leica probably makes the finest 35mm camera, but Nikon, Canon, Minolta and Pentax all are well-known and reliable. However, were I to start over, I would get an Olympus OM-1, the first of the small-format cameras. It's portable, tough and optically good. It started a revolution in camera size and is relatively inexpensive. Olympus (as do all the others) now makes models that do everything but herd sheep and drive you home when you get drunk, but the OM-1, which demands that the photographer know at least the elementary relationships between shutter speed and lens openings, is a bargain. I don't own one, so I can say this based on my knowledge of the machine, not because I got one free or got paid to say this.

Now, a man ought to own a standard lens (usually 50mm), a set of extension tubes that match the camera's built-in light meter and a zoom lens of medium range. With the extension tubes you can boost magnification of the long lens or use the standard lens for extreme closeups. Vivitar makes a set of three for about $60. Vivitar also makes an 80–210mm zoom lens that is good enough optically for any but the most demanding pro. It sells for about $280. The OM-1 lists for about $250.

PERMITS

Finally, a word about permits. First, make sure you have one, then make sure it's the right one. Be sure to investigate buying the permit ahead of time.

Some states allow nonresidents to buy permits by mail. Write the state conservation department. Once, after a seventeen-hour drive to extreme northern Minnesota, three of us had to visit several permit outlets before we found one with nonresident permits—and we got the last three.

Think ahead. If you happen to arrive after store closing hours, the best you can hope for is a couple of lost hours the next morning while you track down a permit. The worst is that you won't find any. If you can't buy ahead, find out where permits are likely to be available along your route and begin searching as soon as you cross into your hunting state.

When you're writing for information, whether it's to the state agency or private individuals, include a self-addressed, stamped envelope. The state can afford the return postage, but the impression you make on whoever gets saddled with your request is better if you're thoughtful enough to pay the freight.

Also, consider spending a few bucks to have personalized stationery printed. If you belong to The Ruffed Grouse Society, National Wildlife Federation, Audubon Society, Izaak Walton League, Sierra Club, Ducks Unlimited, etc., mention it on the letterhead. Make your letterhead simple—name, address, telephone number, perhaps an outdoor motif (a woodcock, pheasant, quail, etc.). Don't brag about what a joiner you are. Just let it be known you do care about the outdoors.

30

The Wild Feed

I, in company with those oft-embarrassed hunters who are prone to brag about their shooting prowess, have had to eat crow often. It's a figurative meal. We all know what the phrase means—or at least its implication.

But who among us literally has eaten crow? Wild game cookery is the oldest form of flesh preparation; there were no domesticated saurians in the Miocene Epoch and if a man wanted a hot sandwich, he necessarily had to stalk and kill it first. Yet, nowhere in my admittedly slender library of wild game cookbooks is there a recipe for crow. Surely somewhere in the literature is a formula for "Pan Fried Crow" or perhaps "Crow *avec Sauce Hollandaise.*"

The most voluminous cookbook I've seen, *Cooking Wild Game,* by Frank Ashbrook and Edna Sater, published in 1945, lists 432 recipes, but goes directly from Crawfish to Deer.

Cy Littlebee, whose faithful recipe contributors ate everything from groundhogs to muskrats, ignored crows studiously. So there apparently is no one dedicated to the delicate preparation of griskin of crow. Surely if people can eat snails, which I equate directly with the garden slug I once stepped on barefoot, they can eat crow without humiliation, indeed with satisfaction.

But, as it stands, the crow is the only animal written about in this book that does not regularly get taken home and eaten.

Game cookery, I have a gut feeling (no pun intended), is an art that has declined in recent years—or at least narrowed its scope. Maybe it's my imagination, but it seems that wild game feeds confine themselves more to the glamour species these days—deer, quail, turkeys and the more succulent of the grouses. No more the coon roast, nor the potted possum. Eat a groundhog! Sooner munch on a wharf rat!

Part of the problem is the life we lead, prepackaged and pasteurized. A plant isn't food until it has been ripped from the good earth by a ham-fisted machine, run through fourteen drenchings with gases and chemicals designed to enhance its color, preserve its texture and, for all I know, change its molecular structure. We get it after it has been shrouded in plastic and shipped halfway across the country.

When I was about seven years old, I watched my aunt preparing chickens for the table. The process did not consist of unwrapping the bird and removing the neatly packaged giblets from the body cavity. No, these birds were packaged in their feathers and there was a lot of blood and squawking connected with the event. It was not a pretty sight, but those birds, self-raised on a hardscrabble farm, had a flavor rarely matched on my table since.

They scratched in the dust with an enormous tom turkey who regarded young boys as fair game and terrorized me all one summer. Summer belonged to him, but Thanksgiving dinner belonged to me and whether the flavor of the bird was better because I knew I was extracting the ultimate revenge on my old enemy or not, I do know the bird was far superior to the superprocessed stuff of today.

Farm turkeys then were about one jump behind wild turkeys and the wild turkey is so far removed from the steroid-stuffed cardboard turkeys found in today's markets that there literally is no comparison. A generation of Americans have grown up celebrating Turkey Day without really knowing what a turkey tastes like. Their holiday bird never scratched for bugs, never ripened his flavor with acorns and shoots of native grass. Maybe that constant diet of pasty meat, hothouse tomatoes and exotic additives has turned us into a nation of eaters with no grit in our craw.

I'm not purist (or gourmet . . . or crazy) enough to eat woodcock with the guts intact, the way historic gourmands did, but wild meat holds no terrors for me. Save when some hunter's awkward knife marinates my venison steak with bile or coats my squirrel stewmeat with hair, I *like* wild meat. I've had bear chili and moose stew, deer steak and antelope sausage, eaten nearly all the edible game birds. I liked them.

Not that there aren't dishes that give me pause—I once ate a raccoon and the pieces seemed to expand in my mouth and go down as if I were swallowing golf balls. Perhaps that was because I'd kept raccoons in my home and the thought of eating one was sort of like dining on one of my Brittanies. I try not to be sentimental about wildlife. After all, the rattlesnake fails to see how cute and cuddly a baby rabbit is as he swallows it butt-first.

Speaking of rattlesnake, I once ate a piece of one that incautiously slithered beneath the moving tire of a car driven by one of our turkey camp hunters. Despite a lifetime of reading that rattlesnake tastes like chicken and is a delicacy, I must report it tasted like old garden hose and like to made me head for the bushes. Alligator tail, however, is superb.

I don't think I could handle possum or groundhog, though I'm not averse to trying if a real squatter-shack chef prepares it, and I doubt there is anyone alive who can fix a coot and make it edible. I have one mudhen to my credit, if that is the word (and it isn't), but it was a case of mistaken identity—the bird was a teal in the air, a coot when it hit dead in the water.

I've heard stories about how coots are wonderful eating "if you fix them right." One widely advertised recipe involves marinating the bird in Jack Daniels, throwing away the coot and eating the gravy.

Cy Littlebee, a wonderful old codger who was the alter-ego of Werner Nagel, one of the country's pioneer wildlife and conservation experts, once compiled a book of the favorite wild game recipes of Missouri's housewives for the Missouri Conservation Department. The book has been a steady seller for nearly thirty years. Among the recipes is one from "Miz Ann Vance from around Macon."

That was my mother and, having grown up eating goosemeat cooked by the recipe (and, on rare occasions, supplying the raw material), I can testify to the book's dedication to superior eating. Still, I approach with trepidation "Fried Coot and Gravy" or "Breast of Whitebill on Toast."

There is no lack of guidebooks to wild game preparation. Later on, I'm going to set up my ideal meal. It may not be yours. In fact, it may not always be mine either—but for someone bereft of imagination, without access to any cookbook, with a fistful of feathered creatures and a powerful hunger, it may turn a moment of despair into a memorable meal.

There is more to a wild game dinner than the wild game. Gnawing on naught but bird is the stuff of which cavemen are made, but not gourmets. Side dishes add scope, depth to your meal.

If you want to go entirely wild, you need Euell Gibbons' *Stalking the Wild Asparagus* (McKay, 1962) which has been through so many editions and price changes that you need a current price quote. Another standard is Bradford Angier's *Feasting Free on Wild Edibles* (Stackpole, 1972). Jan Phillips, a St. Louis schoolteacher, has written a fine book, *Wild Edibles,* which is available from the Missouri Conservation Department for $4.50. Most cooks will limit the wild part of the meal to the meat. So be it. But most of the wild edibles are relatively easy to identify and, I trust, no one is going to eat any given weed without a fair idea of its palatability or its toxicity.

However, many bird dishes fairly cry out for mushroom accompaniment. There's no problem if you stick with button mushrooms from the store. But there are some absolutely luscious mushrooms growing in the outdoors and most of them pop up during some bird season.

Even as I deliver encomiums about the wonders of mushrooms, I hasten to warn that they can kill you. According to reports (not from the survivors, since there rarely are any), the two deadliest mushrooms, called with chill accuracy the Destroying Angel and the Death Cup, are right tasty. But they cause an especially unpleasant death, involving such cheerful symptoms as cramps, vomiting and distorted vision. The liver falls apart and the victim dies in excruciating pain. The death rate is about 70 percent, considerably higher than that from rattlesnake bite, even more than the rate from the Indian krait, one of the world's most deadly snakes. Untreated, the death rate from black mamba bites is 100 percent—but you can treat the bites with antivenin. About all you can do for a victim of one of the deadly *Amanita* mushrooms is tell him jokes.

There are some fifty species of *Amanitas* growing in the United States, about half of which are poisonous, and often they grow cheek-by-jowl with edible mushrooms, which they sometimes resemble as well. Mushroom poisoning goes far back in history. Euripides wrote before Christ of a mother, daughter and two sons "destroyed by pitiless fate" after they ate mushrooms and "strangled by eating of them." The Emperor Claudius, stepfather of Nero, was supposedly a mushroom victim. Nicander of Colophon wrote about a cure potion which contained, among other items, the burned dung of domestic fowl. After you take that, you stick your finger down your throat and "vomit for the baneful pest." A case where the cure seems about as dreadful as the affliction.

Meadow mushrooms, wild cousin of the common commercial button mushroom, look much like *Amanitas,* but have pink or brown gills. *Never* eat a white-gilled, button-type mushroom. In fact, simply enough, never eat any mushroom you haven't identified thoroughly.

The reason I dwell on mushrooms is that they coexist with many game birds during much of the hunting season. Spring is the time of the morel mushroom, most delicious (and harmless) of all the wild mushrooms. No one who ever has seen a true morel can mistake it (even the poisonous false morel doesn't look enough like the true morel to be much of a problem). We Missourians hunt only a half-day for turkeys in the spring and that leaves the afternoon for mushroom hunting. Many a camp meal has been elevated by a mess of fresh-gathered morels.

And in the fall, through September and most of October, the woods are alive with the many fall mushrooms. Among them are meadow mushrooms, shaggy manes, puffballs, chanterelles—all eminently edible; all enough like poisonous varieties that you'd better know what you're doing. Orson K. Miller Jr.'s *Mushrooms of North America* (E.P. Dutton paperback, 1978, $8.95) is by far the finest of all the mushroom guide books.

While some side dishes to our wild meal could throw you a gastronomic knuckle ball, there is one case where the bird itself could give you the gastrointestinal gollywobbles. Grouse eating mountain laurel are reputed to become poisonous and Pennsylvania once banned from the market grouse that had fed on mountain laurel leaves. Dr. N. Schumaker, in the *North American Medical and Surgical Journal* in the 1870s, reported two cases of poisoning resulting from eating a ruffed grouse in the craw of which laurel leaves were found. The symptoms were nausea, temporary blindness, pain in the head, pallid countenance, cold extremities and a very feeble pulse. There's no doubt grouse can pack away mountain laurel leaves—it's a favored food. One grouse had a half pint of them jammed in his craw. The poison is andromedotoxin, which has caused death in livestock, though it doesn't bother grouse a bit. And it doesn't bother humans, either, the good Dr. Schumaker notwithstanding. Gardiner Bump, senior author of *The Ruffed Grouse* (New York Conservation Department, 1947), which is the definitive scientific book on the grouse, once ate two grouse that had been fed nothing but laurel leaves as part of an experiment. He suffered no ill effects and concluded that the claim of laurel leaf poisoning was false.

FIELD CARE AND PREPARATION

Quail expert Charley Dickey thinks it makes no difference whether you field-dress quail or not—he often leaves the ungutted birds in his game bag all day, even overnight if he's tired. He claims it makes no difference in the taste of the flesh. I've done it myself—but I still have some sort of esthetic reluctance to leave perforated intestines in a bird any longer than I need to, especially in hot weather. It takes all of fifteen seconds to field-dress a game bird. I have a knife with a bird hook on it. You're supposed to insert the hook in the bird's anus, twist it, and pull the intestines out with no muss, no fuss. Well, my experience is that the guts break, resulting in a bigger mess. Cut a slit in the skin just below the breast, being careful not to slice any organs, reach in with your fingers and pull out everything you can get hold of. Usually, this is the intestines, liver, gizzard. Don't worry about heart, lungs, whatever—they'll keep until you get home. Carry a cooler in all but the chilliest weather. Put the birds in sealed plastic bags and ice them down.

Comes time to further disrobe your hard-won quarry. Think of it as a seduction, a passionate, slow undressing that will lead you and your bird to a rapturous consummation at the dinner table orgiastic enough to bring a blush to the scandalized cheeks of Julia Child.

There probably are multiple ways to relieve a bird of unwanted parts, but here's the way I do it on everything from a dove to a turkey.

Take off the feet. On smaller game birds, break the leg bone where the feathering starts and cut off the leg from the shin down. Larger birds require cutting between the shinbone and the tarsus. This leaves you with the familiar drumstick.

If you extend the bird's wing, you'll find a web of skin on the forward edge of the wing between the shoulder joint and the next one out (what corresponds to the human elbow). Cut through the web to the elbow joint and remove the wing, either by twisting it off on smaller birds or cutting through the joint, as you did with the legs. (Leg and wing removal is an excellent way to cut yourself seriously, so be careful.)

Next, twist or cut the bird's head off. Most birds give you their heads rather easily; turkeys don't. Remember, in some states, when you're transporting game you are required by law to leave something attached—a wing, head or foot, for example—so the bird can be identified as a legal one if you're stopped.

I gave up picking birds long ago. I skin them. It's far less mess. I don't enjoy the skin that much. I don't think it necessarily leads to dry meat or loss of flavor or any of the familiar charges levied by those who consider a skinned bird an abomination. Picking is easier if you dunk the bird in hot (not boiling) water. Birds are pretty easy to pick when they're freshly killed, but most people prefer to hunt.

If you're going to skin the bird, start in the stomach region. Cut below the breastbone (the same cut you make to gut the bird). Most birds are thin-skinned enough that once you have a cut large enough to get your thumbs in, you can peel to either side, away from the ridge of the breastbone, toward the wings. Work the skin over the wing stubs and over the thighs. The back generally holds the skin most closely and you may tear skin or leave a feathered chunk of skin. Pull it off.

Rinse off any residual feathers. I usually remove the neck and tail stub. I also cut or strip off any heavy fat deposits. Almost inevitably, you'll find feathers driven into the flesh by shot. Pull or dig them out (and the shot, too, if you can find it).

Cut out any heavily bruised meat or make a relief cut to drain any hemorrhaged areas. Cut off any contaminated meat. Rinse the bird thoroughly. Use a finger or thumbnail to dig out lungs. Larger game bird livers are worth saving for use in gravy or, especially, with rice if you have a way to store them.

Freeze smaller birds—quail, doves, woodcock—in water. It's impractical to do so with larger birds, so plan to eat them within three to four months or they'll likely suffer freezer burn.

Tell you what. Some winter night, after the bird seasons have closed, invite your friends for a wild game dinner. Don't discard your bird-hunting buddies, but remember they are no strangers to wild game. Make a special effort to invite your non-hunting friends. Make a social event out of it. We did that last season—pooled wild game and held a dinner. There was venison, pheasant, quail, sharp-tailed grouse, dove and woodcock. It was a cold, sharp January night. The woodstove pulsed heat and the teakettle atop it whispered hot rumors.

We had home-grown music, scarcely less untamed than the simmering dishes on the table. Guitar, banjo, mandolin and the gut bucket, our washtub bass with a broomstick for a neck and a boot lace for a string.

There was venison stew and casseroled woodcock. The china was good, long in the family, its finish reticulated by the years. Rich aromas chased around the house, more ambitious than the hunting dogs who, now that season was done, lay near the stove, great canine sponges, soaking up heat and twitching their paws in somnambulant salute to hazily remembered hunts.

A lot went into the meal—long, leg-busting treks over the Dakota prairie, an icy morning in an Iowa cornfield, a moment of rare magic when the crosshairs settled on a fat young buck's shoulder, steaming days in the itch and glare of a dove field—plus the love and attention of the fine cooks who converted the meat to a meal. It was an earned meal. Browsweat is a fine seasoning.

The woodcock recalled the day Chip made the lovely point in the sycamore thicket . . . and . . . and . . . remember the Big Hole where the sharptails flushed wild? And . . . and . . . how hot it was the day we got the doves (and how, considering the cost of shells and the way we didn't shoot, each bird cost about $5). And . . . and . . . this pheasant is as fat as you'd expect an Iowa cornfed bird to be. Lordy, how the roosters poured out of that standing corn!

Memories. A fine sauce, seasoned with the fine dust of the prairies and the thin cold snow of the late season. And the dogs twitch in their warm sleep, noses astir with the scents from the kitchen.

So we put away the musical instruments and pick up plates and implements and the scents swirl around the kitchen and the fire hisses and the snow touches the window with feathery caress and the dogs search the shadows of their minds for the ghosts of yesterday's birds. . . .

Now comes the moment you have dreaded as if it were a hungry cannibal and you a casserole on the hoof. You are faced with a pile of naked dead birds and in a few hours will be feeding the mayor, whose wife just last week declared ringingly she thought it was disgusting and barbaric to eat wild meat; the minister, whose last sermon (that is, the last one you attended, just before the hunting season opened) was about the brotherhood of man and animal; the new neighbor lady who, as she sunbathed in the back yard late last summer just after she moved in, caused you to walk into the overhang on the dog pen and open a nasty three-stitch gash on your forehead.

In other words, it's a meal where you want to make a good impression. The suggestions to come assume you are entirely bereft of imagination, yet I hope there are few hunters who can't carry their sport into the kitchen or at least turn over the produce to their mates and have something good come of it.

If it is to be an intimate meal, use only one of the bird recipes with appropriate side dishes. George Bird Evans, in his fine book *The Upland Shooting Life* (Knopf, 1971), has several recipes for *grouse à deux,* as well as a choice of appropriate wine and even the proper Mahler symphonies (Second and Fifth) as dinner music.

But for a large group, a buffet with each of the birds prepared a different way seems appropriate.

RECIPES

LIBBY SCHWARTZ'S SMOKED TURKEY. Salt the bird inside and out. Use a smoke-cooker, preferably one with a built-in water pan so you don't have to open it to baste the bird (each time you do, you lose the smoke). Hickory, either green or cured hickory chips soaked in water, creates the delicious smoke. The turkey should be plucked, not skinned. The smoke-cooking should take about twelve hours for an average wild gobbler of eighteen pounds. Turn the bird once or twice and baste if necessary. When the bird's leg easily breaks back from the body, it's done. The skin will be black and disgusting-looking on the surface, but oh! that moist, pink inner meat will make both you and the preacher get religion. We like Durkee's Famous Sandwich and Salad Sauce as a dip for bite-sized pieces (use your fingers— God will forgive you). But you also can serve the turkey as a main course with barley or wild rice (see recipes) and any of the other side dishes. Have plenty of crisp white wine.

IRENE STARR'S PHEASANTS. Two pheasants, soaked overnight in salt water in the refrigerator. Drain and wash in cold water. Piece the birds and bone the breasts. Coat well with flour, salt and pepper to taste. Brown on both sides in medium hot oil. Remove from frying pan, put in roaster. Pour one can of cream of mushroom soup and one-third cup of water over the pieces, cover and bake at 350 degrees for one hour.

ELLIE JOHNSON'S DOVE. (This will work equally well for woodcock or snipe.) Dove gravy for twenty-four doves is made like this: Use enough bacon grease to cover the bottom of a nine-inch skillet one-half inch deep. As it heats, add enough flour to make a thick mixture (about two cups, sifted a little at a time, stirred constantly) until the mixture has a rich, dark-brown color. Set aside to cool, and ready birds. Salt and pepper each bird and place around the bottom of a dutch oven. Cut up two or three medium-sized onions to add to gravy. After gravy has cooled, reheat and add water a little at a time until desired consistency is reached (it should be thick, as doves thin it out some). Add onions, salt and pepper to taste, to hot, bubbling gravy mixture, then pour immediately over birds. Cook in oven at 325 degrees for about three hours. Add potatoes and carrots to dinner abut 1½ hours before removing from oven. If this is your only bird dish, allow three doves per guest. Consider a hearty red wine, since this is a lusty-flavored meal.

MARTY VANCE'S QUAIL IN CASSEROLE. Season six quail (doves, woodcock, snipe, etc.), either breasts or whole birds, with salt, pepper and any other desired seasonings. Place in a casserole dish with chopped onions and long-grain rice. Combine one can mushroom soup with ½ can of water and ½ can of sauterne wine. Pour over birds. Bake in low oven, about 250 degrees, for 2½–3 hours.

MARTY VANCE'S GROUSE IN A BAG.   Place two or three grouse in a large cooking bag (or separate them into smaller bags. Season with salt and pepper and a package of dry onion soup mix. Add ½ cup water and ½ cup sauterne wine. Close bag and place in deep pan. Place in oven at about 275 degrees and bake about three hours.

LIBBY SCHWARTZ'S BARLEY.   Cheap, tasty replacement for expensive wild rice. Use quick-cooking, not pearl barley. Cook according to recipe on box. Then, in a frying pan, melt ¼ pound oleo. Mix in diced onions, sliced mushrooms, sauté mixture a little. Add barley (or wild rice). Season with nutmeg, poultry seasoning, salt, black pepper and garlic salt. Be liberal. Barley is bland. Get mixture good and hot and serve with any of the birds.

WILD RICE.   Buy only genuine wild rice, not black paddy rice. Preparation is involved, but necessary. Wash rice thoroughly. Ten to twenty-four hours before serving, cover one cup rice with quart of boiling water. Let stand until about one hour before serving. Drain and cover again with boiling water, let stand twenty minutes. Drain, add boiling water to cover and two teaspoons of salt. Just before serving, drain thoroughly, season to taste.

VEGETABLES.   Give thought to pleasing colors as well as taste. Cranberries are superb with most game birds and add color as well. Green vegetables likewise add color, but some, such as broccoli, are tough to prepare. Lima beans are easy and tasty. Carrots (not diced) are good.

SALAD.   Rather than a green salad, which can overpower the taste buds, try a Jello salad with fruits (cranberries, oranges, especially) and nuts. Waldorf salad also makes a nice side dish.

IRENE STARR'S APPLE PIE.   Eight to ten apples, depending on size. Core and slice. Mix with one cup sugar, one teaspoon cinnamon, 2½ teaspoons corn starch, ½ teaspoon salt, ½ jigger bourbon whiskey. Put in pie crust, bake at 400 degrees until crust is brown, turn oven back to 375 and bake till apples are cooked—45 to 50 minutes. Top pie either with thin slices of good cheddar cheese or with vanilla ice cream.

WINES.   Find your own favorites (that's half the fun). Only injunction is that cheap wines are no bargain. I'm no wine expert and never will be, but good wine makes food taste better and adds immeasurably to a special evening. Riesling and chablis go well with bird meat. Fruity red wines are good with dark-meated, stronger-flavored birds. Dessert wines should be tartly sweet.

COFFEE.   We are believers in the coffee concentrate method—steep a pound of coffee in cold water for twelve hours, drain the resulting concentrate through a filter, then mix to taste with boiling water. There are several brands of such concentrators and the coffee is rich and free of acid taste.

What more can I say? Having gotten this far, you and your guests are replete. The Mayor's wife is back at the sideboard for thirds. The preacher wants to go hunting with you and the lady next door keeps licking her lips when she looks at the turkey . . . or at *you*.

Bon appetit!

31

The Decline and Fall
of the Hunting Shack

It has taken me a long time to get to old codgerdom, but I think I've finally made it. The smooth, unlined face that I peer blearily at each morning over the washbasin, that noble physiognomy that reminds one of Robert Redford with, perhaps, a sprinkling of Paul Newman (the ''one'' it reminds being me) showed up the other day in a harsh, grainy 11-by-14 photograph looking like Arthur Hunicutt with a fair sprinkling of Gabby Hayes pitched in like a forkful of barn stall residue.

Well, if I gotta be one, I'm gonna enjoy it.

Old codgers get to grump and grumble a lot—it's in the charter—and allow as how things ain't what they used to be. I'd like to get stiff in the joints, but the problem is that most of the joints I used to get stiff in have been torn down to make way for supermarkets.

There is an American prejudice against anything old, especially if it also is decrepit. Since I am approaching both of these conditions at flank speed, it worries me. Thinking back over the years, if I discount familial high points (marriage, five births, getting a new bird dog pup), and a couple of parties that stand out clearly in my memory, at least until about 11 p.m., it seems that much of the fun of my life has taken place in and around hunting shacks. And ''They'' are flattening my old shacks—or, worse yet, upgrading them.

Kids today don't even fish with solid steel casting rods. They're overloaded with gadgets like double-barreled shotguns where one barrel slipped and fell under the other one, instead of laying there side by side the way God intended it to be.

Today's kids just don't know what it's all about. They don't have hunting shacks. Oh, they may call them hunting shacks if they have some fancy place out in the woods, but what they call a shack is not what I call a shack. There is shag carpet on the floor which, admittedly, soaks up beer a good deal more effectively than cracked linoleum. But our old shack had the advantage of senility sag, so that a beer spilled anywhere in the room would run to the center, the lowest spot, where it could be mopped conveniently or, as happened more often, completely ignored until it dried to a sticky paste that caught stray feathers and lint.

The real hunting shack is a very special place. It has aromas (some call them odors and realists call them smells) and atmosphere that are not to be found anywhere else on earth.

Some of my old hunting shacks simply have collapsed, victims of architectural arthritis. Others have been razed to make way for rows of soybeans while one, my favorite, has been rejuvenated and turned into, good Godalmighty, a home! A home, where normal humans live in comfort, where the stove works and there are no muddy footprints on the floor. There are no quail feathers eddying in the dust that lies windrowed along the baseboards. In fact, there's no dust at all.

How can it continue to be a hunting shack without being dirty? I don't mean squalid dirty, but dirty-crusted with the mud of duck marshes, the gumbo of quail fluids. The true hunting shack is stuccoed together with the healthy muds of a thousand days afield. As unkempt as they are, you'll not find festering disease, nor plague-ridden vermin in a hunting shack. I don't believe I ever saw a rat or a mouse in one of them, though they may be there, carrying on their clandestine activities circumspectly, never quite eating or defecating their way into public view.

There are other things you'll not see in an authentic hunting shack—someone taking a bath, a made bed, low-calorie food, full bottles of anything, elementary kitchen sanitation, people without long underwear on, new guns, or a television set that shows anything other than Lawrence Welk apparently entertaining in a Dakota blizzard, calendars with anything other than (1) a hunter and a setter reacting to a covey rise or (2) a nubile maiden wearing a brilliant smile and nothing else.

God alone knows how wives think their husbands exist on trips to the old hunting shack. No one can explain the magic of holing up in a shack so disordered a Mississippi sharecropper would recoil in disgust. My wife and I have shared many wilderness experiences, including a traumatic anniversary date to view a male ruffed grouse drumming. The outing was made traumatic by the fact that we got lost. We have backpacked and canoed together and she'll do to take along—but not to my hunting shack. Call it male chauvinism if you wish, but I can't visualize my wife or any other Miss/Mrs/Ms of my acquaintance crouched around an old library table that lists so badly that if you set a martini olive on the high side, it will roll onto the floor on the other side. Of course, there are no martini olives in my hunting shack on which to test this theory. Anyone who would drink martinis in a hunting shack also would wear pink underwear.

Supermarket beer and very good bourbon curried with water pumped cold from a fifty-year-old dug well is what we use to chew out the inside cockleburrs. Sometimes we share nice wine.

Hank Snow and Roy Acuff sing of rural romantic distraction, life and death in the red clay hills—the same songs they were singing on the first Saturday night I ever came in from a quail hunt, exhausted and at peace with my troubled teenage soul, with a blueblack shoulder and a couple of lightly nicked birds. Hank Snow and Roy Acuff are welcome constants in a world of shifting sand.

Once in a while I step outside and take a couple of deep breaths. The outside air is charged with frost that tingles in the nose like champagne. It carries the sweet-smelling hint of fresh cow manure and of the warm, stolid animals themselves, of old hay and of the warm old coat that keeps the cold off me. The stars glitter with needle-pointed life over the Green Hills of Adair County. You can't see them in the city. This smog of ambient light is called "fugitive light" and it robs the heavens of their stars, veils the mystery of night. It comes from a million man-made sources—parking lots, windows, streetlamps and, most disagreeable of all, the harsh security lights that turn quiet farms into rural industrial complexes. And we gnash our teeth at energy shortages and wonder how it all happened. The stars prickle in the skies unseen. So, I let the cold of the night air into my lungs and watch its warmed fog whisper into the night. Then I shiver and go back inside to Grandpa Jones and his tribute to a damned fine dog named Rattler.

The biggest problem in our hunting shack is who will do the cooking. In twenty-five years of quail hunting, I have not known a single hunter who could boil an egg. I have choked down meals that would gag a Stone County goat. When your breakfast eggs swim across the plate toward you, looking like Jerry Colonna's eyeballs, it is time to complain—except for one universally true situation:

He who gripes about the food in a hunting shack gets to do the cooking from then on. "You think you can do better!" cries the erstwhile cook, as outraged as a spinster to whom an especially vulgar (and subconsciously attractive) proposition has just been made by a darkly handsome stranger. "You cook then!"

And there you are, facing a stove more independent than one of the Missouri mules now so rare in my home state, a quart can of solidified cholesterol and five packages of food brought by you and the other four guys from five different home sites. Try combining a pound of rat cheese, side meat, a dozen oranges, Hotter'n Fire Chili and beef stroganoff into something Jim Beard would slobber over.

Of course you have heard the classic story about the hunter who complained about the cooking and instantly was elected the new cook. He brooded about his terrible fate, since cooking cut into his hunting time, and the next day as he sat on a deer stand, he glanced down and spied a moose flop. It was possibly the most stupendous moose flop ever left by a moose. It was enormous, a real steamer. Inspiration struck the hunter-cook. "I will make a moose flop pie for the rest of the hunters," he whispered, chortling, "and the first guy that complains about it gets to do the cooking."

So he rolled the moose flop back to camp and leaned it against the hunting shack while he whipped up the lightest, fluffiest pie shell ever concocted, for he now was an inspired cook. He had motivation. Then he tenderly laid the moose flop in the shell, careful not to chip or crumble its classic, natural outline, and he garnished it with little strips of dough and made a delicate tracery of design on it with a fork.

And he baked that moose flop pie and set it, steaming, on the rickety table. The first hunter in, hungry as an Ozark coonhound, dropped into a chair and chopped himself a whopping piece of moose flop pie. He shoveled in an enormous bite, paused in mid-chew, threw down his fork and roared, "*Good Godalmighty! That's moose flop pie!* . . . it's good, though."

We used to operate out of an old farmhouse overlooking the Chariton River in north-central Missouri. There was a covey out by an enormous old red barn, a little bunch of birds we could count on for a final covey flush at day's end. We have been snowbound there and have listened to sleet rattle off the century-old eaves. The upstairs was unheated, but the beds were equipped with enough quilts to smother Alex Karras and we slept warm. Sliding out in the dark of dawn with breath hanging in the gray light was a terrible test of a man's desire to hunt quail.

The dogs slept in what once was a smokehouse. Dogs who had been virtual house pets all spring, summer and crisping autumn suddenly found themselves booted into a few inches of mouldy straw along with a couple of smelly, uncouth strangers, on a night so cold that the telephone wires sang and you could hear a coon squall four miles away.

Those brittle nights inside the old farmhouse were especially fine, for the stout building exuded a gentle reminder of a hundred years of woodsmoke and home-canned vegetables, of drop biscuits and honey, of smoke-cured sausage and spattering side meat frying on a Warm Morning wood stove. No matter that those smells were the ghosts of meals cooked at least a quarter of a century before. They were benevolent spirits and they soothed.

In the old farmhouse, in its glory days as a hunting shack, a pot of water simmered on the heat stove—not to brew tea, but to put enough moisture in the arid heat to give it punch and keep the rickety furniture from falling apart. Wallpaper seams gaped like a fat man's vest. The flooring was wide pine planks, sagging tiredly, and the ceilings reached to the skies. Yellow bulbs dangled on frayed tethers, shining obscurely over burbling pork that was cooking in gallons of melted fat, in a fry pan which had coddled tons of greasy pig in its time.

Looking down the length of the ancient couch by the heat stove was like looking at a distant mountain range. Suggestions of humps, unscalable peaks, crevasses and fertile valleys, created by broken spring ties, internal fractures and the crush off a billion butts. This was my bed, by the gently whispering teakettle atop the stove. Pale moonshine sometimes slipped through the window at my head, diffused by the frost layered there, to paint the sagging floorboards with magic.

The second night out was the one that sticks in memory. The first night we hadn't yet hunted, but the second night was after we'd trudged wearily home at dark, coming out of the Chariton River bottoms up the long hill to where the yellow lights of the old farmhouse smiled into the night. Frozen clods tripped and twisted legs numbed by seven hours and miles of slogging after elusive bobs. But the several birds in the shell vest made a comfortable weight. The dog, his frisk and fire long since cooled in the wane of evening, plodded ahead, dreaming perhaps of his straw-filled smokehouse and a dish of dog food. The two of us made our way through a herd of stolid Angus cows, resignedly bracing themselves for the brittle night ahead.

This second night was the night that a bourbon and well water, a meal of side meat and hot beans was the end-all. Then the lumpy old couch felt like the soothing love of a good woman. The bloody briar scratches had dried to dark threads on abused shanks. Rabbits of memory sported in brushy draws and copper-colored fencerows, and there was the convulsive afterpulse of covey flushes, the frozen tick of time when a cock's black and white head and shining eye were as vivid and sharp amid roaring wings and confusion as if he'd stopped in midair. There was the sodden, cold memory of knee-high brush, laden with frostmelt, the dogs tense, vibrantly on point.

And then the down comforter began to give me back my body heat and the old couch reached out to enfold and warm me and the moon washed through the window and the coons squalled in the brittle night and the sky was velvet, sparkled with starshine and the world was still.

Bibliography

This is just a partial list of books I poked into. Many of them are out of print; some may be unavailable to the general reader because of their rarity.

Reading is no substitute for doing, but it's a fine companion to it. And doing often is no more than an experience which can be helped by the perceptions of others. We don't always know just what we saw or did until someone tells us.

Akehurst, Richard. *Sporting Guns*. Octopus Press, London, 1972.

Allen, Durward (ed.). *Pheasants in North America*. Stackpole, 1956.

Bailey, Hogg, Boothroyd, Wilkinson (eds.). *Guns and Gun Collecting*. Crown, 1972. Fascinating gun history.

Bell, Bob. *Hunting the Long-Tailed Bird*. Freshet Press, 1975. The best pheasant hunting book I've found.

Betten, H. L. *Upland Game Shooting*. Penn Publishing, 1940. A fine old anecdotal book, illustrated by Lynn Bogue Hunt.

Brusewitz, Gunnar. *Hunting*. Stein and Day, 1969. History and methods in Europe. Well-written and fascinating.

Butler, David. *The Shotgun Book*. Winchester Press, 1973.

Curtis, Paul A. *Guns and Gunning*. Knopf, 1943.

Dalrymple, Byron W. *Doves and Dove Shooting*. Putnam, 1949. Standard dove hunting book.

Davison, Verne E. *Bobwhites on the Rise*. Scribners, 1949.

Davis, Henry E. *The American Wild Turkey*. Samworth, 1949. A great book by a great turkey hunter. A classic.

Dickey, Charles. *Bobwhite Quail Hunting*. Oxmoor House, 1974. The best quail hunting book.

Edminster, Frank C. *The Ruffed Grouse*. Macmillan, 1947. Standard popular reference on grouse.

Elliott, Charles. *Turkey Hunting*. McKay, 1979. Another great hunter with a fine book.

Elman, Robert. *The Hunter's Field Guide*. Knopf, 1974. Great gobs of good information, well-written.

Errington, Paul. *Of Predation and Life*. Iowa State Press, 1967. Fine philosophy and scientific value.

Evans, George Bird (ed.). *The Woodcock Book*. Amwell, 1977.

_____. *The Grouse Book*. Lovely volumes, superb illustrations.

Greener, W. W. *The Gun*. Crown, numerous editions. Standard book on gun development. More than 800 pages.

Hatcher, J. S. et al. *NRA Firearms and Ammunition Fact Book*. National Rifle Association, 1964.

Heacox, Cecil. *The Gallant Grouse*. McKay, 1980. Ranks with Burton Spiller's grouse expertise.

Hinman, Bob. *The Golden Age of Shotgunning.* Winchester, 1971. Tour through double-barreled shotgun history.

Holland, Ray. *Shotgunning in The Uplands.* A. S. Barnes, 1944. Classic hunting book.

Hunting, Dwight. *Feathered Game.* Bickers & Son, London, 1903.

Johnsgard, Paul A. *Grouse and Quails of North America,* 1973. University of Nebraska Press.

————. *North American Game Birds.* University of Nebraska Press, 1975. Both superb looks at birds we hunt.

Keith, Elmer. *Shotguns by Keith.* Stackpole, 1950.

Latham, Roger. *Complete Book of the Wild Turkey.* Stackpole, 1976.

Laycock, George, *The Alien Animals.* Natural History Press, 1966. Stories of how all those pests got here.

Lewis, Elisha J. *The American Sportsman.* Lippincott, 1863. Whatever it costs to get a copy (probably $20–$30) it's worth it. Utterly fascinating reading.

Luggs, Jaroslav. *A History of Shooting.* Spring Books, England, 1968. Comprehensive look at shooting—even including magic and witchcraft in shooting prowess.

Madson, John. *The Mourning Dove.* Winchester, 1962.

————. *The Ring-Necked Pheasant.* Winchester, 1962.

————. *The Ruffed Grouse.* Winchester, 1969. These three books synthesize nearly everything known about their subjects. Written by my nominee as the best outdoor writer in history.

Maxwell, Aymer. *Pheasants and Covert Shooting,* 1913. Amam and Black, London.

McIlhenny, Edward. *The Wild Turkey and Its Hunting.* Doubleday, 1914. Another Elder of the Clan.

McIntosh, Michael. *Best Shotguns Ever Made In America.* Scribners, 1981. My hunting pard tells more, more accurately about doubles than anyone yet.

Norris, Charles. *Eastern Upland Shooting.* Lippincott, 1946. The Elisha Lewis of his generation. One of the best.

Popowski, Bert. *Crow Shooting.* A. S. Barnes, 1946. The book on hunting crows.

Rosene, Walter. *The Bobwhite Quail.* Rutgers University Press, 1969. This book and Stoddard tell you all you ever conceivably would want to know about bobwhite quail.

Schley, Frank. *American Partridge and Pheasant Shooting,* 1877. Arno Press, 1967 facsimile edition. He means quail and grouse respectively.

Schorger, A. W. *The Wild Turkey.* University of Oklahoma Press, 1966. A standard work on turkey biology, life history, and management.

Sisley, Nick. *Grouse and Woodcock.* Stackpole, 1980. Good hunting tips book.

Spaulding, Edward S. *The Quails.* Macmillan, 1949.

Stoddard, Herbert L. *The Bobwhite Quail.* Scribners, 1936. Most famous quail book in history.

Trench, Charles Chenevix. *A History of Marksmanship.* Follett, 1972. Fine book on history of powder, shot, and wingshooting.

————. *The Poacher and the Squire.* Longmans, Green & Co. Ltd., London, 1967. Great book on the eternal war between the gamekeeper and the poacher.

Trueblood, Ted. *Hunting Treasury.* McKay, 1978. Fine book by a legendary hunter. Helpful and super reading.

Index